How Everyone Could Be Rich, Famous, Etc.

By Lewis S. Mancini

Order this book online at www.trafford.com
or email orders@trafford.com

Most Trafford titles are also available at major online book retailers.

Print information available on the last page.

ISBN: 978-1-4120-7517-6 (sc)
ISBN: 978-1-4122-0617-4 (e)

Trafford rev. 09/24/2015

www.trafford.com
North America & international
toll-free: 1 888 232 4444 (USA & Canada)
fax: 812 355 4082

A Potential Business Item (A brief potentially money-making idea or note to anyone purchasing one or more copies of this book)

In case I am ever effectively treated for my severe obsessive-compulsive disorder, other emotional difficulties, relieved of various learning disabilities, etc. and thereby enabled to return to a lifestyle of being gainfully employed, by dint of making/having made this purchase, you might be possibly getting in on the "ground floor level" of any publishing or medical devices company that I might be involved with in the future. Therefore, please retain proof of purchase in a secure location, for possible future reference.

Please consider that I have already had six articles published in international, peer-reviewed medical and scientific literature and have already worked in a laboratory on the research and development (R&D) of a medical device (as a research assistant on the "Artificial Vision for the Blind" project, under the auspices and guidance of Dr. William H. Dobelle).

L.S.M.

Author's Biography

The author, a psychiatrist with additional background in biophysics and bioengineering and electroencephalography (EEG) technology, turned 54 this year (2005). He has been afflicted with various learning disabilities since childhood and disabled with severe obsessive-compulsive disorder (OCD) since 1985.

The potential business item (contained herein) bespeaks his writing and medical devices' design aspirations. He is a graduated of St. George's University School of Medicine (1983). And previously, in late 1974, worked briefly (as a research assistant) on "Artificial Vision for the Blind", under the auspices of Dr. William H. Dobelle in the Neuroprotheses and Artificial Organs Divisions of the Bioengineering Department at the University of Utah. Dr. Dobelle is cited in the 2005 Guinness Book of World Records under the headings of Medical Phenomena and the "earliest successful artificial eye", on page 20.

The author also won an award for "academic and technical excellence" in EEG technology from Graphic Controls Corporation and has had six articles published in Speculations in Science and Technology and Medical Hypotheses.

One of his goals is to play whatever role he can in the conceivable implementation of brain-stimulation mediated learning facilitation (LF) and work skills facilitation (WF), enhancement and diversification

A Potential Business Item (A brief potentially money-making idea or note to anyone purchasing one or more copies of this book)

In case I am ever effectively treated for my severe obsessive-compulsive disorder, other emotional difficulties, relieved of various learning disabilities, etc. and thereby enabled to return to a lifestyle of being gainfully employed, by dint of making/having made this purchase, you might be possibly getting in on the "ground floor level" of any publishing or medical devices company that I might be involved with in the future. Therefore, please retain proof of purchase in a secure location, for possible future reference.

Please consider that I have already had six articles published in international, peer-reviewed medical and scientific literature and have already worked in a laboratory on the research and development (R&D) of a medical device (as a research assistant on the "Artificial Vision for the Blind" project, under the auspices and guidance of Dr. William H. Dobelle).

L.S.M.

150 word

synopsis for hardcover (?) submission of

<u>How Everyone could be Rich, Famous, etc.</u>

Anyone purchasing one or more copies of <u>How Everyone could be Rich, Famous, etc.</u> might be getting in on the ground floor level of any publishing or medical devices company the author might become involved with if he is ever effectively relieved of his learning disabilities, obsessive-compulsive disorder and related difficulties. Please see the potential business item on page _____.

Via mental activation *(neuromodulation)* or brain stimulation, all learning/work activities might have their effort/"work" eliminated/minimized by becoming intensely pleasurized/de-effortized, whereby anyone could quickly learn to competently perform any employment-related activities, thereby earning a high wage/salary. Similar methods/technologies might facilitate sexual liberation, freedom from pain, suffering, etc.

World-wide fame and immortality for everyone might be achieved through the concept that each person is an animated/consciousized particle bonded to a relatively large (human) body who could be unbonded and circulated among the world's entire (voluntarily-participating) particle-person population.

200 word

Back cover marketing copy for

How Everyone could be Rich, Famous, etc.

Anyone purchasing one or more copies of **How Everyone could be Rich, Famous,**

(Immortal), etc. might be getting in on the ground floor level of any publishing or medical

devices company the author might become involved with if he is ever effectively relieved of his

various learning disabilities, obsessive-compulsive disorder and related difficulties. Please see

the potential business item on page _____.

By using some form of brain stimulation *(possibly, pleasurable)* or other kind(s) of mental activation, *neuromodulation,* (entailing

electromagnetism, sound waves, focused particle beams, transdermal or intravascular nanobots,

microminiature robots or computer components, targeted biotechnological, medicinal or other

chemical agents, solar energy or conceivably, even focused, safely-contained strong or weak

nuclear forces, gravitational waves, dark energy/matter, etc.) to intensely pleasurize/de-effortize

all learning and working-related processes, any individual(s) could thereby quickly become well-

educated and knowledgeably competent to perform any employment-related activities and

thereby earn a valuably high wage/large income. Such methods might also facilitate sexual

liberation, freedom from pain/suffering, etc.

Everyone could possibly become world-renownedly famous (and immortal/eternally

death-free) via the hypothesis that each person is actually an animated or consciousized

subatomic particle (attached to a relatively large, complicated body) and then, intermittently,

circulating each person-particle throughout the world's entire (voluntarily-participating)

population.

BOOK SUMMARY

The primary purpose of this book is to raise public awareness of a) the book's two central ideas as well as b) the potential benefits of usefully implementing these ideas. The two ideas are as follows:

1. When and if, by means of pleasurable brain stimulation (**OR** SOME **OTHER** BIOLOGY-CHEMISTRY-MATHEMATICS-PHYSICS-ENGINEERING-SCIENCE-**TECHNOLOGY-MEDIATED MENTAL ACTIVATION**), it becomes possible to enable virtually **any** person to readily and quickly learn virtually **any** new job skill(s), then unemployment, poverty and financial stress might readily and quickly become problems of the past.

2. If every **individual** (entity) has a corresponding individual, unitary physical basis or foundation, then every **individual** (i.e., person) must, in underlying essence, be a unitary physical **mind PARTICLE** or discrete, self-cohesive energy/**matter** bolus, the size of which might be highly variable. And the invisibility of this particle might be due to either small size or to this particle's being hidden in a **currently**, but **not** necessarily **permanently**, inaccessible spatial dimension. This particle is a person who is bonded to a relatively stable-sized complicated (human) body made up of quadrillions of different things (molecules, atoms, subatomic particles, etc.) as opposed to **just one** unitary **individual** thing/entity. It might be helpful to keep in mind that **"matter is,"** essentially, just **"condensed energy"** ($E=mc^2$). (Please see reference to **Hyperspace**, directly below.)

   Then by scientifically/technologically implementing this idea (via brain stimulation, biomedical engineering, biotechnology, particle physics, mind particle circulation, global positioning systems, GPS, etc.) not only might everyone become forever famous, but also everyone might become permanently, painlessly and, more or less, continuously (i.e., deathlessly, as opposed to intermittently) immortal. It may or may not be too optimistic or too bold to say that it might prove possible to cure all diseases and death itself. Nevertheless, in view of the mind particle concept, etc., it might prove possible, sooner or later, to cure or effectively treat all diseases, aging, etc. and render everyone permanently healthy.

The potential market would be adults, teenagers and even some preteenagers/younger children. And, although this is a manuscript about scientific ideas (mostly, but not entirely), nevertheless, because it contains a potential business item that might interest various and diverse kinds of people (not necessarily only scientifically-minded people), for this reason, the potential market would seem to encompass a general readership much more widely than just a scientific readership.

Reference

1. Kaku M. Hyperspace: A Scientific Odyssey through Parallel Universes, Time Warps, and the 10th Dimension: Doubleday, Anchor Books, 1994: 359 pages; please see pages 87-88.

Caption for the drawing on the cover: an example of one (of many possible) schematic illustrations(s) of a combined brain stimulator and mind particle circulator, detector and accelerator. CO = circulation directed outward, CI = circulation directed inward, CCC? = central circulator and consciousizer with question-answering mechanism, WLO = work or learning output modality, LWI = learning or work input modality, OS = operant stimulus mediator, OR = operant response mediator. Drawing done in 1980.

Acknowledgements and Thanks

Grateful Acknowledgements and Thank-You Notes are hereby extended to:

C. Timothy, Gloria,

Michael, Cathie,

Nick, Anna,

Tom, Tom,

Ray and

Bernice

and also to:

Robert J.,

Patricia, Mike,

David, William,

Akhlesh, Seymour,

Betty, Amanda,

Denise and

William

Dedication:

This book is dedicated to:
Herbert, mary, Grace and Robert

Herbert (c.1955) Mary, Grace and Robert on the next 3 pages

Dedication continued:

Early photo of Mary;
B.S. in Education, Buffalo State College,
M.S. in education, State University of NY at Buffalo,
Certified Teacher of the Deaf, Canisius College and State
Univ. of NY at Buffalo

Dedication continued:

Early photo of Grace;
B.S. in education, Buffalo State College,
Certified Teacher of the Deaf, Canisius College and State
Univ. of NY at Buffalo

Dedication continued:

Recent photo of Robert;
M.D., Harvard; Ph.D. in biophysics, State University of NY at Buffalo

Author's photo, aged 52 (D.O.B. 6/29/51)

Curriculum Vitae

LEWIS S. MANCINI

EDUCATIONAL BACKGROUND

B.S. - 1973 – Psychology Major, Trinity College (Connecticut), 1969-73

- Coursework in Master's of Natural Sciences Program at State University of New York at Buffalo (S.U.N.Y.A.B.), 1973-74

- Coursework in undergraduate electrical engineering at the University of Utah, 1975-76

- Coursework in Bioengineering Master's of Engineering program *(M.E.)* at the University of Utah, 1977-78

M.D. - 1983 – St. Geroge's University School of Medicine (S.G.U.S.O.M.), Grenada, West Indies, 1978-83

Certificate of Psychiatric Residency – 1985 – S.U.N.Y.A.B. Affiliated Hospitals
Psychiatric Residency Training Program, 1983-85

A.A.S. - 1988 – (with high distinction) Associate in Applied Science in Electroencephalography (EEG) Technology from Niagara County Community College (N.C.C.C.) (program co-sponsored by S.U.N.Y.A.B. School of Medicine), 1986-88

- Independent study in genetics (Life Sciences Department) at N.C.C.C. under Dr. Nicholas LoCascio, 1988

- Tutorial in Biophysics at S.U.N.Y.A.B. under Dr. Robert Spangler, 1989

- Writing class with editor, Denise Sterrs and editor/novelist, William Appel (author of Whisper…he Might Hea You, The Watcher Within, etc.), 1991

- Independent Studies in Biophysics at S.U.N.Y.A.B. under Dr. Robert Spangler, 1992

PROFESSIONAL BACKGROUND

1994	Visited Drs. Scott Lukas of Harvard, Richard Pavelle, Zeb Hed of Massachusetts Institute of Technology (MIT), Mr. Dick & Mrs. Eleanor Grace of Brain Research Institute on Cape Cod, and Dr. Conan Kornetsky of Boston University
1993	Guest speaker at seminar at the Pennsylvania State University, Department of Engineering Science and Mechanics, topic: "Noninvasive Brain Pacemaker or a Real-life Thinking Cap" (21-5 to 2-17)
1992	Visited Drs. Joie P. Jones and Patricia C. Rinaldi, Departments of Radiology, Surgery and Neurosurgery, School of Medicine, University of California at Irvine, to observe experiments in ultrasonic brain stimulation (6-22 to 6-27)
1989	Guest speaker at EEG technology lecture, Erie County Medical Center, Topic: "Psychiatry and the EEG" (December)
1988	Visited Dr. Reza Jalinous at Massachusetts General Hospital and Dr. Vern Gugino at Brigham and Women's Hospital, Boston, Massachusetts, to observe and serve as unofficial experimental subject for noninvasive magnetic brain stimulation using MAGSTIM-200 and Cadwell MES-10 devices (7-10 to 7-15)
1986-88	Hospital rotations as EEG technology student
1983-85	Psychiatric Resident in the State University of New York at Buffalo Affiliated Hospitals Program
1981-83	Clinical Clerkships at Niagara Falls Memorial Medical Center

LEWIS S. MANCINI

PROFESSIONAL BACKGROUND (continued)

1978   Exemption via Qualifying Test and Teaching Assistantship for Biomedical Psychology course during fall semester at S.G.U.S.O.M.

1978   Research Assistant in psychophysiology Lab at VA Hospital working on project aimed at correlating EEG with psychological variables (especially depression) under auspices of University of Utah, Bioengineering Department, Salt Lake City, Utah

1976   Psychosurgeons Conference in Gottingen, West Germany (mid-July)

1974   Research Assistant in Artificial vision for the Blind Project, Artificial Organs Program: "The Artificial Eye," University of Utah (autumn) *under the auspices of Dr. William H. Dobelle, who is cited in the 2005 Guinness Book of Records for "earliest successful artificial eye" (page 20, "Under Medical Phenomena").*

1972   Participant in Psychophysiology experiments involving EEG and feedback at the Institute of Living in Hartford, Connecticut

1971   Volunteer Remedial Reading Tutor for disadvantaged children in Hartford

1970   Discussion group leader at Red Cross Training Camp at Manilus, New York (summer)

1969-70   Remedial Reading teaching assistant during summer sessions at the Park School of Buffalo

1969   Employed as Remedial Reading tutor for elementary school student with reading difficulties

PUBLICATIONS, *copyrighted and (hopefully) yet-to-be published articles and essays*

~~1969, '73~~ *1973*   Unpublished initial manuscript done as 'senior thesis' (actually Open Semester term paper) Open Semester Project, Spring, 1973: Practical Implications of Learning and Cognitive Facilitation Theory; 119 pages. Done under the auspices of Dr. George W. Doten, Chairman of Psychology Dept. at that time at Trinity College (Hartford, Connecticut)

1982   How Learning Ability might be Improved by Brain Stimulation, Speculations in Science and Technology, 5 (No. 1): 51-53.

1986   Brain Stimulation to Treat Mental Illness and Enhance Human Learning, Creativity, Performance, Altruism and Defenses against Suffering, Medical Hypotheses, 21:209-19.

1990   Riley-Day Syndrome, Brain Stimulation and the Genetic Engineering of a World Without Pain, Medical Hypotheses, 31: 201-7.

1992   Ultrasonic Antidepressant Therapy might be more Effective than Electroconvulsive Therapy (ECT) in Treating Severe Depression, Medical Hypotheses, 38: 350-1.

1992   A Magnetic Choke-Saver might Relieve Choking, Medical Hypotheses, 38: 349.

1993   A Proposed Method of Pleasure-inducing Biofeedback using Ultrasound Stimulation of Brain Structures to Enhance Selected EEG States, Speculations in Science and Technology, 16 (No. 1): 78-9.

1995   Waiting Hopefully, Western New York Mental Health World, 3(4), Winter: 14. Written under pen name Nemo T. Noone.

2004   Copyrighted but yet-to-be published/unpublished book manuscript titled: **How Everyone Could Be Rich, Famous, Etc.**

2001   *How Everyone could be Rich, Famous, Painless, Deathless, Well Educated, Sexually Liberated etc; copyrighted in 2001 but (hopefully) yet to be published etc*

OTHER

1.   National Merit Certificate of Merit, 1969; New York State Regents Scholarship, 1969; Merit's Who's Who Among American High School Students, 1968-69; Advanced Placement in American History and English, 1969-70

OTHER (continued)

2. Member of the American Society of Electroneurodiagnostic Technologists (ASET), 1987. Intend to renew for '96.

3. Member of the American Medical Association.

4. Graphic Controls Corporation EEG Technology Award, 1988.

5. Student Representative to the EEG Technician Curriculum Advisory Committee at N.C.C.C., 1988-89.

6. Member, EEG Technician Curriculum Advisory Committee, 1989-92.

7. General Member of the American Institute of Ultrasound in Medicine (A.I.U.M.), 1993. (Was invited to join on the basis of publication #4, listed above.)

8. Member of the American Mensa, Ltd.

9. Member's Presentation, no Saturday, May 28, 1994, at Western New York Mensa Society annual regional gathering, Radisson Hotel, Niagara Falls, New York; Subject: "Non-Invasive Brain Pacemaker…a Real Life Thinking Cap."

10. Guest/Alumni Speaker, on Thursday, February 8, 1996, at the Park School of Buffalo, Snyder, New York, subject: Book in Progress, Title of Synopsis; How Everyone could be Financially Stress-Free, Famous, Sexually Liberated, Effort-Free, Well-Educated, Healthy, Deathless, Unselfish, Etc. via Electromagnetic, Ultrasonic or other kinds of Brain Stimulation/Pacemakers and Internet of Mind Particles, Genetic Self-Engineering, Etc.; Title of Book: How Everyone could be Rich, Famous, Sexually-Liberated, Etc., Etc.

11. Donated Oil painting, 4'x5', done during summer, autumn & winter, 1970-71 entitled, "To be Whatever We Want to Be," to Trinity College, Hartford, Connecticut in early 1971. Displayed in front hallway of Life Sciences Building for approximately ten years.

12. Historical Committee member, St. Louis Catholic Church, 1995 →.

13. Member, Father's Rights (Organization) of W.N.Y., 1994 → (daughter born 12/29/83).

14. Member, Society for the Scientific Study of Sex, 1989; renewed '97.

15. Member, Inventors' Alliance of Canada/America, 1997.

16. Member's Presentation for Inventors' Alliance, "How Learning and Work could be made both Thoroughly Effortless and Intensely Enjoyable: via Noninvasive (i.e., non-surgical, non-implanted, external, extra-cranial) Brain (Pacemaker) Stimulation, April 2, 1997.

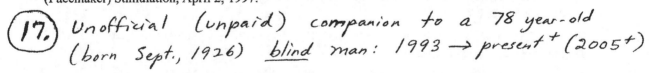

17. Unofficial (unpaid) companion to a 78 year-old (born Sept., 1926) _blind_ man: 1993 → present + (2005+)

Correspondence, SST, Vol. 5, No. 1 (1982)

HOW LEARNING ABILITY MIGHT BE IMPROVED
BY BRAIN STIMULATION

LEWIS MANCINI

Received: 28 November 1980

It would be necessary to determine an electroencephalographic characteristic, designated as the learning-linked characteristic (LLC), which always and only occurs during learning. The LLC would be used as a turn-on signal for an electric circuit which would deliver pleasurable electrical (or conceivably chemical) stimulation to a suitable reward site in the brain by way of an implanted intracranial electrode whenever and only whenever, and only for as long as the student would emit the LLC and hence engage in learning. From the student's standpoint, because learning and the LLC can only occur simultaneously, the learning process itself would be rendered pleasurable. And it would therefore be likely to occur for as long as the student's stimulation appetite remained unsatiated.

Hence the method, which could be referred to as learning facilitation or LF, would entail a prosthetic system consisting essentially of: (1) a *suitable* reward site in the human brain; (2) an intracerebral or scalp-level recording electrode; (3) an electric circuit which would recognize the LLC and use it to initiate and sustain stimulation of the reward site; and (4) an intracerebral stimulating electrode which would convey the stimulation to the reward site.

A practicable LF circuit would be similar to a circuit designed by Butler and Giaquinto[2] which delivered stimulation triggered automatically by electrophysiological events. They were interested in studying brain function in terms of the interplay between stimulated and unstimulated brain sites. Drugs could conceivably be used to maintain the thresholds of excitability of reward sites at low levels. In order to minimize the invasiveness of the system, the LLC would preferably be detectable at the level of the scalp rather than merely intracerebrally.

The workability of LF would depend upon: (a) the existence of one or more *suitable* reward sites in the human brain, and (b) the existence and detectability of one or more LLCs. The LLC might equally adequately be either unique to a particular individual whose learning is to be facilitated or common to that individual and many or all others.

A suitable reward site might be one which subserves pleasure which is inherently nondistracting to or integrable with the learning process. Using this kind of a reward site, the processes of LLC-detection, brain stimulation and learning could all occur simultaneously as implied above.

0155-7785/82/0005-0051$02.50/0

Alternatively, a suitable reward site might be one which subserves pleasure which is inherently distracting to learning but which also has the property that the pleasure does not appreciably outlast the duration of an electrical stimulus which induces it. If the pleasure significantly outlasted the stimulus duration, then, regardless of how brief the stimuli were made, the student would tend to waste time experiencing pleasure as opposed to learning. Because stimulation and learning could not occur simultaneously if this kind of a reward site were used, the electrical circuit would have to be designed in such a way that LLC-detection/stimulation periods would be alternated in time with learning periods. Both types of periods should be brief (for example, on the order of several minutes) because if the former were too long, the student would be wasting time experiencing pleasure as opposed to learning, and if the latter were too long, the student's learning process would effectively not have the benefit of pleasurable motivation.

An unsuitable reward site would be one which subserves pleasure which is inherently distracting to the learning process and which has the property that the pleasure does appreciably outlast the duration of a stimulus which induces it.

Although there is very little question that reward sites do exist in the human brain[1,3], there would be little justification for hazarding any guesses with respect to their LF suitability. There is a wealth of experimental evidence that (at least relatively undetailed, slow-paced) learning can be facilitated in animals by means of rewarding brain stimulation[5,9]. However none of this evidence seems to provide solid suggestions that the reward sites in question might be suitable according to the criteria given above.

Although at this time the question of whether or not the brain emits LLCs may not have a definitive answer, there are experimentally-derived suggestions that it does. Some of these are as follows. Lehmann[4] observed that "decrease of slow wave frequencies and increase of fast frequencies is systematically correlated with better quality of memory". Surwillo[7] found that longer as compared with shorter digit spans (as measured by the WISC digit span backward test) were accompanied by a greater degree of synchrony between the EEGs of the left and right hemispheres of the brain. Subsequently, Surwillo[8] found that tasks utilizing different cognitive modes have differences in their associated patterns of right-left interhemispheric symmetry of the EEG and that these differences, by means of the "central-moments technique of EEG period analysis", are detectable. Stigsby et al[6], confining their attention to the dominant hemispheres of ten normal subjects, compared EEG recordings during auditory rest, an auditory memory task, visual rest and a visual memory task. They observed various increases and decreases in the amplitudes and indices of alpha, theta and delta activity as recorded from the various regions (for example, frontal, temporal, occipital) of the scalp. They concluded that "the two different types of mental activity, i.e. memorization and mental relaxation, induced two different patterns of regional EEG changes". And even if the brain does not, in fact, emit any LLCs which are common to statistically significant percentages of individuals in experimental-sample-sized groups, the LF method may, nonetheless, be workable by virtue of the existence of LLCs which are unique to each individual.

If the LF method should prove workable, it would enable the brain to learn more effectively, rapidly and voluminously by virtue of reliably, rapidly and sustainedly providing large amounts of pleasurable motivational energy which could be used to accomplish the work of performing analyses and forming memory traces for informational perceptions. Additional learning-expediting benefits might be obtained by using LLCs which are specifically associated with very high-speed, detailed learning. LF would also enable anyone to become interested in any subject matter which would otherwise fall outside of that person's natural sphere of interests. It would do so by providing enough pleasurable motivational energy to overcome the pain of boredom, impatience and anxiety.

References

1. Bishop, M.P., Elder, S.T. and Heath, R.G., Attempted control of operant behaviour in man with intracranial self-stimulation, in *The Role of Pleasure in Behavior*, R.G. Heath (ed.), Harper & Row, New York (1964).
2. Butler, S.R. and Giaquinto, S., *Med. & Biol. Eng.*, 7, 329-331 (1969).
3. Heath, R.G., Pleasure response of human subjects to direct stimulation of the brain, physiologic and psychodynamic considerations, in *The Role of Pleasure in Behavior*, R.G. Heath (ed.), Harper & Row, New York (1964).
4. Lehmann, D., *Electroen. & Clin. Neurophysiol.*, 30, 270 (1971).
5. Major, R., and White, N., *Physiol. & Behav.*, 20, 723-733 (1978).
6. Stigsby, B., Risberg, J., and Ingvar, D.H., *Electroen. & Clin. Neurophysiol.*, 42, 665-675 (1977).
7. Surwillo, W.W., *Cortex*, 7, 246-253 (1971).
8. Surwillo, W.W., *Physiol. Psych.*, 4, 307-310 (1976).
9. Guyton, A.C., *Textbook of Medical Physiology*, Saunders, Philadelphia, pp.762-763 (1976).

Editorial Comment

These suggestions of Mancini depend almost solely upon the existence of his postulated learning-linked-characteristic (LLC). I cannot see that such a characteristic can exist in the brain because there appears to be no necessity for this in the EEG wave forms. These wave forms are simply some weighted average of all of the millions of action potential spikes which are occurring in the brain at any one time. The recognition that learning has occurred is not a conscious or even unconscious action because presumably, on the basis of current physiological knowledge, memory is distributed over broad volumes of nerve cells at synapses and consists of a permanent or semi-permanent modification of the condition of those synapses. The idea, however, is a compelling one but this particular idea must concentrate on this matter because reward centres, etc., are quite well known and obvious but do not really bear on the practicality of the scheme Mancini proposes, without having LLC.

P.S. Dr. William M. Honig of the University of Western Australia is wrong about this: there is _now_ an enormous amount of experimental evidence that _LLC does_, in fact, exist.

Plus, it is probably possible at this time to improve anyone's learning abilities (etc.) entirely noninvasively via a combination of focused ultrasound and electromagnetic fields (e.g., TMS = transcranial magnetic (brain) stimulation).

3

Everyone is (potentially) just as Smart, Talented, Creative, Geniustic, Capable andGifted (in All Possible Ways) as Everyone else is or could be

This third update was written on April 20, 2004 and is dedicated to:

Miriam, Diana, Geraldine, Helen, Mary B., William B., Gertrude and Mr. Thomas

Although, based on principles of science and technology, including principles of medicine (especially artificial organs, neurology and psychiatry), psychology, mathematics (especially statistics, geometry and calculus), biology (including cloning, stem cells and biotechnology in general), chemistry (especially bio- and organic chemistry), engineering, computer science, and physics (especially cosmology, particle, quantum and astrophysics), it can be inferred that everyone is **potentially equally** as **gifted** (intelligent, entertaining, charismatic, imaginative, inventive, etc.), **capable** (skillful, mechanically-inclined, physically-strong, knowledgeable, well-educated, practical, etc.), **motivated** (conscientious, diligent, self-disciplined, industrious, etc.), and conceivably **even** as **good, but, probably, with some definite, notable exceptions**, (kind, compassionate, honest, reliable, decent, altruistically-idealistic, unselfish, courageous, etc.) as everyone else is (or could be), the specific concepts, or ideas, that might (surprisingly **readily**) **engender data** that might prove the validity of this multi-faceted hypothesis, are beyond the scope of this book.

However, as an incidental afterthought to this update (and a minimal preview of one aspect of the essence of this book), it should be **pointed out that, regardless** of any person's being able and willing to work hard, due to the prospect of entirely **eliminating** the **effortfulness** from all learning and employment/work-related (and, really, all other) kinds of activities, **it might**, conceivably, (in the not necessarily very distant or, possibly, **even** in the relatively **near future** it could become **unnecessary** for anyone **to work hard** and, therefore, **unnecessary** for anyone **to experience any significant** (or large) amount(s) of learning or work/job-related **stress** or worrisome tension, as **explained** (especially in terms of unlimited, high-paying, new job-creation) **below**, in the ~~two somewhat long~~ *three* essays contained in this book.

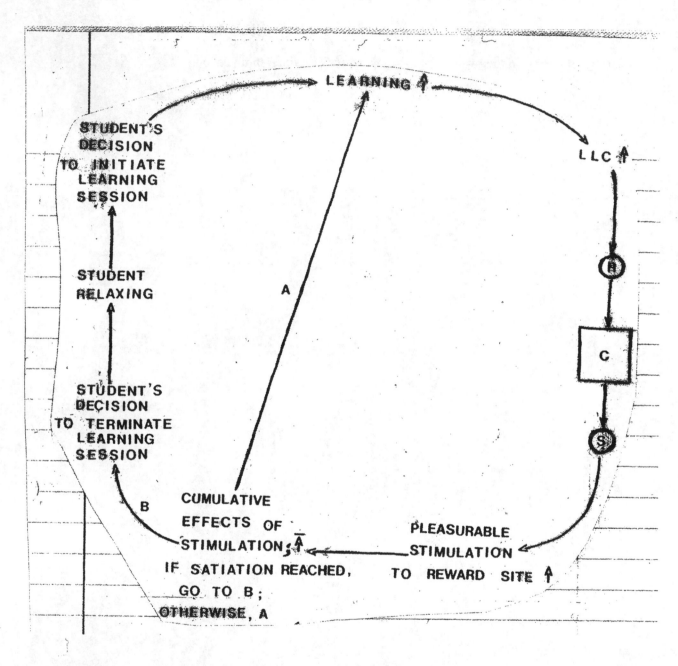

Figure One. Schematic diagram of how human (and animal) learning (and work skills performance) ability might be improved by a subtle variant or modified version of the psychologist, B.F. Skinner's operant conditioning (that is, essentially, a learning/educational-improvement paradigm that might entail instrumentally-mediated brain stimulation or some other kind of probably but not necessarily pleasurable and facilitative) mental activation. LLC = learning-linked characteristic, R = learned/newly-acquired response, C = central consciousizing circuit, S = (pleasurable) stimuli or stimulation.

How everyone might be rich, famous, pain and death free (immortal), well educated, sexually liberated, unselfish, healthy, free of anorexia, obesity, nausea, blindness, deafness, paralysis, insomnia, etc. via brain stimulation, neural prostheses, pacemakers, mind particle internet, circulation, cloning, genetic engineering, conscious computers, etc.

(completed on or before September 7, 2000)

Lewis S. Mancini

SUMMARY

Financial stress might be markedly diminished, while employment-related knowledge, productivity and adaptability might be augmented and diversified by a (preferably, surgically-) **noninvasive** brain stimulator, pacemaker, or other kind of nervous-system-function modifier or neural prosthesis. This device or method would deliver highly enjoyable brain stimulation whenever and only whenever one were to engage in high-level (of complexity or of time-pressure-related intensity, economically-appropriate and sellable) mental or physical activities, as indicated by physiological criteria. Sexual liberation might be achieved through brain-stimulation-mediated enhancement of (a) freely-chosen sexual impulses and suppression of (b) impulses one would prefer not to be compelled by. It may be possible to circulate everyone's **mind particle** (**MP**, the hypothesized biological and physiological basis of each person's individual mind or consciousness) through everybody's **brain-body pair** (i.e., body, including its associated brain), BBP or, simply, BB, so as to enable each consciousness to directly experience and, therefore, be empathetic toward every BB's needs and wants. No longer being confined within one particular BB, each individual mind (particle) would be unaffected by any given BB's death and might always be able to transfer, when necessary, to a viable BBP, thereby avoiding death. A less fascinating, less educationally valuable way to avoid dying would be to simply transfer oneself (i.e., one's mind particle) to a youthful clone of the original BBP one were **born into** each and any/every time the latest-issued clone might become too decrepitly old or otherwise impaired to continue living.

8

UNIVERSITY OF CALIFORNIA, IRVINE

UCI COLLEGE OF MEDICINE   IRVINE, CALIFORNIA 92717
DEPARTMENT OF RADIOLOGICAL SCIENCES
DIVISION OF PHYSICS AND ENGINEERING

June 26, 1992

To Whom It May Concern:

This will confirm that Dr. Lewis Mancini visited my ultrasound research laboratory the week of June 22, 1992. He viewed in some detail the ongoing experiments conducted by Mr. Christos Georgiades and supervised by Dr. Patricia Rinaldi and myself involving the use of ultrasound pulses to alter communication pathways in brain tissue. These experiments, although conducted in-vitro on sections of rat hippocampus, could potentially be applied in-vivo to human subjects. In humans, such experiments could lead to a better understanding of brain function and might someday aid in the diagnosis and treatment of a variety of brain disorders.

During the week of June 22nd, we had extensive discussions with Dr. Mancini concerning the use of ultrasound to affect the way neurons in the brain respond. Our discussions ranged from purely scientific to the very practical. I found Dr. Mancini to be a bright and very engaging person. He is clearly interested in our ultrasound research from both a scientific and personal point of view. I would welcome regular visits by him to our lab and continued discussions with him on a long term basis. I believe such discussions would be stimulating and productive and could well lead to new insights and discoveries of both a scientific, as well as a practical nature.

Joie Pierce Jones
Professor of Radiological Sciences

JPJ:pc

9

UNIVERSITY AT BUFFALO
STATE UNIVERSITY OF NEW YORK

Department of Electrical & Computer Engineering
Faculty of Engineering and Applied Sciences

September 13 1989

To whom it may concern:

This is to certify that I am cooperating with Dr. Louis Mancini in a graduate level independent study and research project concerning the design, development and use of a noninvasive stimulator of focal regions of cns and peripheral nerve tissue. The device as proposed by Dr. Mancini will include highly focal magnetic and ultrasonic field components.

I have reviewed Dr Mancini's background in biomedical engineering and medical sciences and find him thoroughly qualified to participate as a principal in this study at the level commensurate with graduate credit in my discipline (Electrical Engineering).

Sincerely,

Peter D. Scott
Associate Professor

G Graphic Controls

September 26, 1988

Mr. Lewis S. Mancini

Dear Lewis:

Congratulations on being the recipient of the 1988 Graphic Controls Corporation Electroencephalography Award for Acedemic and Technical Excellence.

A commemorative plaque is enclosed to acknowledge this achievement. A One Hundred Dollar U.S. Savings Bond has been sent to you.

We at Graphic Controls are pleased to provide this award for your distinguished achievement.

Very truly yours,

Al Barber
Product Marketing Manager
Patient Data Supplies

AB/dc:3925u

ENGINEERING SCIENCE & MECHANICS SEMINAR

presents

SPEAKER: LEWIS S. MANCINI
State Univ. of New York at
BuffaloSchool of Medicine
Biophysics/EEG Program

TOPIC: *"Non-Invasive Brain Pace Maker or a Real-Life Thinking Cap"*

DATE: Wednesday, February 17, 1993

TIME: 3:35 P.M.

LOCATION: Room 314 Hammond Bldg.

REFRESHMENTS WILL BE SERVED IN ROOM 226 HAMMOND BEGINNING AT 3:00 P.M.

PENNSTATE

Department of Engineering Science and Mechanics

The Pennsylvania State University

Akhlesh Lakhtakia
Associate Professor

February 23, 1993

Dr. Lewis Mancini,

Dear Lewis:

It was my sincere pleasure to have met you last week and listened to your ideas on the ultrasonic stimulation of the human brain. This is potentially exciting idea that needs more work on. If it is succesful, I am quite sure it will lessen performance anxieties and thereby lessen conflicts between people.

Please keep me occasionally informed about your work. With my best wishes, I remain

Sincerely yours,

Akhlesh Lakhtakia
Fellow, Optical Society of America
Fellow, Leonhard Center for Innovation
Editor-in-Chief, Speculations in Science and Technology

An Equal Opportunity University

14

 niagara falls memorial medical center

December 13, 1982

C. Timothy Golumbeck, M.D.
Director of Residency Training
Department of Psychiatry
Erie County Medical Center

Re: Lewis Mancini

Dear Doctor Golumbeck:

I have known Dr. Mancini since early October, 1981, when he came for a six-week psychiatric rotation at our inpatient unit of Niagara Falls Community Mental Health Center. He came back for another rotation in late October, 1982, for a period of four weeks. He apprently has been interested in the field of Psychiatry for a long period of time and he states that he was involved in, or ran, Research concerning this field.

He impresses me as a very conscientious young man, having a high moral standard, and very energetic and enthusiastic about certain areas which he is interested in. He is also immaculate and punctualistic. He also willingly admits some of his weaknesses, which may have influenced him to be more interested in the research area than direct patient care.

I am particularly impressed by his openness and some fascinating ideas he can come up with. With further training and support, I'm sure that he will be able to contribute to the better understanding and further development of Psychiatry in the future, particularly in the field of Psychiatric Research.

I wish him to be accepted into the program for which he wants to be trained.

Sincerely,

NIAGARA FALLS COMMUNITY
MENTAL HEALTH CENTER

J. S. Rhee, M.D.
Psychiatrist

JSR:ve

15

DIVISION OF LIFE SCIENCES

September 15, 1988

TO WHOM IT MAY CONCERN

Lewis Mancini, MD has recently completed an AMA accredited Electroencephlography Program that is jointly sponsored by Niagara County Community College and the State University of New York at Buffalo, School of Medicine. As a student in the EEG Program, he was academically the highest in the class. He is the recipient of the Graphics Control Award in Neurodiagnostic Technology (1988) for Clinical and Academic Excellence. Dr. Mancini holds a Bachelor of Science degree from Trinity College (Hartford, Connecticut) and an MD degree from St. George's University School of Medicine (Grenada, West Indies).

His interests appear to lie in the areas of bioengineering, neurology, and psychiatry. Lewis completed a special independent project on Riley-Day Syndrome, resulting in a paper entitled "Riley-Day Syndrome, Brain Stimulation, and the Genetic Engineering of a World Without Pain of Any Kind." Some thought-provoking ideas emerged from this study. He has recently published an article in Medical Hypotheses entitled "Brain Stimulation to Treat Mental Illness and Enhance Human Learning, Creativity, Performance, Altruism, and Defenses Against Suffering".

Dr. Mancini always dressed in a neat and conservative fashion, always came to class on time, was well prepared, and contributed actively to the discussions. In the context of his rotations at the four hospitals in the EEG Program, he had a uniformly positive rapport with both clinical personnel and patients.

I feel he has both the academic qualifications and professional maturity to engage in independent research and I whole-heartedly support this endeavor.

If I may be of further assistance relative to Dr. Mancini's credentials, please do not hesitate to call or write.

Sincerely,

Nicholas J.T. LoCascio, Ph.D.
Assistant to the Vice President of
    Academic Affairs - NCCC
Clinical Instructor, Neurology
    State University of NY at Buffalo
    School of Medicine

**Indianapolis Center for
Advanced Research, Inc.**

May 27, 1987

Lewis S. Mancini, M.D.

Dear Dr. Mancini:

Your survey of articles pertinent to the possibility of focal excitation of CNS seems to have been both perceptive and accurate. Since what you are proposing to accomplish is a much sought after and worthwhile goal it is appropriate to applaud your persistence and analysis. No noninvasive method to my knowledge has yet been shown to accomplish what you seek to do.

My first comment is to state that I think it is only a matter of time before the goal is achieved. It may be achievable with careful experimental application of known technology which you have reviewed in your letter. The size of the stimulated volume with present technology if it works would undoubtedly be limited to several cubic millimeters.

One would of course not start out to prove a given methodology if it involved ultrasound by leaving the skull in place in experimental animals. Once the method was proven the skull complication could then be addressed. This is my answer to your first question.

Since the second question requires a high degree of speculation I prefer to answer question one in as firm and positive manner as I can and hope that you can take definitive steps to carefully apply basically known technology to demonstrate feasibility. I would place the probability of a reasonable measure of success in the hands of careful experimenters as well over 50%.

Sincerely,

Francis J. Fry
Senior Scientist

FF:kk

Date composed on: February 14, 2005

Copy designated for your receipt on: ~~March ___, 2005~~

Dear _____:

I am a disabled physician whose afflictions include obsessive-compulsive disorder (OCD) (first diagnosed by a psychiatrist – Dr. M.R.P. – in 1985 at age 34; first symptoms apparent in 1963 at age 12) and various learning disabilities since earliest recollectable childhood (beginning around ages 2 to 4), most notably entailing deficiencies in ordinary mechanical abilities and general information. My Wechsler Adult Intelligence Scale (W.A.I.S.) performance IQ is only 105-109, but this does not seem to be my biggest problem.

Impaired attention and concentration and their joint consequence: extreme slowness of ordinary work-speed are also among my functional afflictions and apparent (?) limitations. However, on rare occasions, when my motivational wherewithal is unusually high, my work-speed can be at least average.

On the plus side, my strong egalitarian, humanitarian and altruistic concerns provide a (hopefully significantly) strong motivational undercurrent that (a) might compensate somewhat for the above-stated problems and challenges and (b) seem to have engendered/brought about the writing of a (now) complete (since July 20, 2004; approximately 235 page-long) book manuscript with a short-title, as follows: How Everyone Could be Rich, Famous, Etc. and a full-length title as follows: How Everyone Could be Rich, Famous, Painless, Deathless, Well Educated, Sexually Liberated, Disease Free, Etc. This manuscript contains a potential business item that reads, as follows:

A Potential Business Item (A brief potentially money-making idea or note to anyone purchasing one or more copies of this book)

In case I am ever effectively treated for my severe obsessive-compulsive disorder, other (related) emotional difficulties, significantly relieved of various learning disabilities, etc. and thereby enabled to return to a lifestyle of being gainfully employed, by dint of making/having made this purchase, you might

possibly be getting in on the "ground floor level" of any **publishing** or **medical devices company** that I

might be involved with in the future. Therefore, please retain proof of purchase in a secure location, for

possible future reference.

As indicated within the manuscript, I have already been involved *as a research assistant,* (though, thus far, only briefly)

in ~~the~~ *a context of* research and development of medical devices. That was in 1974 at the University of Utah, under

the auspices of Dr. William Dobelle *, who is* (listed in the (2005) **Guinness Book of World Records** *under the category of the "earliest* ~~for the~~ "earliest

successful artificial eye" *The* ~~whose~~ focus *there* was on the prospect of providing useful brain-stimulation-/

neuromodulation-mediated eyesight to blind individuals via the "Artificial Eye" Project within the ~~context~~

~~of the~~ "Artificial Organs" division of the Bioengineering Department at that university.

Moreover, I have been fortunate to have had (a) six articles published in the peer-reviewed,

international literature (including the esteemed **Medical Hypotheses and Speculations in Science and**

Technology, between 1982 and 1993, and subsequently received 194 reprint requests from 25 or 30

different countries) as well as (b) one short autobiographic article (in 1995) published in the **Western**

New York Mental Health World newsletter. This most recent article was written under the pseudonym

indicated above (i.e., Nemo T. Noone). Article titles and other items and information (including possibly

copies of the articles themselves and letters of recommendation from Drs. Scott, Jones, Rhee, Spangler,

LoCascio, Lakhtakia, etc.) are contained along with my resume within the Appendix to the book

manuscript or may be enclosed herewith. My educational background and strongest interests are in

neuropsychiatry, psychometrics, bioengineering, biophysics, astrophysics-cosmology, and

electroencephalography (EEG) technology. Hobbies include mineralogy/gemology, rock and country

rock music.

My intention would be to **divert** a significant percentage of any monetary proceeds (consequent

to the book manuscript's-potential-publication and sales that would be somehow commensurate with the

degree of success of the book) toward a **variety of different charities.** Better yet, **perhaps** a first edition of a published version of the book (manuscript) should **possibly** be entirely free, that is, entirely a **gift** from my own personal perspective(?).

My choice of 'Nemo Tee Noone' as a pen name follows from 'Nemo' being the Latin word for 'no one or nobody,' 'Noone' being a contraction of 'no one,' the Buddhist notion that "To be Everyone is to be No One and to be No One is to be Everyone" (which I appreciate the subtle validity of despite my Christian faith) and the impression that 'Tee' fits in harmoniously with the overall pseudonym.

Computer illiteracy seems to figure conspicuously into the underlying pattern of my learning disabilities. I would need one-on-one tutoring to overcome this problem. But, so far at least, my lack of computer and word-processing skills has been well compensated for by (and thanks to) the meticulous work of Mrs. Gloria G. Zachary, etc. In any case, it should be **relatively easily** possible to reorganize the book manuscript in such ways as to adhere to almost any guidelines of organization and format. For example, an Introduction could quite readily be composed and chapter numbering assignment could be provided.

If you can kindly be of ~~nay~~ any assistance to me in my drive to get the book published, distributed and effectively sold, that would be greatly appreciated not only by me directly, but also, indirectly, but hopefully significantly, by anyone and everyone else who might (charitably or potential-business-item-relatedly) benefit from any short-term or long-term proceeds that might be generated thereby. Thank you.

Sincerely,

Lewis S. Mancini

P.S. Part of why I wrote the book in question is because I suffer from an intermittently agonizing low back pain problem that could easily be relieved with the technology in question. This is a "slipped disc" problem. There have been approximately twenty episodes (of four to six days each) between 1993 and the present. Actually, they have become less frequent in recent years, perhaps due to a better-balanced daily exercise regimen.

SMH 547
UNIVERSITY OF ROCHESTER
STRONG MEMORIAL HOSPITAL
LABORATORY OF
ELECTROENCEPHALOGRAPHY
ROCHESTER, NEW YORK

UNIT NO. ___1215057___

NAME ___Kanelni, Dr. Lewis___ AGE 33 DIV Out Pt. DATE 5/31/85

Requested by ___Dr. Privitera___

Type of EEG ___Nasopharyngeal___ Channels: 8 ___ 16 x

Technical comments The patient was sedated with Chloral Hydrate to a total of 1 gm.

Description:

Well formed 10 cps activity is seen bilaterally in the background of the resting record, without undue further slowing or disorganization of the alpha activity during overbreathing. Some nonrhythmic 4 - 5 cps left temporal slowing is seen at this time, and returns as the patient drifts in and out of drowsiness. In the nasopharyngeal linkages, no new focal or discharging abnormalities were seen.

Impression:

Abnormal EEG due to paroxysmal slowing from the left temporal region.

43 -16

21
Signed _Maurice R. Charlton, M.D._

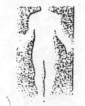

**NorthTowns
Imaging**

NAME: MANCINI, LEWIS

CT: **40-00-79-37 (YOUNGS)**

DATE: 5/2/01

AGE/DOB: 6/29/51

REF.PHYS.: DR. W. KUEHNLING

CT SCAN OF THE LUMBAR SPINE:

CLINICAL HISTORY: 49-year-old male with the history of back and neck pain since 1993.

TECHNIQUE: Axial CT scans through the lumbar spine are obtained.

FINDINGS: The L3-4 disc level demonstrates diffuse annular bulge and a right paracentral focal broad-based disc protrusion causing a moderately severe degree of acquired spinal stenosis.

At L4-5 level, there is noted diffuse annular bulge and a left paracentral broad-based disc protrusion causing indentation on the thecal sac and causing a moderate degree of acquired spinal stenosis. The foramina bilaterally are normal, and the facet joints are normal at this level.

At L5-S1 level, there is noted diffuse midline broad-based disc bulge causing some indentation on the thecal sac.

IMPRESSION:

1. MODERATE DEGREE OF SPINAL STENOSIS AT L3-4 LEVEL AND A RIGHT PARACENTRAL BROAD-BASED DISC PROTRUSION AT THIS LEVEL CAUSING INDENTATION ON THE THECAL SAC.
2. MODERATELY SEVERE DEGREE OF SPINAL STENOSIS AT L4-5 LEVEL AND A LEFT PARACENTRAL BROAD-BASED DISC PROTRUSION AT THIS LEVEL.
3. MIDLINE DISC PROTRUSION AT L5-S1. FURTHER EVALUATION WITH MRI IS RECOMMENDED.

THANK YOU FOR YOUR KIND REFERRAL.

Jayant G. Kale, m.d

MAY 0 4 2001

JAYANT KALE, M.D.
JK:lw
Preliminary report until verified by signature.

22

Background Information about the author

The initial reason why, beginning in the early 1970s, as a second-year college student, I became very interested in neural (especially, brain) stimulation was that its prospects seemed to suggest potentially effective ways to alleviate my own mental and behavioral (work-speed-related) slowness, attention-deficit disorder, learning disabilities, and pervasive high-intensity, ambient or "free-floating" anxiety and **very** high-intensity (skilled-behavior or goal-oriented) **performance anxiety** (which can be considered analogous to some substantial part of the portion of the "activation energy" in a chemical reaction that can be diminished by a catalyst, refs. 1, 2) in relation to learning in general, especially learning connected or coupled with implementation of **practically-applicable**, such as **manual skills**, as noted below.

According to the diagnoses of my two regularly-visited psychiatrists and a clinical psychologist, whom I have seen sporadically, I am severely disabled with **obsessive-compulsive disorder** (OCD). This diagnosis was first affixed to me in early 1985, when I was overwhelmed by a combination of work-related and marital difficulties.

The diagnoses of **attention deficit disorder (ADD)** and several specific learning disabilities are, admittedly, **self**-diagnoses. But the psychiatrists, psychologist and a psychometrist (the latter of whom, consistent with the nature of her area of expertise, administered a number of standardized, psychological tests) all **seem** (albeit **tacitly**, according to the best of my inferential ability), to agree, based on test results (if nothing else), with their appropriateness as descriptive labels.

The specific learning disabilities mostly center around the fact or condition of being profoundly mechanically **dis**-inclined. For example, learning to tie shoelaces and neckties, learning to ride a bicycle, to drive a car, to carry out instructional laboratory experiments in science classes, etc. have all required exceptional efforts on the part of teachers, lab partners and other helpful people in order to achieve even marginally adequate levels of competency. Furthermore, my mental processes and work speed, in virtually all respects, are so slow as to nearly always incur marked impatience, annoyance and, sometimes outright wrath, expressed by a definite majority of people thereby affected.

My educational background, albeit very sketchy and inadequate in a number of ways, is mostly in psychiatry and biophysics. I am generally passable when it comes to basic vocabulary, reading, math and liberal arts in general. But, when it comes to practical matters, **especially**, **mechanical** endeavors, such as plumbing, carpentry, construction work, gardening, yard work, car maintenance, cooking, housework, electrical wiring, repairs of household appliances and other equipment (in short, in relation to home and other physical-environment or place-related maintenance in general) and also in terms of giving road/highway-transportational directions to other people), I'm embarrassingly unknowledgeable. Regarding computers, suffice to say, I'm hampered by a phobia about them or, in other words, I'm **computer-phobic**, which is far more problematic than simply being computer-illiterate. I would need **one-on-one** teaching/tutoring to overcome my computer phobia and computer illiteracy.

The circuits I built in electronics laboratory classes **never** seemed to work **properly** and, more often than not, did not work at all. However, I passed anyway, thanks to the kind helpfulness and technical capability of my laboratory partner. And I would not have passed high school chemistry had it not been for the assistance of another kindly and capable laboratory partner. My anxiety and resultant impatience with mechanical devices, practical mechanisms and gadgets in general is so notably extreme that the term 'gadgetaphobia' seems applicable. Nevertheless, brain stimulation, as suggested in the context of this essay might possibly cure me of my gadgetaphobia and could conceivably cure or, at least, more or less effectively or significantly **treat** virtually any person in relation to their/our specific phobias, attention deficit disorders and learning disabilities, including dyslexia.

In general, my grades were satisfactory (mostly 'B's), but, sometimes, they were quite unsatisfactory. For example, I never did get my master's degree in bioengineering, due to my having failed the engineering graduate students' Comprehensive Examination. And I passed my medical school Final Examination only on a 'make-up' basis, having failed it the first time.

Also, it took approximately 170 applications, to various medical schools, just to clinch two acceptances (both from outside of the U.S.). And it took me five years, instead of the standard four-and-a-half-year curriculum, just to finally graduate from the one actually attended. The reason for the prolongation of my course of study was a decision (made in consultation with faculty members and administrators) to spread out and slow down the pace of my workload in order to minimize the distinct (and, at the time, apparently very probable) possibility of failing out (of the programs' course of training) altogether.

Regarding standardized testing, intelligence quotient/IQ and psychometrics (mental measurement methods) in general, a number of test scores have been somewhat disappointing, including a performance <u>IQ</u> score of ~~105~~ *105-109* on the **Wechsler Adult Intelligence Scale** (W.A.I.S.), which I understand is approximately average but may be somewhat **below average** among college attendees and graduates, and a mere (standardized test score of) 425 (only the **22nd** percentile) as an overall score on the **Psychiatric Residents In-Training Examination**, together with/including an unusually low standardized test score of 308 (only the 5th percentile and the lowest test score achieved by anyone in the entire residency training program) on one major section of this psychiatric knowledge assessment examination.

And, regarding competitive games of any kind, whether mental, physical or both, especially athletic and sports-related types, my end-of-game status has been remarkably consistent as that of indisputable "loser."

Although always, or as far back as is within grasp of memory, an excessive worrier, my symptoms did not become totally incapacitating until late 1984, which marked the beginning of an extremely bitter series of divorce-related battles that plunged me into an anxiety-riddled, depressive state of markedly exacerbated slowness **and** ineptitude, from which there often seems to be no way to recover and no possibly valid hope of recovery.

Or perhaps, for me at least, the most feasible way to recover might be by way of brain pacemaker stimulation or, **preferably**, (surgically-) noninvasive focused brain stimulation. Virtually every medication known or reputed to reduce OCD symptoms has been tried on me. Not only have they all failed to relieve my symptoms, but in a number of cases, they have entailed markedly unpleasant side effects, such as moderately severe depression, headaches, nausea and insomnia. Behavior modification techniques have also been found **not** to be effectively or adequately therapeutic in my case.

Nevertheless, despite all of the afflictions, shortcomings, failures, and limitations, only **some** of which are described above, it is conceivable that my conceptual wherewithal or inclination might possibly be helpful and useful in relation to significant endeavors in an appropriate and medical-device-development-conducive research setting. Hence, my only realistically, foreseeably possible role in such a medical-device-development-related project might be that of a **volunteer** research consultant.

Therefore, it is clear that the principal investigator(s) and technologists would, without a doubt, **need** to be **other** people. Locating and persuading qualified investigators to fulfill crucially important roles, those of the practical, **real doers** and implementors, would be problematic but, in any case, would require and be facilitated by **adequate financial backing**.

Some Other Relevant Circumstances

On Saturday, August 10, 2002, a somewhat odd and ironic situation emerged while I was waiting (along with several other people, as noted above, in the dedication) in the emergency room of an apparently ordinary local hospital. We were waiting for a medical decision on whether or not to hospitalize Bernice, the 100-year-old mother of my friend and neighbor, Herb (Herbert).

During the eight or nine hours we spent there, a couple of apparently widely acceptable, popular magazines (refs. 3, 4) on a nearby table-top captured my attention. Several articles within them, intended for the regular, non-medically-trained reader, dealt with several (seemingly widely acceptable, though, arguably) "futuristic," therapeutic modalities such as **brain pacemakers, vagal nerve stimulation** (VNS) and **transcranial magnetic** (brain) **stimulation** (TMS) that are **being** (or already have been) **designed** and clinically implemented in order to treat a number of medical and psychiatric conditions, including depression and obsessive-compulsive disorder (OCD).

In December, 2000, a friend and former instructor of mine (a clinical instructor in an electroencephalography, EEG, technicians' training program) who had been extremely supportive and encouraging in relation to my writing and getting several medically-and-science-and-technology-related articles published in the medical and technical literature between 1980 and 1995 (refs. 5-11) gave as his reaction and response to a 100-page (copyrighted, but yet-unpublished) manuscript (ref. 12) the contention that the ideas suggested in that relatively long essay were too futuristic to be tested in the foreseeable future.

With all due respect and appreciation for his record of helpfulness and encouragement, contradictory evidence seems to suggest that both the medical as well as the other scientific (such as physics-related) ideas expressed in the manuscript could be tested at the present time and many (or most) of the medical ideas could actually be put to use at this time.

Consequently, the **irony** (and, I believe, the incorrectness) inherent in the following two facts: (1) (on the one hand) I casually came across two popular, contemporary magazines (refs. 3, 4) (in a commonplace, down-to-earth setting of an Emergency Room in an apparently adequate but unremarkable hospital) that matter-of-factly discuss such topics as **brain pacemakers,** vagal nerve stimulation (VNS), transcranial magnetic (brain) stimulation (TMS), etc. and (2) (on the other hand) a friend/former instructor (who has been most helpful in the past has said that the ideas expressed in the 100-page-long manuscript/essay (ref. 12) are too futuristic to warrant or justify their being published even as theoretical items amounts to an erroneous irony or twist of reason which has as its size a magnitude too large to be inconspicuous from my viewpoint. The essay in question is included in this book as Essay number one.

I have always been significantly disconcerted by my being notably mechanically disinclined. For example, the Master of Engineering (M.E.) degree in bioengineering was denied to me on the basis of my miserably failing the biomechanics section of the bioengineering graduate students' comprehensive examination (having received a score of zero (0) on that section of the exam).

However, despite this disinclination, I did work briefly (for about three weeks' time, in 1974) within the context of the "Artificial Eye" or "Artificial Vision for the Blind" Project, within the Neuroprostheses/Artificial Organs and the Microcircuits Division/Laboratory of the Bioengineering Department of the **University of Utah.** After three weeks of working with and under the auspices of Dr. William Dobelle, then the Director of the Artificial Eye Program, I realized that the background in engineering and technology that would be necessary in order for me to contribute and participate in a constructive and helpful way in relation to this project/program was something lacking in my education and training and, therefore, dropped out of/resigned from the Artificial Eye project and instead started taking undergraduate electrical and other engineering-related courses, etc.

My occupation with Dr. Dobelle (my former boss) was a **research assistantship** and, therefore, substantial disappointment afflicted me in connection with the loss of this position. Nevertheless, my ex-boss/ex-supervisor and his work are referred to in both the 2001 and the 2002 editions of the Guinness Book of World Records (for the "first artificial eye" – 2001 – and the "best artifical eye" – 2002) (refs. 13, 14). *also, 2005* In the References section, an Artificial Vision article, published in the journal, **Science**, and co-authored by my former boss/supervisor is cited (ref. 15) as an additional item. Another (one-of-his-work-related items, in particular, a) newspaper-clipped article is further coupled therewith (ref. 16). And a one-page write-up in Newsweek magazine also contributes to his credit (17).

Also noted in the References section (ref. 18) is another clipped-out-of-the-newspaper article, on the subject of Dr. Willem J. Kolff, inventor of the "artificial kidney" or dialysis machine. He is currently, at the age of 91, working on an "artificial lung" device, intended to help people who have badly impaired pulmonary/respiratory functioning. He was working within/in connection with the Bioengineering Department at the University of Utah at the same time as I was a student there, in particular, in 1974, including the brief period during which I was working on "artificial vision for the blind."

Within the context of this recent newspaper clipping, reference is made, in the course of delineating Kolff's career, to his involvement, during the 1970s, with the University-of-Utah-connected, U. of U's first artificial heart (care of Dr. Robert Jarvik of the "Jarvik hearts" renown, who was also, at that time, affiliated with the Univ. of Utah Artificial Organs program). And in this same career-delineating context, reference is similarly made to Kolff's involvement with the relatively early stages of the "Artificial Eye/Artificial Vision for the Blind" project. Moreover, I recently had the pleasure of meeting Wilson Greatbatch, inventor of the **cardiac** pacemaker, etc. at a meeting of the Inventor's Alliance of America/Canada. One of my brothers, in connection with an initiative taken by my late father, had the privilege of working on a project with Mr. Greatbatch when this brother was a student at New York University.

Despite my mechanical disinclination, with the conceivable benefit of being in an environmental frame of reference of a competent and adequately diversified research and development (R & D) team, **it might finally** (after having supplemented my education and training in a hopefully-significant way since my Dobelle-days and), after the passage of approximately thirty years' time, it might **conceivably** be possible for me (when and **if** equipped with sufficient financial backing and wherewithal) to actually play some small role in the R & D suggested herein.

Figure Two through Eleven (cartoons by Erica-Joani, circa 1990-1992): Schematic depictions of individuals enjoying and benefiting from learning-abilities-improving and/or work-skills-enhancing/teaching-facilitative mental-sharpening equipment (such as, for example, brain stimulators) that also serve(s) as a mind (or, synonymously, a mind **particle**) circulator that might mediate interactions with other individuals' minds/mind particles, perhaps via satellite-mediated global positioning systems (GPS) or other kind(s) of mind (-particle) circulation-empowering devices or gadgetry, as conceptually explained in the longer of this book's two main essays.

Figure Two. A young man organizing his thoughts and putting his ideas down on paper.

Figure Three. Three men **calmly** sharing their thoughts with each other. They could be engaged in a process of highly significant and sensitive negotiations. Please note the relatively great distances between the contact-free brain stimulators/mental activating equipment and the three gentlemen on whom these remote neuroprostheses are respectively focused.

Figure Four. A woman and man **calmly** experiencing the benefits of couples' counseling.

Figure Five. Three athletes experiencing the joys of motivational enhancement.

Figure Six. An agitated, potentially violent individual being calmed down and somewhat relaxed so that he can deal with his problems in a relatively rational way.

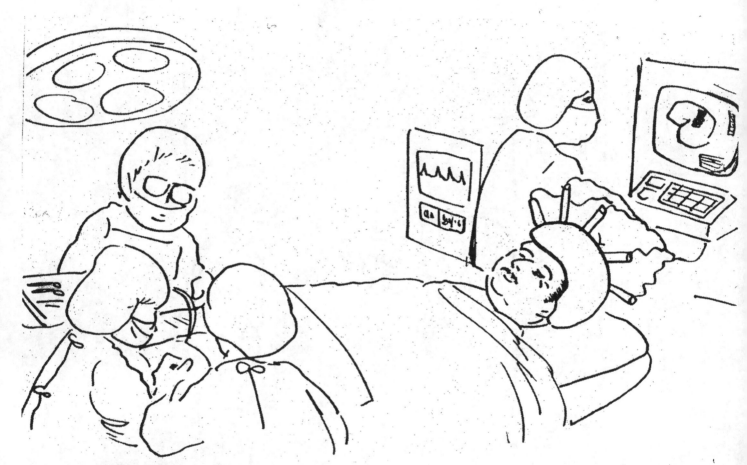

Figure Seven. Pleasurable-mental-activating/brain-stimulating painlessness/analgesia being enjoyed by a patient while he is undergoing surgery.

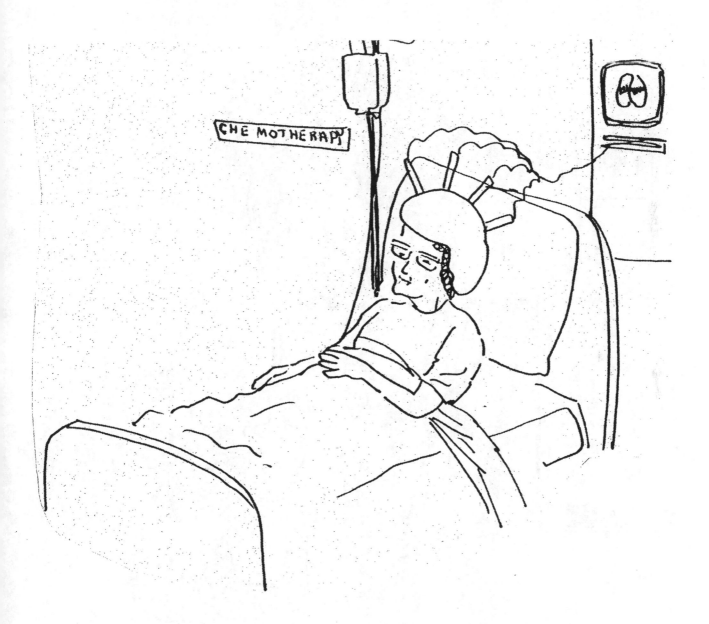

Figure Eight. Pleasurably-brain-stimulated, hedonic-calculus-maximized and, mentally-activated freedom from side-effects associated with medical-therapeutic treatment(s) for an individual's illness/medical problems.

Figure Nine. A young man enjoying pleasurable brain stimulation or other possible mode(s) of rewarding mental activation in a context of learning-facilitation or work-skills' knowledge augmentation and diversification.

Figure Ten. A young woman enjoying learning-facilitation and work skills' enhancement and diversification.

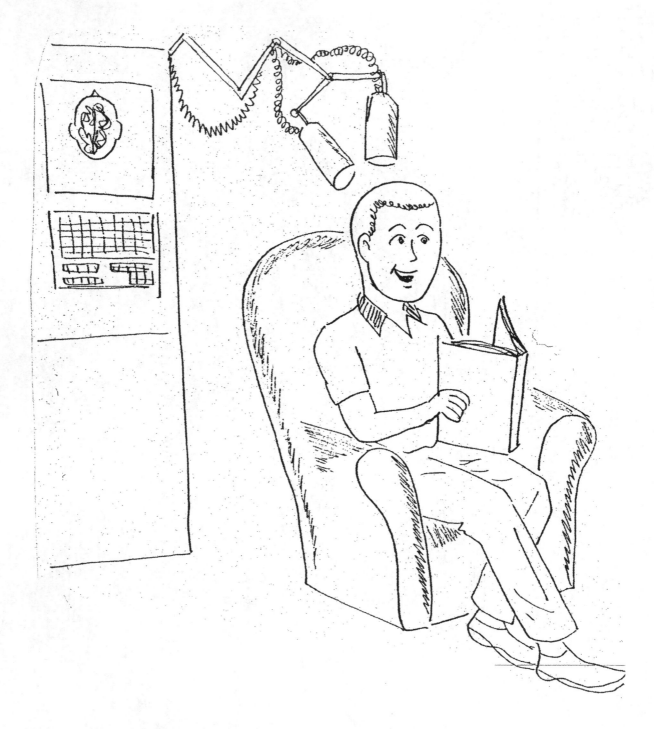

Figure Eleven. A young man who is simultaneously deriving entertainment, educational, vocational/occupational and employment-related value and enhancement via rewarding brain stimulation/mental activation.

Medical Hypotheses 21: 209-219, 1986

BRAIN STIMULATION TO TREAT MENTAL ILLNESS AND ENHANCE
HUMAN LEARNING, CREATIVITY, PERFORMANCE, ALTRUISM, AND
DEFENSES AGAINST SUFFERING

Lewis Mancini

ABSTRACT

Any mental/emotional state or process (MESP) which is considered
(a) highly desirable (e.g., sustained concentration, memorization of
important facts, empathy) or (b) undesirable (e.g., paranoid delusional-
ism, delirium) could be, respectively, (a) facilitated or (b) deterred
by means of an external (i.e., extracranial, or at least extracerebral,
and extracorporal) brain stimulation circuit designed in such a way as
to deliver rewarding stimulation as often and only as often as and for
as long and only for as long as an electroencephalographic or other kind
of brain function characteristic, which uniquely identifies the occurrence of the MESP in question, were being emitted by the individual's
(i.e., the subject's) brain, with the intensity of the stimulation at
every point in time being proportional, respectively, (a) to the simultaneous magnitude or (b) to the reciprocal of the simultaneous magnitude of the MESP-identifying characteristic. Approaches a and b are
generalized examples of a number of hypothetical stimulation paradigms
presented below that might be used to treat mental illness, enhance
learning, etc. (as in the title). Explanations of the psychodynamic
mechanisms whereby these paradigms might exert their intended effects
are given in most cases.

INTRODUCTION

The methodology herein proposed is predicated on the inference that
can be drawn from substantial experimental evidence (1, 2, 3, 4, 5, 6,
7) that any given mental/emotional state or process that one might want
to either induce or suppress has characteristically and uniquely associated, detectable electroencephalographic and other kinds of measurable
brain-function features (and a corresponding underlying, uniquely characteristic configuration of excited and inhibited neuroanatomic circuits) which could be used by an external circuit to automatically detect the occurrence of that MESP. Such features, which are characteristically linked with a particular MESP, may be thought of as linked
characteristics (LCs) of that MESP. This methodology would require
merely that each person's LCs be essentially time-invariant for her or
him so that, for example, whenever person A engages in high-level concentration (MESP-CONC), A's brain reliably emits one or more particular

LCs (LC-CONCs). It would make no difference whatsoever whether A's LCs were completely different from anyone else's or not.

What is meant by stimulation is the production or suppression of impulses or action potentials within minute volumes of brain tissue, for example, a sphere or "focal spot" with a diameter of 1mm (8) or less, without any direct production or suppression of action potentials in surrounding tissue. For any given application in any given case, the stimulation might consist in a continuous waveform or (more probably) in successive discrete waveforms, that is, pulses. The technical implementation of such a system might entail the use of electroencephalographic, ultrasonic, and/or electromagnetic techniques, such as MRI, for LC determination, detection, and magnitude monitoring. According to Brown and Kneeland (9, p. 495), "More powerful magnets offer the possibility of monitoring phosphorus^{31} and therefore cell energy metabolism" and therefore the possibility of monitoring MESP-specific cerebral activity as reflected in LCs. Stimulation that would be nondestructive might be affected either invasively (but hopefully not), e.g., via surgically implanted electrodes, or (preferably) noninvasively or minimally invasively (e.g., invasively with respect to the skull, such as with an ultrasonic irradiator implanted therein, but noninvasively with respect to the brain) by means of focused electromagnetism and/or ultrasound as is discussed in some detail in another paper (10).

The types of brain stimulation that might be used are (a) pleasurable (PLE), i.e., rewarding, (b) sedating (SED), (c) alerting (ALERT), (d) specific-MESP-excitatory (SMESPEX), (e) specific-MESP-inhibitory (SMESPIN), and (f) otherwise characterizable. Stimulation could be any one of, more than one of, or even all of the above in nature, with its nature in every instance being determined both by the particular neuroanatomic site(s) focused upon and the particular stimulation parameters used. Distressing, i.e., aversive stimulation should never be used.

The essential principle of the methodology, stated in the most general terms possible, is that, by means of an ideally wholly external prosthetic system, the individual would receive brain stimulation of one or more kinds as often as and only as often as and for as long as and only for as long as (and with intensity either directly or inversely proportional to the magnitude with which) the individual would emit a predetermined LC and, hence, would be either facilitated or inhibited with respect to indulgence in the MESP corresponding to that LC. Hence, the delivery and the intensity of the brain stimulation would be dependent upon the magnitude of one or more LCs and, hence, could be referred to as linked characteristic-dependent brain stimulation(LCDBS). Each LCDBS system would consist essentially in:
1. An LC detection and magnitude-monitoring component.
2. An LC-magnitude/stimulation intensity proportionalizing circuit.
3. A stimulating component.

RESULTS OF SOME (NON-LCDBS) BRAIN STIMULATION EXPERIMENTS

Sem-Jacobsen (11,p.379) reported that "We have been able to obtain feelings of comfort, relaxation, joy, and intense satisfaction.... In the ventromedial part of the frontal lobe, regions of pleasure and relaxation are lower and more internal than those mediating anxiety and irritation. The responses of relaxation and comfort obtained from stimulation of the frontal lobe are so intense that psychotic episodes have been broken up in less than one minute on several occasions.... Stimulation of the ventromedial part of the frontal lobe has a calming effect, as does stimulation of the central region of the temporal lobe."

Heath (12, p.224) found that "With septal stimulation the patients brightened, looked more alert, and seemed to be more attentive to their environment during, and for at least a few minutes after, the period of stimulation.... Expressions of anguish, self-condemnation, and despair changed precipitously to expressions of optimism and elaborations of pleasant experiences, past and anticipated. Patients sometimes appeared better oriented; they could calculate more rapidly and, generally, more accurately than before stimulation. Memory and recall were enhanced or unchanged." Moan and Heath (13) also reported sexual feelings to be associated with self-stimulation of the septal region.

The observations of Higgins, Mahl, Delgado, and Hamlin (14, p.418) that "after one stimulation..." of the "frontotemporal" area, which they define in neuroanatomic detail, a young male subject "...said, without apparent anxiety, 'I'd like to be a girl'", whereas "In the last interview, when he came close to expressing a similar idea under pressure by the interviewer but in the absence of stimulation, he became markedly anxious and defensive" suggest that stimulation of that area could be useful in the treatment of the personality disorders intrinsic to which is the ostensible incorrigibility of maladaptive defense mechanisms. Hence, the neuroanatomic areas explored by these investigators might include appropriate stimulation sites for the applications discussed herein. The septal region in particular may contain utilizable sites (15, 16).

LCDBS AS TREATMENT FOR MENTAL ILLNESS

Examples of paradigms or modi operandi of LCDBS systems designed to treat mental illness and/or affect prophylaxis for antisocial including criminal behavior are as follows.

1. Treatment of Mental Illness Type I, that is, psychosis (including schizophrenia), which may be defined here simply as a phenomenon consisting in gross disorganization of mental processes and/or distorted perception of reality:

   PLE stim. int. inc. in prop. as mag. LC-PSYCH dec.
   and
   PLE stim. int. dec. in prop. as mag. LC-PSYCH inc.

where PLE stim. int. = (i.e., abbreviates) pleasurable stimulation intensity, inc. = increases, dec. = decreases, in prop. as = in proportion as, mag. = magnitude of, and LC-PSYCH = an LC which identifies the occurrence of a psychotic process or state entailing, for example, hallucinations and/or delusions, and/or looseness of associations. Hence, the less psychotic an individual's mentation would become, the more intense the pleasure which he or she would obtain from the system (and the

43

more psychotic, the less pleasure), so that the individual would be strongly motivated to discard psychotic processes and states. Antipsychotic SMESPIN stimulation paradigms might entail the use of inhibitory stimulation directed at some of the same sites in the brain as where antipsychotic drugs exert their therapeutic effects (17).

2. Treatment of Mental Illness Type II, that is, mental pain (MP), including all forms of neurosis. The three basic kinds of mental pain: (a) anxiety (grading up to terror), (b) depression (grading up to hopelessness), and (c) anger (grading up to rage) pervade all forms of mental illness, especially the anxiety, depressive, personality, and adjustment disorders.

    PLE stim. int. inc. in prop. as mag. LC-MP inc.
    and
    PLE stim. int. dec. in prop. as mag. LC-MP dec.

where LC-MP = an LC which identifies the occurrence of one or more kinds of mental pain. The rationale of this modus operandi would be that, inasmuch as the brain's reward (i.e., pleasure) and punishment (i.e., aversion or pain) systems are reciprocally inhibitory with respect to each other (18), the more intense the mental pain a person is experiencing, the more intense would be the pleasure needed to nullify, that is, inhibit, suppress, or relieve that pain. And the less intense the pain, the less intense the pleasure needed to nullify it. Hence, by dint of this modus operandi, mental pain would be automatically nullified by an intensity of pleasurable stimulation commensurate with it.

3. Treatment of Mental Illness Type III, that is, maladaptive and/or destructive pleasure (MDP), such as constitutes the motivational or affective essence of drug (including alcohol) abuse, sadism, some forms of sexual deviance, and mania:

    SMESPIN-MDP stim. int. inc. in prop. as mag. LC-MDP inc.
    and
    SMESPIN-MDP stim. int. dec. in prop. as mag. LC-MDP dec.

where SMESPIN-MDP stim. = stimulation of one or more neuroanatomic sites which specifically causes inhibition of a particular kind of MDP and LC-MDP = an LC which specifically characterizes that kind of MDP. Hence, the greater the intensity of MDP (and, correspondingly, the greater the magnitude of LC-MDP), the higher the intensity of MDP-inhibitory (i.e., SMESPIN-MDP) stimulation that would be needed and automatically delivered to nullify it.

4. Treatment of Mental Illness Type IV, that is, pathological unconcern for others; facilitation of empathy, compassion, and altruism (ECA):

    SMESPEX-ECA stim. int. inc. in prop. as mag. LC-ECA dec.
    and
    SMESPEX-ECA stim. int. dec. in prop. as mag. LC-ECA inc.

where SMESPEX-ECA stim. = stimulation of one or more neuroanatomic sites which specifically causes excitation of ECA toward others and LC-ECA — an LC which specifically characterizes the process or state of being empathic and/or compassionate and/or altruistic. Hence, the lower the intensity of an individual's ECA (and, correspondingly, the lower the magnitude of LC-ECA) and, correspondingly, the greater the degree of appropriateness of an increase in the intensity of that individual's ECA, the higher the intensity of ECA-excitatory (i.e., SMES-PEX-ECA) stimulation that would be automatically delivered in order to affect that increase. And the greater the intensity of spontaneous ECA, and the less the degree of appropriateness of an increase in ECA, the less SMESPEX-ECA stimulation would be delivered. One or more of approaches 1-4 and/or 1-4-like approaches would be appropriate for prophylaxis of antisocial including criminal behavior.

In cases in which the rudiments of and hence the potential for ECA were so pervasively lacking as to be noninducible by virtually any means, then it might be possible to affect prophylaxis of antisocial behavior by means of what could amount to arresting LCDBS affected by implementation of the phenomenon of cortical suppression (19), that is, suppression of spontaneous electrical activity of cortical area 4 (i.e., the motor cortex) and hence suppression of all movement by dint of the stimulation of specific suppressor areas of the cerebral cortex all of which have been demonstrated to project to the caudate nucleus. And inasmuch as when certain stimulation parameters were used, stimulation of the caudate in humans was found to be rewarding (20, 21), one might surmise that such movement-suppressive stimulation could be made both pleasurable and arresting. Whenever more than one LCDBS system were required, e.g., whenever criminal behavior is motivated by both sadism and anger or whenever a schizoaffective patient suffers from both active psychosis and depression, the two or more appropriate circuits would simply be operated in parallel with respect to each other.

EXAMPLES OF LCDBS SYSTEMS TO ENHANCE COGNITION AND PERFORMANCE

5. To improve learning ability or affect learning facilitation (LF) (22):

> PLE stim. int. inc. in prop. as mag. LC-LTM inc.
> and
> PLE stim. int. dec. in prop. as mag. LC-LTM dec.

where LC-LTM = a linked characteristic which always and only occurs during the formation of a long-term memory trace (LTM) in the individual in question, i.e., the subject. If it were not readily possible to identify the occurrence of an LC-LTM, then a more generalized kind of learning-linked characteristic (LLC) such as an LC-CONC which always and only occurs in the subject in question during high-level, sustained concentration, which might more readily be identified, could be used in place of LC-LTM in this paradigm, by dint of which the process of long-term memory trace formation (or the state of high-level, sustained concentration or some other learning-linked MESP) would become intensely pleasurable for the subject and therefore likely to occur readily, rapidly, and sustainedly. LF LCDBS methods would be based on the idea that if learning could be made intensely pleasurable, for example, at

least as pleasurable as eating and sexual activity are for most of us
after long periods of deprivation of these modes of gratification, we
would be able to tap into what for most of us are our greatly underde-
veloped intellectual potential. Even our IQ scores might gradually
rise, though probably not as rapidly or markedly as our actual demon-
strable learning ability. In view of the realization that some individuals are far more nearly hedonistically optimized with respect to
the learning process, that is, have far larger appetites for informational details than others do, it stands to reason that some individuals far more nearly attain to what may be considered their upper biological limits of intellectual functioning than others do. Hence, one
would not necessarily predict a very high correlation between pre- and
post-LF IQ scores. LF might prove to be of value not only for intel-
lectually normal individuals but also, as a treatment modality, for the
mentally retarded and for neurologically impaired individuals such as
aphasic stroke victims (in particular vis-a-vis relearning language
skills) and those afflicted with dementing processes such as Alzheimer's
Disease.

6. To create new interests or affect interests' diversification in a
person:

> PLE stim. int. inc. in prop. as mag. LC-ATUN inc.
> and
> PLE stim. int. dec. in prop. as mag. LC-ATUN dec.

where LC-ATUN = a linked characteristic which characterizes the process
of _attending_ (AT--) to details of a kind, for example, details of car
mechanics, robotics, or a foreign language, which would naturally, that
is, without LCDBS be _uninteresting_ (--UN) to the particular subject in
question. Hence, by dint of this modus operandi, attending to and processing information of a kind which would otherwise bore the individual
would become intensely pleasurable and therefore likely to occur.

7. To enhance performance of skills or affect performance enhancement
(PE):

> PLE stim. int. inc. in prop. as mag. LC-METT inc.
> and
> PLE stim. int. dec. in prop. as mag. LC-METT dec.

where LC-METT = an LC which characterizes metticulousness (METT).
Hence, the process of being metticulous would become intensely pleasurable and therefore likely to occur. By virtue of PE, working (like
learning, by virtue of LF) could be rendered as pleasurable as eating
and sexual activity are for most people. Consequently, productivity in
the context of work might dramatically increase.

8. To enhance creativity:

> PLE stim. int. inc. in prop. as mag. LC-CR inc.
> and
> PLE stim. int. dec. in prop. as mag. LC-CR dec.
> operated together with

SMESPIN-CRIN stim. int. inc. in prop. as mag. LC-CRIN inc.
and
SMESPIN-CRIN stim. int. dec. in prop. as mag. LC-CRIN dec.

where LC-CR = an LC which characterizes one or more creative processes such as might occur during dreaming when, unfortunately, under natural circumstances, that is, without brain stimulation, the individual's capability of converting concept into actuality is minimal, because he or she is immobilized by the sleep process. And SMESPIN-CRIN stim. = stimulation of neuroanatomic sites which specifically causes inhibition of the inhibition of these creative impulses which naturally occurs during the waking state in most people and is inherent in the perceptual and cognitive rigidity imposed by the conscious mind. And LC-CRIN = an LC which characterizes the naturally inhibited state of these impulses during the waking state.

THE ABOLITION OF SUFFERING WITHOUT COMPROMISE OF ADAPTIVENESS

The following example, entailing the simultaneous use of paradigms 9-11, suggests ways in which any and all suffering (e.g., anxiety, dyspnea, nausea) could be abolished without any compromise of its naturally associated adaptive value.

9. SMESPIN-POA/MP stim. int. inc. in prop. as mag. LC-POA/MP inc.
    and
    SMESPIN-POA/MP stim. int. dec. in prop. as mag. LC-POA/MP dec.
    together with, i.e., operated in parallel with
10. PLE stim. int. dec. in prop. as mag. LC-POA/MP inc.
    and
    PLE stim. int. inc. in prop. as mag. LC-POA/MP dec.
11. SMESPEX-AVOID stim. int. inc. in prop. as mag. LC-POA/MP inc.
    and
    SMESPEX-AVOID stim. int. dec. in prop. as mag. LC-POA/MP dec.

where POA = pain and other forms of bodily aversiveness, SMESPIN-POA/MP stim. = stimulation of neuroanatomic sites which causes inhibition of POA and MP. And SMESPEX-AVOID stim. = stimulation of neuroanatomic sites which causes excitation of avoidance or withdrawal behavior. LC-POA/MP = an LC which characterizes one or more kinds of POA and/or MP. With LCDBS systems 9 through 11 operating in parallel with respect to each other, the more closely a person's body were to approach or be approached by a noxious (i.e., LC-POA/MP-inducing) stimulus, the more strongly his or her POA and/or MP would be inhibited by paradigm 9, so that he or she would experience no pain (23, 24, 25), other bodily aversiveness or mental pain, and the less pleasure he or she would be gratified with by 10 (so that the person would be motivated to promptly move away from the noxious stimulus to a more highly gratifying distance from it), and the more strongly (what would effectively be reflex) avoidance or withdrawal behavior would be excited by paradigm 11.

One might object that the nullification of all pain and other aversiveness would undermine the diagnostic skills of internists and surgeons. A rebuttal to this objection is entailed in the realization that LC-POA/MP recording devices, LC-POA/MP-based alarm systems, etc.

could be used to monitor and record the time course of the intensity and anatomical distribution of POA- and MP-engendering pathophysiological processes (so that physicians would have precise and accurate records to refer to) and to inform physicians instantaneously of dangerously high intensities of these processes without the patient ever having to actually _experience_ any of the POA or MP.

Pharmacologic and LCDBS approaches could readily be made therapeutically complementary to each other as is suggested by the observations that some pharmacologic agents facilitate self-(administered-brain-) stimulation behavior (26). Some LCDBS systems might even entail a pharmacologic component in the form, for example, of an implanted reservoir of some medication from which a minute quantum thereof would be released with each pulse or after every predetermined number, e.g., 10 or 100, of pulses of brain stimulation. It is clear that precautions against overdosing would have to be built into such prosthetic systems.

CONCLUSIONS

If, at times, in what will hopefully prove to be the relatively utopian future, we should want to nullify all selfishness, egocentricity, and loneliness and render all of us (or as many as would want to participate) optimally altruistic, that is, precisely as concerned about each other as about ourselves, we could accomplish this by telemetrically interconnecting every reward and punishment site in every participant's brain with its neuroanatomic counterpart in every other participant's brain. We would thereby affect interindividual cerebral telemetric interconnectedness, IICTI, by virtue of which we could all truly and thoroughly share our joys and sorrows (if there were still any of the latter despite LCDBS and possibly other aversiveness-annihilatory approaches) with each other.

Ideally, the neurobiological basis of the capability of experiencing distress of any kind, that is, possibly, for example, modes of functioning of certain intraneuronal structures in certain areas of the brain, might be prevented from ever developing as such by means of the individual's brain's being subjected at one or more ontogenetically opportune times to certain drugs, electromagnetic or ultrasonic waves, recombinant repressor genes, antibodies, other immunological entities, or some combination thereof, directed against this neurobiological basis. Such prevention of development would be ideal because it would preclude even the potential for suffering.

The mind recognizes that there is a common denominator among the experiences of reading a book one enjoys, eating a food one enjoys, engaging in a favorite hobby or pastime, having sexual relations with a preferred partner, achieving a goal, etc.. That common denominator, of course, is pleasure. The fact that the mind experiences pleasure as a distinct entity despite the great diversity among the numerous contexts and forms in which it can occur, suggests that there is an electrophysiological process common to all of these contexts and forms which could be objectively detected and quantified as an LC for pleasure (LC-PLE). This LC could be used as a measure of any and all of the various kinds of pleasure one can have to enjoy such as happiness (which may be defined in the present context as pleasure which is consonant with one's idealism and/or aspirations), joy (which may be defined as pleasure which is anxiety-free and exhilarating), bodily or sensual pleasure, etc.. Hence, LC-PLE, cumulated or averaged over time or in some other form, could be used to derive a concept and a value of a person's positive aspects of subjective state of being.

Analogously, one would expect that all distressing or aversive experiences could be quantified in terms of an LC-AVERS which could serve as a measure of a person's negative aspects of subjective state of being. The measure of a person's overall subjective well-being (SWB) would be a function of both LC-PLE, which, being a positive quantity, would add to its value, and LC-AVERS, which, being a negative quantity, would subtract from its value. The standard deviation of the distribution of all of the SWB scores (SD-SWB) of everyone in the world or universe could serve as an index of the equitableness of the distribution of happiness and other aspects of SWB among the members of the population of the world or universe and, hence, as an index of the degree of actualization of the democratic principle. Inasmuch as from an objective standpoint each individual's SWB is equally as important as every other individual's SWB, the smaller the value of SD-SWB, the more equitable the distribution of SWB among the population.

Consistent with Bentham's ideal (27) of "the greatest happiness of the greatest number"' the quality of our world or universe (QW) could be assessed in terms of the ratio or quotient of the magnitude of the sum total of the SWB scores of everyone in the world or universe (SWB-TOTAL; the larger its value, the better) divided by SD-SWB (the smaller its value, the better).

$$QW = \frac{SWB\text{-}TOTAL}{SD\text{-}SWB}$$

In a similar way as the Dow Jones Index provides a means of assessing broad-based economic strength, this ratio, the QW, would provide a means of assessing broad-based (ideally universal) happiness and other aspects of SWB. It might also serve as a means of determining whether or not the lot of humankind were actually improving over time, that is, whether or not the changes which will come about in the world will actually be constructive. The larger the value of QW, the more worthwhile, humanistic, and heavenly we could consider our world to be.

REFERENCES

1. Flor-Henry P, Yeudall LT, Koles ZJ, Howarth BG. Neuropsychological and power spectral EEG investigations of the obsessive-compulsive syndrome. Biological Psychiatry 14(1); 119-130, February 1979.

2. Morihisa JM, Duffy FH, Wyatt RJ. Brain electrical activity mapping (BEAM) in schizophrenic patients. Archives of General Psychiatry 40; 719-728, July 1983.

3. Shagass C, Roemer RA, Straumanis JJ. Relationships between psychiatric diagnosis and some quantitative EEG variables. Archives of

General Psychiatry 39: 1423-1435, December 1982.

4. Stevens JR, Livermore A. Telemetered EEG in schizophrenia: spectral analysis during abnormal behavioral episodes. Journal of Neurology, Neurosurgery, and Psychiatry 45(5): 385-395, May 1982.

5. Stigsby B, Risberg J, Ingvar DH. Electroencephalographic changes in the dominant hemisphere during memorizing and reasoning. Electroencephalography and Clinical Neurophysiology 42(5): 665-675, May 1977.

6. Tucker DM, Stenslie CE, Roth RS, Shearer SL. Right frontal lobe activation and right hemisphere performance: decrement during a depressed mood. Archives of General Psychiatry 38(2): 169-174, February 1981.

7. Wogan M, Moore SF, Epro R, Harner RN. EEG measures of alternative strategies used by subjects to solve block designs. International Journal of Neuroscience 12: 25-28, 1981.

8. Gavriloy LR. Use of focused ultrasound for stimulation of nerve structures. Ultrasonics 22: 132-138, May 1984.

9. Brown RP, Kneeland B. Visual imaging in psychiatry. Hospital and Community Psychiatry 36(5): 489-496, May 1985.

10. Mancini L. The prospect of a noninvasive brain stimulator. In progress.

11. Sem-Jacobsen CW. Effects of electrical stimulation on the human brain. Electroencephalography and Clinical Neurophysiology 11: 379, 1959.

12. Heath RG. Pleasure response of human subjects to direct stimulation of the brain: physiologic and psychodynamic considerations. p 219-243 in The Role of Pleasure in Behavior (RG Heath, ed) Harper & Row, New York, 1964.

13. Moan C, Heath RG. Septal stimulation for the initiation of heterosexual behavior in a homosexual male. Journal of Behavior Therapy and Experimental Psychiatry 3(1): 23-30, March 1972.

14. Higgins JW, Mahl GF, Delgado JMR, Hamlin H. Behavioral changes during intracerebral electrical stimulation. A.M.A. Archives of Neurology and Psychiatry 76: 399-419, 1956.

15. Holt L, Gray JA. Septal driving of the hippocampal theta rhythm produces a long-term, proactive and non-associative increase in resistance to extinction. Quarterly Journal of Experimental Psychology: Comparative & Physiological Psychology 35B(2): 97-118, May 1983.

16. Heath RG, Walker CF. Correlation of deep and surface electroencephalograms with psychosis and hallucinations in schizophrenics: a report of two cases. Biological Psychiatry 20: 669-674, 1985.

17. White FJ, Wang RY. Differential effects of classical and atypical antipsychotic drugs on A9 and A10 dopamine neurons. Science 221: 1054-1057, September 1983.

18. Stein L, Belluzzi JD, Ritter S, Wise CD. Self-stimulation reward

pathways: norepinephrine vs dopamine. Journal of Psychiatric Research 11: 115-124, 1974.

19. Carpenter MB. Human Neuroanatomy (7th ed) p 589. Williams & Wilkins, Baltimore, 1976.

20. Heath RG. Electrical self-stimulation of the brain in man. American Journal of Psychiatry 120(6): 571-577, 1963.

21. Bishop MP, Elder ST, Heath RG. Intracranial self-stimulation in man. Science 140 (whole no. 3565): 394-396, 1963.

22. Mancini L. How learning ability might be improved by brain stimulation. Speculations in Science and Technology 5(1) (correspondence): 51-53, 1982.

23. Boivie J, Meyerson BA. A correlative anatomical and clinical study of pain suppression by deep brain stimulation. Pain 13(2): 113-126, June 1982.

24. Hosobuchi Y. Periaqueductal gray stimulation in humans produces analgesia accompanied by elevation of beta-endorphin and ACTH in ventricular CSF. Modern Problems in Pharmacopsychiatry. 17: 109-122, 1981.

25. Plotkin R. Deep-brain stimulation for the treatment of intractable pain. South African Journal of Surgery 19(4): 153-155, December 1980.

26. Jacques S. Brain stimulation and reward: "pleasure centers" after twenty-five years. Neurosurgery 5(2): 277-283, 1979.

27. Rader M. Ethics and the Human Community, chapter 3 p 91. Holt, Rinehart, & Winston, New York, 1964.

Medical Hypotheses

Medical Hypotheses (1992) 38, 350–351
© Longman Group UK Ltd 1992

Short Note
Ultrasonic Antidepressant Therapy Might be More Effective Than Electroconvulsive Therapy (ECT) in Treating Severe Depression

L. S. MANCINI

ECT is widely acknowledged as an effective treatment for severe depression (1), but its drawbacks of entailing a seizure, general anesthesia, post-ictal confusion and memory disturbance can be problematical to the extent of preventing some patients from undergoing the treatments often enough to sustain relief. According to Higgins et al (2), stimulation of specific points on the surface of the temporal lobes reliably produces a pleasure response without causing a seizure, confusion or memory impairment. Due to reciprocal inhibition between the brain's reward and punishment pathways (3), such a response might be expected to relieve depression. Work done by Velling and Shklyaruk with animals, specifically rabbits, (4) suggests that much stimulation could be produced in humans through the intact skull and scalp by using ultrasound focused from outside of the head. Ultrasound transducers contained in water-filled, bag-like stimulators, like those used by Gavrilov (5) to stimulate auditory nerves through intact skull, when placed in contact with the outside of the head, would eliminate the need for conductive gel, which can be messy. Since there would be no pain or other tactile sensation, anaesthesia would be unnecessary. Hence, externally-focused ultrasound could provide the same benefit as ECT, that is, relief of depression, without

any of the drawbacks. And since the frequenc treatments would not be limited by these complic factors, the therapeutic effects could be better tained over time and, therefore, more effective. A tionally, the basic approach of Velling and Shkly could possibly be adapted for many other analg and therapeutic clinical applications such as treatr of pain, nausea and insomnia.

Acknowledgements

The author wishes to acknowledge with gratitude the encoui ment and support of Drs Robert A. Spangler, Michael R. Privi Nicholas J. LoCascio, C. Timothy Golumbeck, Louise A. Jai son, Elizabeth Kelly-Fry, Robert J. Lanigan, Richard T. Mil Anthony A. Pace and Erica E. Wanecski.

References

1. Ahuja N. What's wrong with ECT? American Journal of I chiatry 148, 5: 693–4, 1991.
2. Higgins J W, Mahl G F, Delgado J M R, Hamlin H. Bel ioral changes during intracerebral electrical stimulation. AI Archives of Neurology and Psychiatry 76: 399–419, 195€
3. Stein L, Belluzzi J D, Ritter S, Wise C D. Self-stimulation ward pathways: norepinephrine vs dopamine. Journal of F chiatric Research 11: 115–124, 1974.
4. Velling V A, Shklyaruk S P. Modulation of the functional st

Date received 8 November 1991
Date accepted 10 February 1991

of the brain with the aid of focused ultrasonic action. Neuroscience and Behavioral Physiology 18, 5: 369–75, 1988.

5. Gavrilov L R. Use of focused ultrasound for stimulation of nerve structures. Ultrasonics 22, 3: 132–8, 1984.

Medical Hypotheses

Medical Hypotheses (1992) 38, 349
© Longman Group UK Ltd 1992

Short Note
A Magnetic Choke-Saver Might Relieve Choking

L. S. MANCINI

When a person is choking on a piece of food and there is acute obstruction of the airway so that s(he) cannot breathe, the Heimlich maneuver or procedure can be effective in relieving the emergency (1). However, if someone were choking while dining alone or not in the company of anyone adequately skillful in the application of this maneuver, the problem might be solvable by means of a slight modification of a magnetic device (2) which is currently used in neurology, pneumonology and urology. It is used in these three fields, respectively, to assess disorder of the motor system, to measure diaphragmatic strength and to assess bladder and pelvic floor function. The device is a magnetic nerve stimulator which can stimulate deep or otherwise inaccessible nerves painlessly, contactlessly and without any need for removal of clothing. The stimulating coil is merely held in place either next to or a few millimeters away from the area of the body to be stimulated. With as little as perhaps 20% more power than that provided by currently available models, the stimulating coil could relieve choking by stunning the neuromuscular apparatus of the pharynx or larynx in such a way that it would momentarily relax and thereby release the food bolus and allow it to become reoriented so as to either be ejected, pass on down through the esophagus to the stomach or, in the worst case, down through the trachea into the lungs, in which case it would subsequently have to be removed in a clinical setting, perhaps by a nonsurgical,

noninvasive technique involving suction. In any case, the emergency of being in danger of choking to death would be relieved as a result of application of the coil to the neck area. One way of demonstrating that the suggested method would be effective would be to test it on animals with obstructed airways whose temporal lobes were being pleasurably stimulated with ultrasound, as described in another paper (3), through the intact skull and scalp, so they would experience none of the distress or pain a human feels when s(he) accidentally chokes.

Acknowledgements

The author wishes to acknowledge with gratitude the encouragement and support of Drs Robert A. Spangler, Nicholas J. T. LoCascio, Catherine Hall LoCascio, Michael R. Privitera, Erica E. Wanecski, Anthony V. Ambrose, Kenyon A. Riches, William and Denise Appel and his family.

References

1. Heimlich H J. A life-saving maneuver to prevent food-choking. JAMA 234: 398, 1975.
2. Barker A T, Freeston I L, Jalinous R, Jarratt J A. Magnetic stimulation of the human brain and peripheral nervous system: an introduction and the results of an initial clinical evaluation. Neurosurgery 20, 1: 100–9, 1987.
3. Mancini L S. Ultrasonic antidepressant therapy would be more effective than electroconvulsive therapy (ECT) in treating severe depression. Medical Hypotheses 38: 350-1.

Date received 22 November 1991
Date accepted 10 February 1992

Medical Hypotheses

Medical Hypotheses (1990) 31, 201–207

0306–9877/90/0031–0201$10.00

Riley-Day Syndrome, Brain Stimulation and the Genetic Engineering of a World Without Pain

L. S. MANCINI

Abstract — Riley-Day Syndrome, a genetic disorder in which there is impaired ability or inability to feel pain, hot and cold, is cited as an example of evidence that the commonplace notion that life cannot be painless is not necessarily valid. A hypothesis is presented to the effect that everything adaptive which is achievable with a mind capable of experiencing varying degrees of both pleasure and pain (the human condition as we know it) could be achieved with a mind capable of experiencing only varying degrees of pleasure. Two possible approaches whereby the human mind could be rendered painless are a schematically-outlined genetic approach, which would or will probably take thousands of years to implement, and a brain stimulation approach that could be effected by means of a noninvasive, contactless, transcranial, deep-neuroanatomic-site-focusable, electromagnetic and/or ultrasonic (and/or, conceivably, other kind of) brain pacemaker which could be developed within a few years. In order to expedite the relief of all kinds of suffering and the improvement of the human condition in general, it is advocated that prompt and concerted research effort be directed toward the development of such a brain pacemaker.

Introduction

In this article the concept of pain should be construed in its broadest sense. It should be thought of not merely as bodily suffering but rather as any unpleasant or distressing experience, whether it be of bodily pain, nausea, dyspnea, pruritus, hunger, thirst, fear (anxiety), depression, anger, etc. Most people seem to regard pain as a necessary evil of life. Such rationalizations as 'no pain, no gain', which are widely invoked, may be adaptive in terms of helping one to deal with life's current reality, but this does not mean they are or will prove to be insurmountably valid for all time. On the contrary, one will find that the people who are the most productive and efficient at their work tend to be the ones who enjoy it the most.

Or people will ask, 'How would you be able to recognize pleasure if you never experienced pain?' On the contrary, one does not need to have been tortured in order to enjoy fine music or fine dining. Or people will contend that happiness is a matter of free will. In effect, those who are happy are so because they choose and work to be. Those who are unhappy are so because they do not choose or work to be happy. However, in view of the now well-documented biological and, in some cases, hereditary bases of many of the depressive, anxiety, and psychotic disorders, to say nothing of adverse external circumstances such as the occurrence of natural disasters, over which one cannot possibly (except, conceivably, superstitiously) have any control, any self-deterministic theory of happiness level seems seriously flawed or altogether incredible.

Or people will rationalize: 'If you were happy all the time, then you would be bored'. On the contrary, this statement makes no sense, because happiness and boredom are mutually exclusive states. If one were to consider only the happiest (the most enthusiastic and contented) one or two percent of the human population, it would be surprising if one would find that these people spend even a small fraction of their time being bored. Hence, even given the existing state of affairs, it is not necessarily humanly impossible to be happy most of the time. Some electrophysiological ways in which pleasure and pain could be measured and quantified are suggested below.

Riley-Day Syndrome

A rare genetic disorder known as Riley-Day Syndrome or familial dysautonomia, i.e. FD (1, 2, 3, 4), which has an autosomal recessive means of transmission, was first identified in 1949. It occurs almost exclusively in descendants of the Eastern European Ashkenazy branch of Judaism, although it has been diagnosed occasionally in members of other religious, ethnic, and/or racial groups.

The syndrome is evident from the time of birth in terms of difficulty in feeding, episodes of unexplained fever and pneumonia, and failure to thrive. Its symptoms and signs as a life-long disorder include defective lacrimation with an inability to shed tears when crying, corneal ulceration, absent corneal, axonal, and tendon reflexes, unstable blood pressure with episodes of hypertension and postural hypotension, unstable body temperature, vomiting spasms, profuse sweating, sialorrhea, impairment of vestibular function, repeated infections, an initial delay in mental development (with the subsequent achievement of intellectual parity with one's peers by age 4), difficulty or inability to suck or chew with impaired pharyngeal and esophageal motility, esophageal and intestinal dilation, absence of taste buds or fungiform papillae with inability to taste food, a marked tendency to develop symmetric blotchy erthematous skin rashes, especially in connection with eating or emotional stress, emotional lability with a nervous system which is unstable in the sense that strong emotions, whether pleasing or distressing, frequently lead to episodes of loss of consciousness, stunted growth and, most significantly from the standpoint of this article, an impaired ability or *inability* to feel pain, and an impaired ability or inability to feel (or distinguish between) hot and cold, although there is relative preservation of pressure and tactile sense.

The syndrome is considered to represent a disturbance of both sensory and autonomic functions, both parasympathetic and sympathetic. Compared to individuals who are not afflicted with the syndrome (i.e., neurologically normal individuals), there is a diminution in the number of sympathetic and parasympathetic ganglion cells and, to a lesser degree, in the number of nerve cells in the sensory ganglia. There is a paucity of small myelinated and unmyelinated nerve fibers, which explains the impairment of temperature and pain sensation. There is increased excretion of homovanillic acid and decreased excretion of vanillylmandelic acid and methoxyhydroxyphenylglycol. There is also an abnormally low concentration of serum dopamine beta-hydroxylase, the enzyme that converts dopamine to norepinephrine.

There are about 300 known cases in the United States, but the true incidence, which would amount to a larger number, among American Jews, is estimated to lie between 1 in 10 000 and 1 in 20 000 with a carrier frequency of 1 in 50 to 1 in 70. According to Bundey and Brett (1), 25% of afflicted children are dead by age 10 and 50% by age 20, usually as a result of pulmonary problems secondary to bronchial hypersecretion or inhalation of stomach contents during attacks of vomiting. Apparently due to consciousness-raising brought about by the New York based Dysautonomia Foundation and the concerted efforts of a pediatrician, Dr. Felicia Axelrod (2), who has centered her life's work on FD, improved supportive and symptomatic treatment has resulted in more afflicted children surviving to adulthood. Nonetheless, so far no one known to have this condition has survived beyond the fifth decade of life. There is, as yet, no definitive treatment.

Although FD probably originated well before its date of initial identification (1949), it is at least ironic that a genetic condition involving an inability to experience bodily pain would emerge primarily among a group of people who had been subjected, unfortunately and unpardonably (over a period of centuries or millennia), to extraordinary amounts of pain (which culminated) only a few years earlier, during the heinous period of Nazi domination connected with World War II (2, 3, 5).

The underlying implications of Riley-Day Syndrome

Although from a superficial standpoint the existence of FD as a disease entity may seem to underscore the indispensability of pain to the processes whereby an organism adapts to its environment, closer scrutiny will reveal that this indispensability may be more illusory and circumstantial than it is real and immutable. The most important point to be deduced from FD is that life without a phenomenon which most of us assume is an unavoidable part of life (that is, the capability of experiencing bodily pain) is not only conceivable but actually occurs in some cases. If FD did not exist, it would be easier for anyone to claim that life without the capability of experiencing bodily pain is an impossibility.

If the genetic modification which underlies FD can result in a life without bodily pain, then it is quite conceivable that other genetic modifications could result in lives devoid of the capabilities of experiencing any and all other forms of pain, including everything from nausea to frustration and hostility (variants or subtypes of anger).

In fact, there is another condition, even rarer than FD, known as congenital indifference to pain (1), in which the individual does recognize a painful stimulus as such but perceives it as no more distressing than a touch or a tickle, that is, not distressing at all. These patients can learn to take precautions that will minimize the possibility of trauma. So far, the nervous systems of such individuals have not been shown to be abnormal in any way (1). Nonetheless, this condition of lifelong unreactivity to pain does appear to adhere to a genetic pattern of inheritance, in some cases autosomal dominant, in others autosomal

recessive. Because it appears to be possible to compensate adaptively for this condition, it would appear to be a better candidate for genetic modeling for a painless world than FD, but it too leaves much to be desired, both because it tends to be maladaptive and because it does not preclude forms of pain other than the distress of bodily pain.

How life could be painless without being maladaptive

Let us now broach the question of how, in psychodynamic terms, we could go through life as adaptively (or more so, and certainly more enjoyably) without the capability of experiencing any kind of pain as we do in our current condition of being equipped with that capability. For example, if we did not have anxiety — specifically, the fear of getting killed — what would prevent us from driving our cars into the oncoming traffic? An answer is as follows. We would not want to genetically engineer ourselves so that we would be rid of the anxious impulses that deter our driving into traffic without putting anything adaptive in their place. However, what could adaptively be put in place of these anxious impulses would be pleasure-diminishing impulses with or without the added adaptive benefit of reflexly avoidant impulses. Hence, rather than producing pain (anxiety), the thought or anticipation of the possibility of driving into oncoming traffic would produce a marked diminution of the high level of baseline pleasure, with or without an accompanying unconsciously motivated reflexive avoidance response, which would prevent the injurious behavior just as reliably as the anxiety currently does. The option of having unconscious reflex avoidance associated with any perception of potential danger, while not strictly necessary in terms of protective motivational wherewithal, might facilitate faster reaction times (because less interneuronal processing would be entailed) than would pleasure diminution alone associated with any perception of danger.

Furthermore, a proportional factor could be built into the system (the genetically engineered mind) so that the more dangerous the situation (for example, the closer one's actual position to the oncoming traffic), the more marked the diminution of pleasurable impulses (and, possibly, the stronger the unconsciously-motivated avoidance responses) would be.

By generalizing from this example, it is

possible to appreciate that everything adaptive which can be achieved with a mind capable of experiencing varying degrees of both pleasure and pain (the current human condition) could be achieved with a mind capable of experiencing only varying degrees of pleasure or a mind capable of experiencing such pleasure simultaneously with varying intensities of unconsciously mediated avoidance behavior. The possibility of leading a strictly painless yet adaptive life would constitute an improved human condition.

This improved condition could be achieved in either one of two different ways, with each of them having its respective pros and cons. One way in which it could possibly be achieved would be with a contactless, noninvasive, transcranial brain pacemaker which could also be called a noninvasive neuroprosthesis or brain stimulator. The essence of the method whereby brain pacemaking or brain stimulation could be used to effect the improved human condition is delineated in another paper (6) and, therefore, need not be repeated here.

Brain stimulation experiments done on animals confirm the widely acknowledged point that 'stress kills' which is to say that the unpleasant aspect of stress or distress affects organisms adversely not only in terms of the quality of life, but also in terms of the duration of life. Prolonged unconditional, unavoidable stimulation, lasting 24 hours or more, of areas within an animal's brain which cause the animal to show all of the signs of extreme distress (i.e., 'punishment centers', areas to which an animal will promptly terminate stimulation if given the means to do so) has been observed to actually cause the animal to become severely ill and die (7). Perhaps needless to say, such experiments are horrendously cruel and, while carrying out such experiments even once is unconscionable regardless of the extent to which scientific knowledge might be augmented thereby, certainly should never be done again.

How genetic engineering could be used to effect a painless improved human condition

There is currently a good deal of speculation and controversy regarding the prospect of mapping and sequencing the entire human genome. Dr. Leroy Hood, a pioneer in the field of biotechnology (8), estimates that 'it will take us at least

hundreds of years to decipher the multitude of messages contained in the human genome.'

We know that some people have a low threshold of pain and other people have a high threshold of pain. And this would seem to be true regardless of what kind of pain we are talking about. It is also quite likely, as is exemplified by FD, that there is a strong genetic basis for the height of a person's threshold for any kind of pain. Let us consider two different kinds of people. The first kind of people become greatly distressed when confronted with adverse circumstances and only tolerably placated when confronted with favorable circumstances. Let us describe these people as *pain-dominated* (PAD). The other kind of people become only mildly displeased when confronted with adverse circumstances and become greatly elated when confronted with favorable circumstances. Let us describe these people as *pleasure-dominated* (PLD).

The majority of most present-day populations would fall somewhere in between the two extremes of being PAD and PLD. However, let us suppose that for any given person there is some electrophysiologically discernible characteristic (of the computerized-spectral-analyzed electroencephalogram or EEG, magnetoencephalogram or MEG, electromyogram or EMG, or whatever) which can be detected whenever the person is experiencing any kind of pleasure. This characteristic can be referred to as the pleasure characteristic (PLC). Because the mind gives the same 'pleasurable' label to all different kinds of pleasure (in other words, the mind is aware of both the differences and the fundamental *similarity* among the various different kinds of pleasure), it makes sense that there would be some potentially electrophysiologically-detectable, common denominator of all of them. Similarly, suppose that for any given person there is some electrophysiologically discernible characteristic which can be detected whenever the person is experiencing any kind of pain. This can be called the pain characteristic (PAC).

Then, by measuring any person's amplitudes, duration, and frequency of occurrence of PLC and PAC, one could determine whether the person is more PLD or more PAD. If we were to measure and record the PLC and PAC values for every person in a population over a period of time, we would then be able to identify both those who are extremely PLD and those who are extremely PAD. Suppose the 1% of the population who are most PLD (1%-PLD) and the 1% who are most PAD (1%-PAD) have been isolated. One would probably then be able to verify that the 1%-PLD and the 1%-PAD groups, respectively, (approximately, at least after individual differences in stress exposure have been taken into account) constitute or at least correlate positively with the 1% of the population with the highest and lowest pain thresholds. Using some arbitrary scale of pain threshold, suppose the average pain threshold value of the 1%-PLD group is 100 and the corresponding value for the 1%-PAD group is 10. After the task of having sequenced the entire human genome has been completed, suppose we move on to the task of sequencing each person's entire genome or, at least, for the purpose in question here, the task of sequencing the genome of each person in either of these two 1% subpopulations.

One should then look for systematic differences between the DNA sequences of the 1%-PLD group and the 1%-PAD group. The likelihood seems high that there would be at least one common denominator, or possibly a number of different patterns of common denominator(s), of DNA sequencing among the 1%-PLD group (PLD-DNA) and at least one common denominator (different from PLD-DNA) of DNA sequencing among the 1%-PAD group (PAD-DNA). Then, by noting the trend of differences between the DNA-sequence common denominator patterns for the pleasure-dominated group and the DNA-sequence common denominator patterns for the pain-dominated group, one could possibly extrapolate a DNA sequence common denominator that would characterize people with an ultra-high pain threshold of, for example, 1000. Let us refer to this extrapolated sequence as a super-pleasure-dominated DNA or super PLD-DNA sequence. Anyone with such a DNA sequence in her or his genome would have a very high (possibly higher than any level or value which nature, unassisted, has bestowed upon anyone) threshold of pain, perhaps comparably as high for all kinds of pain as the thresholds for mechanical and thermal pain of the prototypical FD sufferer, which could mean unreachably high for all kinds of pain.

Any individual with the extrapolated DNA sequence in his or her genome might actually still be mildly pleased (or have a neutral affect) when confronted with adverse circumstances and would undoubtedly be joyously elated when confronted with favorable circumstances. Such an individual

could never experience any pain. Her/his mood could only vary between neutral affect when confronted with catastrophic circumstances (but the pleasure-seeking nature of all organisms, regardless of height of pain threshold, would still motivate such a person to do whatever possible to calmly undo or compensate for catastrophic circumstances), and joyous elation when confronted with even the ordinary homeostasis-conducive circumstances, such as the pervasiveness of ample amounts of oxygen for the purpose of breathing, which most of us take for granted.

Then, one could implement in vitro genetic engineering by microinjecting every fertilized human egg with the recombinant super PLD-DNA sequence(s) that would replace the existing homologous (mediocre) PLD-DNA and/or PAD-DNA sequence(s) so that all humans born after the perfection of the recombinant super PLD-DNA sequence microinjection technique would have a pain threshold of approximately 1000 and be unable to experience pain of any kind.

Or, when and if in vivo genetic transformation techniques are ever perfected, whereby every cell in the body of a living organism at any stage in its life span can simultaneously undergo homologous insertion of any desired recombinant DNA sequence encoding for any desired gene(s) coupled with the deletion of the homologous less desirable DNA sequence encoding for any less desirable gene(s), then all individuals alive at the time of the achievement of such technical capability, regardless of their age at that time, could be converted from being PAD or PLD type people to being super-pleasure-dominated people incapable of experiencing pain of any kind.

But what if these elation-prone, super-pleasure-dominated genetic transformers with unreachably high pain thresholds prove to be aimlessly and recklessly euphoric, like many present-day psychiatric patients who are afflicted with mania, as in manic-depressive illness? Such individuals would have little or no inclination toward concerted, constructive, and productive activities (i.e., learning and working; work that is of value to society), and a marked inclination toward consumptive or libidinal activities such as wild spending sprees, gambling, alcohol abuse, sexual indiscretion, overeating, etc. Even though they would be incapable of suffering, they would be relegated to relatively unfulfilling, hence dull, minimally pleasurable lives, because nothing and no one would reward them for their unproductivity. Their lives would be devoid of a sense of purpose, which is essential to happiness. They would be a burden to society and to themselves. Their problems could be solved by implementing methods whereby their vast potential pleasure could be actualized and harnessed or channeled into constructive, productive, adaptive activities and pursuits.

One way of doing this would be by implementing the brain stimulation paradigms delineated in another paper (6), whereby learning and working could be made at least as pleasurable and probably (by dint of the intrinsic pleasurableness of diversification of knowledge and skills) more pleasurable than consumptive or libidinal activities.

Another way, a genetic way, of accomplishing this would be by looking for and isolating common denominators of DNA sequencing that characteristically are present within the genomes of individuals (regardless of whether they are PLD or PAD) who do function productively and adaptively. And then, by in vivo insertion of the productivity-/adaptiveness-characteristic DNA sequences into every cell in the bodies of these unproductive, maladaptive super PLD individuals, which would effect homologous replacement of DNA sequences encoding for unproductive, maladaptive tendencies with DNA sequences encoding for productive, adaptive tendencies, they could convert themselves from pleasureless, painless, unproductive members of society into elated, productive members thereof. Hence, the goal of adaptive, painless, and pleasurable living could be achieved genetically as well as by brain stimulation.

The pros and cons of the two different approaches

The genetic engineering approach to achieving painless living would be the definitive one, far superior to brain pacemaking, primarily because, with the former, the individual would not have to be dependent upon or encumbered with external gadgetry or subject to conceivable side effects of long-term brain stimulation. However, the drawback of the genetic approach is that it may take a very long time, perhaps thousands of years, to implement. Such amounts of time would certainly make sense on the time scale of Dr. Hood. In sharp contrast to this greatly extended time scale, noninvasive, contactless brain stimulation or pacemaking, which could be used to accomplish essentially the same goal, that of

painless yet adaptive living, could be developed within a few years. Dr. Robert G. Heath, a pioneer in the use of surgically implanted electrodes to effect neuropsychiatrically relevant brain stimulation, has indicated that an ultrasound-emitting device could be built (ostensibly as early as any time between the present moment and the early part of the 21st century) which could activate the brain's 'pleasure centers' without having to go inside the skull. And, in line with his claim is a prediction that, by the year 2005, family physicians will be using such a device on a routine therapeutic basis (9).

All of the technological ingredients that would have to be brought together in order to construct such a device already appear to exist. The combined use of electromagnetism and ultrasound (as opposed to ultrasound alone), as suggested by W. J. Fry (10) and affirmed by his brother, F. J. Fry (11), might more readily facilitate the goal of developing a contactless, noninvasive brain pacemaker capable of exciting or suppressing any small or large area(s) in the living human brain. The principal drawbacks of brain pacemaking would be that it would entail the possibility of periodic equipment failure or malfunctioning, the burden (even if a very small, light-weight one) of having to carry around a pacemaker wherever one wanted to go while still having the benefit of its use, and the possibility of some as yet undetermined side-effect(s) which, according to the observations of Barker et al (12), are unlikely to prove prohibitive.

Genetic engineering could enable each person to be whatever s(he) wants whenever s(he) wants

Dr. Hood also predicts (13) that 'It isn't that [through genetic engineering] we'll be able to design individuals whose intelligence is increased by a factor of three. It isn't that we'll be able to change physical attractiveness or emotional stability.' Given the virtually universal human motive toward self-improvement, it appears doubtful that this prediction will prevail through the extent of time. Let us not think in the authoritarian terms of some individuals genetically engineering the characteristics of others. Instead, let us think in the egalitarian terms of each individual genetically re-engineering herself/himself according as s(he) pleases. What is being suggested here is that in the distant future, by means of in vivo genetic transformation techniques effected with recombinant DNA or some other biotechnological tool(s), it will be possible for any person (or other kind of organism) to be an introverted, academically-oriented, purple-haired, orange-eyed, 10 foot tall white male with an IQ of 160 on any given day and a party-going, humorous, green-haired, green-eyed, three foot tall green female with an IQ of 200 on the next day. Stated in more general terms, it will become possible for each one of us (that is, anyone alive during the future era in question) to be whatever we want to be whenever we want to be. Some of us may choose to take a DNA pill that will cause us to sprout a pair of wings whenever an automobile is not readily available to us. Granted: all of this may be thousands of years away, but compared to the eternity that stretches ahead, the amount of time in question is minuscule.

Some may object that if each of us were able to change our mental and/or physical characteristics at any given time, then the notion of individual identity would be essentially lost. Undoubtedly, the objection is at least partly valid (however, the philosophical implications will not be delved into here), but the advantages of such a greatly augmented arena of potential endeavor would seem to greatly outweigh the disadvantages. In a world equipped with virtually instantaneous, or at least high-speed, self-determined in vivo genetic transformation, no one would ever have any reason to feel inferior to or less fortunate than anyone else, because whatever characteristic(s) one might envy in another person, one could incorporate into one's own being almost as quickly as the envious impulses could emerge. Hence, the ideal of all humans being equal could be realized in terms of each individual having the same (infinitely variable) genetic potential. If this were the case, both egotism and the competitive spirit would become extinct, but their disappearance from the world really would not be a substantial loss; in fact, it would be a gain for everyone.

Conclusion

In the meantime, that is, the intervening thousands of years between now and the successful implementation of genetic engineering techniques which might create the possibility of painless living, it would be advisable to develop a brain pacemaker and then to determine whether or not its drawbacks could be eliminated or minimized to a tolerable level. Moreover, as one of its virtually limitless potential therapeutic applications, it is conceivable that such a pacemaker, by suppressing maladaptive neuronal impulses (such as those underlying the vomiting attacks) and by exciting adaptive impulses (such as those that could underlie better coordinated pharyngeal and esophageal motility during eating), could provide more effective therapy for Riley-Day Syndrome than any that is currently available by minimizing or eliminating such problems as the aspiration of vomitus, impaired eating ability, etc.

References

1. Bundey S, Brett E M. Genetics and Neurology. p 206. Churchill Livingstone, Edinburgh, 1985.
2. Axelrod F B, Sein M E. Caring for the Child with Familial Dysautonomia — a Treatment Manual. Dysautonomia Foundation Inc., New York, 1982.
3. Adams R D, Victor M. Principles of Neurology. 3rd edition, p 991. McGraw-Hill, New York, 1985.
4. Axelrod F B. Report on the Dysautonomia Research Symposium. Dysautonomia Foundation Inc., New York, May, 1987.
5. Chusid J G. Correlative Neuroanatomy and Functional Neurology. 16th edition, p 148. Lange Medical Publications, Los Altos, California, 1976.
6. Mancini L. Brain stimulation to treat mental illness and enhance human learning, creativity, performance, altruism, and defenses against suffering. Medical Hypotheses 21: 209–219, 1986.
7. Guyton A C. Textbook of Medical Physiology. 7th edition, p 680. W. B. Saunders Company, Philadelphia, 1986.
8. Hood L. Biotechnology and medicine of the future. The Journal of the American Medical Association, March 25: 1837–1844, 1988.
9. Clarke A C. July 20, 2019, Life in the 21st Century, p 223. Macmillan Publishing Company, New York, 1986.
10. Fry W J. Electrical stimulation of brain localized without probes — theoretical analysis of a proposed method. The Journal of the Acoustical Society of America 44, 4: 919–931, 1968.
11. Fry F J, personal communication, May 27, 1987.
12. Barker A T, Freeston I L, Jalinous R, Jarratt J A. Magnetic stimulation of the human brain and peripheral nervous system: an introduction and the results of an initial clinical evaluation. Neurosurgery 20, 1: 100–109, 1987.
13. Davis J. Leroy Hood: automated genetic profiles. Omni, November: 116–156, 1987.

REPRINTED FROM

Speculations in

Science and

Technology

Letter to the Editor

A proposed method of pleasure-inducing biofeedback using ultrasound stimulation of brain structures to enhance selected EEG states

Lewis S. Mancini

A non-invasive method of stimulating human brain structures to induce pleasure involving focused ultrasound waves is proposed. Such a device, in combination with an EEG analysed for desirable mental states, could be used to enhance thinking, ameliorate neuroses and treat chronic pain.

The seeking of pleasure and the avoidance of pain are perhaps the root behavioural mechanisms in humans. It is proposed that a device which analyses an EEG for specific patterns and stimulates, through a non-invasive technique, the pleasure centres of the brain when a desired pattern is achieved would be useful in enhancing thought, overcoming neuroses and in treating chronic pain.

The novel mechanism in such a device would be an ultrasound beam focused from outside of the skull onto a key area of the subject's brain. Research in the former Soviet Union by Velling and Shklyaruk[1] has shown that a focused ultrasound beam is capable of selectively stimulating neuron activity in localised areas of animal brains. Velling and Shklyaruk found that ultrasonic waves in the intensity of 1–100 mW cm^{-2} and of a duration of more than one second led to increased bioelectrical activity in the brains of cats and rabbits. The effects were reversible; *i.e.* no permanent damage was detected. It is postulated the mechanism of the ultrasound's action may be a change in the permeability of neuron membranes through elastic deformation of the membranes.

A hypothetical ultrasound setup could be adapted to stimulate the septal area of the human brain, inducing a pleasurable response and an increased level of consciousness. Heath[2] reported that electrical stimulation of electrodes implanted directly in the brains of 54 schizophrenic and epileptic patients led to pleasurable responses in most patients when the septal area was stimulated. Other areas inducing positive feelings were the medial forebrain bundle and the interpenduncular nuclei of the mesencephalic tegmentum. With septal stimulation the patients brightened, looked more alert, and seemed to be more attentive to their environment..." Heath reported.

Heath also found ".... (S)triking and immediate relief from intractable physical pain" when the septal region was stimulated in six patients with advanced cancer. This result suggests that the proposed ultrasound device might be useful in the management of chronic pain. Heath also speculated that stimulation of the septal region might help people with neuroses overcome patterns of experiencing 'emergency' emotions during normal situations.

Ultrasonic stimulation of the septal region would not necessarily be merely a new avenue into meaningless hedonistic play without a serious purpose attached. The author suggests that an electro-encephalograph could monitor the subject's mental state during a task or activity, and a computer analysing the tracings could activate the ultrasound when a desired mental state is achieved. Research has shown correlations between EEG patterns and various mental states, including alertness, concentration and memory retrieval.[3] Such correlations, though, have not been determined to be definitely reliable. Thus, the proposed biofeedback device probably would have to be calibrated for each individual. The device, used in such a manner, would be a powerful tool for enhancing an individual's skills in thinking and learning.

A previous line of research begun in the 1950s and continued in the 1960s involving direct stimulation by electrodes of human subjects' brains has not been followed. Presumably, this is due to two factors: (1) a moral, puritanical objection to such a short-cut to pleasure; and (2) the disturbing prospect of having electrodes implanted into one's brain. It is beyond the scope of this paper to examine the moral problem of pleasure as a phenomenon. However, Heath[2] found that electrical stimulation of pleasure centres in the brain, though perhaps creating a risk of dependence, was not addictive. The second shortcoming of previous research, the implantation of electrodes, would be overcome by the proposed mechanism, as ultrasound waves involve no surgical penetration of the brain tissue.

The potential uses of a non-invasive device for evoking pleasure and erasing pain in a human subject are numerous. It is suggested that research into this thought-provoking area would have significant benefits in the fields of education, psychology and medical pain management.

References

1 Velling, V.A. and Shklyaruk, S.P. 1988. Modulation of the functional state of the brain with the aid of focused ultrasonic action. Neuroscience and Behavioral Psychology, 18(5), 369–75.
2 Heath, R.G. 1964. Pleasure response of human subjects to direct stimulation of the brain: physiologic and psychodynamic considerations. In: Heath, R.G. (ed.), The Role of Pleasure in Behavior, pp.219–243, Harper and Row, New York.
3 Low, M.D. 1987. Psychology, psychophysiology, and the EEG. In: Niedermeyer, E. and da Silva, F.L. (eds), Electroencephalography. Basic Principles, Clinical Applications and Related Fields., pp.541–548, Urban and Schwarzenberg.

Received: 20 May 1992; accepted: 8 June 1992

TABLE OF CONTENTS

c. how everyone might be famous ....

d. Would a clone of You be another You? ....

e. Does one's MPEC age? ....

f. By circulating everyone's MPEC through positions of close proximity with Every other MPEC and literally through every living BBP, everyone would be famous and better able to live in peace ....

g. Would there be any privacy possible for MPECs opting to participate in global MPEC/BBP circulation? ....

h. Every MPEC is inherently, intrinsically and immutably unique ....

i. Another way of every MPEC and every BBP being famous (and peaceful) would be via MPEC-internet ....

j. how everyone might be pain free ....

k. We might currently or eventually render ourselves incapable of experiencing pain or suffering by means of BSNP or (instantaneous) genetic self-re-engineering (IGSRE) ....

l. how we might become death free or immortal ....

m. how everyone might be very well educated ....

n. how everyone might be **extremely** well educated ....

o. how everyone might be sexually liberated ....

p. how everyone might be healthy ....

q. how everyone might be anorexia-, obesity-, insomnia-free, etc. ....

r. to be whatever we want to be, whenever we want to be ....

s. Can computers be conscious? ....

t. how we might all become relatively unselfish ....

18. Appendix containing several letters of recommendation, copies of six internationally published articles, one relatively locally-published article that was written under the pseudonym Nemo T. Noone, a copy of an advertisement/flyer for a seminar given at Pennsylvania State University, a letter of notification of having won an award from Graphic Controls Corporation (1988), and a detailed, descriptive Curriculum Vitae (C.V.)/resume. ....

How Poverty, Financial Stress, Pain, Anxiety, Depression, Insomnia, Cancer, Cardiovascular Disease, Blindness, Deafness, Paralysis, Obesity, Nausea, Choking, Etc. might be Alleviated (or Effectively Treated) by Brain Stimulation, Electromagnetism, Sound (Waves) (e.g., Ultrasound), Particle Beams, Etc.

by Lewis S. Mancini

June 1, 2005

Summary or Abstract

Abstract – Poverty and financial stress might be alleviated by (**preferably**) **noninvasive electromagnetism** – (EM or E), sound- (S), for example, **ultrasound-** (US), **Particle-Beam (PB or P)** – mediated, **possibly perceptibly pleasurable brain stimulation** (PBS) (hence, overall: **EUSPBS or ESPBS**) that might enable virtually anyone to (learning-facilitatedly, **LF**) learn new job skills quickly and seemingly almost effortlessly (work-ing- facilitatedly, WF), so that (preferably) high-paying scientific, high-technology and other kind(s) of employment would be within reach for (almost-?) everyone. Headaches (and all other kinds of aches), (back- and all other kinds of) pain, anxiety, depression and nausea might also be relieved by ESPBS. Insomnia blindness and deafness might be alleviated by stimulation, respectively, of the brain's sleep, vision, and hearing subserving pathways. Paralysis might be alleviated by noninvasive, wireless, electromagnetically-/acoustically-/particle-beam-mediated conveyance/transmission of the brain's motor-cortex-initiated impulses in order to move/change body position via stimulation of the skeletal muscles. Cancer might be effectively treated by noninvasive electromagnetic/acoustical (e.g., ultrasonic) or particle-beam-mediated, highly focused ablation. Cardiovascular disease might be treated via noninvasive dissolution of blood clots, thromboembolic phenomena and atherosclerotic plaques, cauterization of leaky, hemorrhagic areas and noninvasive blood-pumping. Obesity might be alleviated via stimulation of the brain's food-satiety center. And choking might be relieved by relaxing (antispasmodic), inhibitory stimulation of the (bilateral) larynx-controlling areas of the brain's motor cortex.

How Poverty and Financial Stress might be Alleviated

It might be helpful to bear in mind, in the context of this section's perusal that if poverty and **financial** stress could be markedly diminished, then **the broader category of stress** might also be minimized. And if the broader category of stress could be minimized, then the burden of **stress-related mental** and **physical/bodily illness** and **infirmity** might **also** (i.e., consequently) be **minimized.**

Now, turning attention to the potential practicalities of poverty and financial stress alleviation, let us proceed as follows. Whenever a person engages in **learning** or **working** (as opposed to idle rumination) this individual's brain, neural and muscle activity or activation patterns change in detectably characteristic and monitorable ways (1-20). Let us call these changes 'learning-' and 'working-linked **characteristics'**, **LLCs** and **WLCs**. What is being proposed here is that LLCs and WLCs be used as the **necessary** and **sufficient TURN-ON** and **STAY-ON signals** for a (preferable noninvasive) pleasure-mediating brain stimulator (or, synonymously for this context, brain or neural pacemaker, neurostimulator, neuromodulator, neuroactivator or neuroprosthesis).

Accordingly, the student/worker would receive the pleasure (pleasurable brain stimulation) **if** and **only if, whenever** and **only whenever** and **for as long as** and **only for as long as** this individual were (engaging in a process of) learning and/or working, as necessarily indicated and (brain-stimulation-circuit-drivingly) signaled by this person's emission of one or more LLCs and/or WLCs. The subject matter being learned/studied and/or work skills being learned/exercised (virtually regardless of its/their nature) might become **intensely interesting** to the student/worker because of its/their being **simultaneous** (or alternated) with pleasurable brain stimulation. Hence, anyone might readily and quickly develop new interests and areas of knowledge/expertise at any time (21).

It would be necessary to focus on those brain sites or pathways that subserve feelings of well-being and self-confidence (i.e., pleasures of the mind or mental pleasures) (22) as opposed to those subserving physical or bodily pleasures, such as sexual or gustatory arousal or gratification. This would be because physical pleasures tend to distract attention away from rather than potentiate learning and/or working-related processes.

It might be a good idea to use **both electromagnetic** (EM) (fields, waves or lasers) and **sound/sonic/acoustic** (ultrasonic, US, or, possibly, **infrasonic, shock, audible** or otherwise describable kind(s) of acoustical waves, fields (23-25) or **sasers** – please see sasers' description below (26)) phenomena. The focused sound waves (probably ultrasound) would possibly serve to neuroanatomically define the target region in the brain by mechanically stretching, deforming or twisting and thereby **opening** up cell-membrane **channels** in the neural area(s) being focused on. And the focused electromagnetism would possibly provide the (probably ionic) **current-driving mechanism** (27).

"Sasers" can be described as follows. A saser (acoustically analogous to a laser) might be characterized as "bright sound" or "a laser that's made from sound," expressed here in acronym form that abbreviatedly represents the analogous-to-laser concept of "sound amplification by stimulated emission of sonic/acoustic (rather than electromagnetic) radiation." Sasers are currently in early experimental and developmental stages. A diverse assortment of designs are in the process of being conceived and implemented in preliminary ways (26). Both lasers and sasers, because of their potential to facilitate **convergent beam therapy**, might be expected to be helpful with the focusing aspect of targeted pleasurable brain stimulation.

LLCs and WLCs might be spectral-analyzed electroencephalographic (EEG), functional magnetic resonance imaging (fMRI), magnetoencephalographic (MEG), evoked-response potentials (EP), electromyographic (EMG), galvanic skin response (GSR), near-infrared brain-scanning (NIBS), thermal imaging (TI), or some other kinds of **phenomena** that identify the occurrence of learning and/or working (1-20, 28, 29).

Transcranial magnetic stimulation (TMS) (22, 30) **might** (?) emerge as the method of choice for getting focusable electromagnetism into the brain's mental-pleasure- (sense-of-well-being- and self-confidence-subserving) centers and pathways. And the obstacle of the skull bone (a relative obstacle to sound but not at all to electromagnetism) might be bypassable by means of so-called 'time-reversal mirrors' (TRMs) that can be described as follows (31-33).

Acoustic time-reversal mirrors are explained essentially as follows: "…a source emits sound waves…. Each transducer in a mirror array detects the sound arriving at its location and feeds the signal to a computer…each transducer plays back its sound signal in reverse in synchrony with the other transducers. The original wave is re-created, but traveling backward, retracing its passage back through the medium,…refocusing on the original source point."

A relevant observation, as expressed by Mathias Fink (31, pg 97) is that "porous bone in the skull presents an energy-sapping challenge to focusing ultrasound waves on" a relatively small neuroanatomic target (such as a pleasure subserving center, site or pathway). However, "a time-reversal mirror with a modified playback algorithm can nonetheless focus ultrasound (right) through skull bone onto a small target." Time reversal mirrors could possibly be used to focus ultrasound, electromagnetism, electron-, ionic-, such as proton-, or other, such as atomic or molecular kind(s) of particle beams on to any small (or large) target(s) in the brain (or anywhere else in the body).

Consequently, virtually any person, by means of pleasurable brain stimulation, could possibly very quickly become knowledgeable and competent in relation to virtually any (preferably high-paying) work skills. **And poverty and financial stress might** consequently **be expected to become problems of the past if virtually anyone could readily be enabled to do virtually any (kind of) job at almost any time.** At the present time, many high-technology job vacancies "go begging" and do not get filled. That problem might be solved as explained above.

What is being suggested here is really just an adaptation of the late psychologist B.F. Skinner's **operant conditioning**. The only real differences are as follows. Instead of the **operant response** being a **behavioral** one (such as pressing a lever or pushing a button), it would be a **neurophysiological** one (i.e., the emission of LLCs and/or WLCs), coupled with the learning and working experiences (and behaviors) which these LLCs/WLCs signify the occurrence of. And instead of the **operant stimulus** being an externally tangible one such as food, drink or a means of escape from confinement, it would be a purely internally or intrinsically tangible one: pleasurable brain stimulation, which would be a **direct** mental reward or reinforcer.

How Headaches, Pain, Depression and Nausea might be Effectively Relieved

The phenomenon of reciprocal inhibition consists in the mechanism underlying the observation that pleasurable brain stimulation inhibits all kinds of unpleasant mental and physical states (depression, anxiety, anger, pain, etc.) (34-37). Conversely, unpleasant components of a person's subjective experience can observably disrupt what would otherwise be pleasant mental and physical states (contentment, self-confidence, bodily comfort, etc.). So, **reciprocal inhibition** consists in the notion that pleasure inhibits pain and vice versa.

The reciprocal inhibitory relationship between pleasant and unpleasant (mental and/or physical) states has its basis in (a) the interplay between neuroanatomic structures and pathways and (b) neurophysiological processes within the brain and the central nervous system (CNS) as a whole. By means of this phenomenon (of **reciprocal inhibition**), **aches, pains, depression, anxiety,** and **nausea** could all be inhibited, hence, alleviated by pleasurable brain stimulation.

Alternatively, by using different stimulation parameters and by targeting the unpleasant-state-subserving site(s)/pathway(s) (themselves) in the brain with **inhibitory** stimulation, the unpleasant states might be equally well/markedly alleviated, hence treated.

How Insomnia, Blindness and Deafness might be Alleviated

Insomnia, blindness and deafness could possibly be alleviated/minimized by focused noninvasive brain/neural stimulation of the respective sleep-/vision-/hearing-mediating sites and pathways (such as might be neuroanatomically determined or ascertained via fMRI or some other function-determining modality) such as might be targeted within the brain/nervous system, as suggested by the work of William Dobelle (who is cited in the 2005 Guinness Book of World Records for implementation of the earliest successful "artificial eye" for the blind and under whose auspices I worked briefly as a research assistant in late 1974) and others (38-40).

We were working with flat Teflon arrays of platinum-alloyed electrodes that were placed over the primary visual cortex (at the back surface of the brain), underneath a flap of skull-bone. **Noninvasive** stimulation might be expected to be **superior to** (that kind of) a **surgically-invasive** approach for at least two reasons: with a noninvasive approach one would have

1. much less reason to worry about the possibility of wires (that are passing through the scalp and skull-bone) potentially serving as pathways for possible infectious invasion of the meninges and the brain itself and

2. there would be much more (i.e., virtually unlimited) mobility of the stimulation target areas as compared with the situation of positionally-fixed surgically-implanted electrode arrays. And even if you use **wireless**, implanted electrodes, you still have this problem of (at least) relative immobility of targeted stimulation sites.

Moreover, with (highly movable) noninvasive particle-beam/electromagnetic/ultrasonic (or other acoustic) stimulation, it would be possible to activate **any** site(s) and pathway(s) in the sleep-, vision-, hearing-subserving and any and all other neuroanatomic systems, as opposed to being limited (positionally-speaking) to surgical electrode-implantation sites.

How Cancer and Cardiovascular Disease might be Effectively Treated

Returning to the insight of Mathias Fink, here might be another pertinent instance of quoting him: "Time-reversal mirror(s)" (coupled) "with a modified playback algorithm could (noninvasively) focus USs" (or EM, electron-, ionic such as proton- or other kinds of particle-beams) right "through" (the) "skull bones" (and) "onto" any (benign or malignant) "tumor" or cancer cells located (anywhere) in the brain or anywhere else in the human body (31, pg 97). In support of this contention, let us consider that radiofrequency ablation is already being used to destroy cancer cells inside of living patients.

So, focused US, other kinds of acoustic phenomena such as infrasonic, audible or shock waves EM (perhaps mediated by sasers or lasers), or particle beams could possibly be used to kill cancer (and/or benign but problematic neoplastic) cells whenever and wherever they exist (41). Furthermore, speaking from a therapeutic viewpoint of anti-neo-angiogenesis or anti-neo-angiogenically-speaking, these modalities might also be used to therapeutically-destructively target the blood supplies of cancer (or benign neoplastic but problematic) cells or cell clusters (42).

Focused EM and/or acoustic phenomena (e.g., US or shock waves) perhaps in the form of lasers, sasers and/or particle beams might also be used to dissolve and clear away blood clots/thromboembolic phenomena and atherosclerotic plaques (43) as might be blood-flow-obstructingly located anywhere in the cardiovascular system. These same modalities, if mediated via different physical stimulus parameters, might also be useful for cauterizing or sealing off leaky or hemorrhagic areas anywhere within the circulatory system. Moreover, these modalities might be used to effectively pump and circulate blood throughout the entire body, thereby affecting the role of a surgically-noninvasive "artificial heart."

How Paralysis might be Relieved or Effectively Treated

Paralysis might be alleviated by wireless particle-beam-electromagnetically- or –acoustically-mediated transmission of cerebral-motor-cortex-initiated-and-sustained-movement-subserving impulses such as might be conveyed in order to initiate and sustain task-oriented patterns of contraction and relaxation of the task-appropriate skeletal muscles. There has already been considerable success or progress in the implementation of communication of monkeys' and **humans'** movement-intentions to computer cursors, robotic arms, various other external devices and even their own (externally-assisted) paralyzed limbs (44, 45).

How Obesity and Anorexia Could be Minimized

Obesity could be minimized by a) **stimulating** the **satiety-** (as opposed to the appetitive or appetite-) subserving sites/pathways of the brain (including, possibly, the ventromedial hypothalamic nucleus in the tuberal region - ?) (46) or by b) **inhibitingly** (inhibiting by virtue of the choice of stimulus parameters used in) **de-activating** the appetite-subserving sites/pathways in the brain (including, possibly, "portions of") the lateral hypothalamic nucleus - ?) (46). Conversely, anorexia could possibly be treated in neuroanatomically-opposite, but functionally analogous, brain-stimulative (excitatory or inhibitory, depending on stimulus parameters used) ways.

How Choking Could be Readily and Reliably Alleviated

Choking could possibly be alleviated by a) **inhibitingly** stimulating the clenched larynx by applying an electromagnetic, acoustic device directly over the laryngeal area of the neck, b) abruptly and sharply **stunning the** laryngismus-afflicted **larynx into a** kind of 'hands-off/caught-off-guard' or startled, paradoxic, neuromuscularly relaxed state, by means of a noninvasive application (directly over the laryngeal area) of a device such as a more-powerful-than-usual transcranial magnetic stimulator (TMS) device (47) or by c) noninvasively,

inhibitingly stimulating the laryngeal motor cortical areas of the brain (directly over the tops of

both ears) (48) while using appropriate stimulus parameters in such ways as to momentarily relax

the larynx and then either 1) instantaneously induce either projectile vomiting of the food bolus

or other object(s) obstructing the trachea or 2) instantaneously allow descent of the obstacle into

the lungs, from which it could subsequently be suctioned out, after the choking emergency

situation were alleviated.

Vagus or vagal nerve stimulation (VNS) together with pleasurable brain stimulation

might also prove helpful in relieving a choking emergency, because VNS's parasympathetic

energy-conserving (relaxing) properties (49) (together with the consciousness-maintaining

effects of pleasurable brain stimulation) might tend to relax and thereby relieve the spasmodic

condition (i.e., laryngismus) that is associated with choking.

Incidentally, relevant to the overall subject of (possibly-perceptibly-) pleasurable brain-

stimulation-mediated learning-facilitation, **VNS** has been found to have some **possibly**

significantly **memory-enhancing effects** (50, 51).

Conclusion

In the context of the potential economic scenario depicted above, with virtually everyone

being/becoming much **more productive** and **work-skills diversifiable** than we currently are (via

LLC/WLC-contingent pleasurable brain stimulation, that is) via a scenario that might be

described in terms of B.S. or ESPBS-mediated learning facilitation (LF) and work skills'

facilitation (WF), **not only** might we (all of us) humans be unlikely to suffer from either financial stress or poverty **but also** we might become the beneficiaries of **markedly increased** (a) collective-global as well as (b) per-capita wealth.

Consequently, **the cost of frequent** (weekly or monthly- ?) **whole-body scanning** (52) for cancers, atherosclerotic plaques and other (manifestations of) diseases **could be** effectively (relative to (a) and (b)) **driven downward** so low as to facilitate its being/becoming readily accessible to and affordable by the entire population. Such increased accessibility and affordability might bode tremendously well for both public as well as individual-personal health (53).

The essence of what might make the differences between/among the potential(s) of EM, sound/ultrasound (SUS) (54) and particle beams (PBs) (31, pg 97) to a) **detect and image** cancers atherosclerotic plagues, etc., b) **stimulate or activate** brain/neural, muscular and other kinds of tissues and c) **extirpate or ablate** these disease-mediating entities might effectively consist in **differences in stimulus** (i.e., input) **parameters** of these modalities.

In summary, poverty, financial stress, pain, anxiety, depression,…etc. (as listed in the title) might all be effectively alleviated/minimized by the technological methods of approach suggested herein or by some other technologies (that might or might not be noninvasive) that are yet to emerge as being appropriate and useful for the applications suggested in this context. Nanoscale robots or nanobots (55-58) and genetically-engineered therapeutic viruses or viral entities (45) that could travel throughout the bloodstream (or, conceivably, even outside of it) **might** (?) be examples of health-promoting, relatively non-hazardous modalities that might potentially controvert the notion that noninvasive treatment modalities are preferable to invasive ones. **In any case, with there being an apparent superabundance of new technologies** (and new applications of already invented or discovered technologies) (59) emerging at seemingly always accelerating rates, one cannot safely or securely place all of one's confidence in any one technology.

Acknowledgements

The author wishes to acknowledge with gratitude the encouragement and support of
Herb, Mary, Grace, Robert, C. Timothy, Gloria, Michael, Cathie, Nick,
Joani-Erica, Anna, Tom, Tom, Robert J., Patricia, Mike, David, William,
Akhlesh, Betty, Amanda, Denise, William Shirley, Tony, Mary, Louis,
Alice, Eugene, Charlotte, Ellsworth, Ray and Bernice.

References

1. Gevins A.S., Morgan N.H., Bressler S.L. et al, Human neuroelectric patterns predict performance accuracy. Science 1987; 235: 580-585.

2. Williamson S.J. How quickly we forget-magnetic fields reveal a hierarchy of memory lifetimes in the human brain. Science Spectra 1999; 15: 68-73.

3. Walgate J., Wagner A., Buckner R.L., Schacter D., Sharpe K., Floyd C. Memories are made of this. Science & Spirit 1999; 10, 1:7.

4. Connor S. Thanks for the memory. The World in 1999. The Economist Publications, 1999: 110-111.

5. Goetinck S. Different brain areas linked to memorization. The Buffalo News, final edn., Sun., June 13, 1999, Science Notes: H-6.

6. Hall S. S. Journey to the center of my mind, brain scans can locate the home of memory and the land of language. They may eventually help to map consciousness. The New York Times Magazine, June 6, 1999; section 6: 122-125.

7. Neergaard L. Studies shed new light on memory/studies take close look at brain's memory process. The Buffalo News 1999; Fri., Aug. 21: A-10.

8. Sullivan M.M. (Editor). Task-juggling region in brain pinpointed. The Buffalo News 1999; Sun., May 23: H-6.

9. Fox M. Test on rats turns thought into action. The Buffalo News 1999; Sun., June 27: H-6.

10. McCrone J. States of mind, learning a task takes far more brainpower than repeating it once it's become a habit, could the difference show us where consciousness lies, asks J.M. NewScientist, March 20, 1999; 161: 30-33.

11. Gaidos S. Written all over your face, even the coolest criminal can't hide a guilty countenance. NewScientist, Mach 12-18, 2005; 185, 2490: 38-41.

12. Carmichael M. Medicine's Next Level – Improving the memory. Newsweek, Dec. 6, 2004; CXLIV, 23: 44-50.

13. Buderi R. The deceit detector. You didn't lie – your prefrontal cortex did. And Britton Chance is developing infrared-based brain imaging to catch it in action. Technology Review, MIT's Magazine of Innovation, June, 2003; 106, 5: 66-69.

14. Osborne L. Savant for a day. Allan Snyder claims he can turn on a person's inner Rain Man, and then turn it off again, with the flick of a switch. All it takes is a strange set of electrodes – and a radical new theory of autism, genius and the human brain. The New York Times Magazine, June 22, 2003; section 6: 38-41.

15. Thompson C. The lie detector that scans your brain. The New York Times Magazine, Dec. 9, 2001; section 6: 82.

16. Huang G. T. Mind-machine merger. A $24 million government initiative is jump-starting researchers' efforts to link brains and computers. The new push could yield thought-controlled robots, enhanced perception and communication – and might even make you smarter. Technology Review, MIT's Magazine of Innovation, May, 2003; 106, 4: 38-45.

17. Damasio A., Damasio H., Andersen R., Gazzaniga M.S., Haseltine E., Koch C., Kuiken T., LeDoux J., Tallal P., Gould E., Skayles J., Rose S., Hauser M.D., Sejnowski T. Neuroscience, Top scientists pinpoint the critical developments of the last 25 years and predict wonders yet to come. Discover, May, 2005; 26, 5: 72-75.

18. Tancredi L.R. The new lie detectors. Scientific American, May 23, 2005; 16, 1: 46-47.

19. Wilson J. Why we laugh. Popular Mechanics, March, 2003: 40-41.

20. Fox D.S. The inner savant. Discover, Feb., 2002; 23, 2: 44-49.

21. Mancini L. Brain stimulation to treat mental illness and enhance human learning, creativity, performance, altruism and defenses against suffering. Medical Hypotheses 1986; 21: 209-219.

22. Breuer H. A great attraction: magnetically stimulating the brain could lift depression and perhaps even boost creativity, but questions remain. Scientific American (special on the Mind), July 25, 2005; 16, 2: 54-59.

23. Fry W.J. Electrical stimulation of brain localized without probes – theoretical analysis of a proposed method. J. Acoust. Soc. Am. 1968; 44: 919-931.

24. Fry F.J. (brother of the late W.J. Fry; please note the preceding reference), of the Indianapolis Center for Advanced Research, Indianapolis, Indiana, USA, personal communication, May 27, 1987.

25. Spangler R.A., Assoc. Prof., State Univ. of NY at Buffalo, Depts. of Physiology and Biophysics: personal communication, Oct. 18, 1991.

26. Watson A. Pump up the volume, what lasers do for light, sasers promise to do for sound – once you can work out the best way to build one. NewScientist March 27, 1999; 161: 36-40.

27. Spangler R.A. of the Dept. of Biophysical Science and Physiology, School of Medicine and Biomedical Sciences, State Univ. of New York at Buffalo, Buffalo, New York, USA, personal communication, late, '99.

28. Legrand L.N., Iacono W.G., McGue M. Predicting addiction: behavioral genetics uses twins and time to decipher the origins of addiction and learn who is most vulnerable. Scientific American, March-April, 2005; 93, 2: 140-147.

29. Niedermeyer E., Lopes da Silva. Electroencephalography, Basic Principles, Clinical Applications and Related Fields: Urban & Schwarzenberg, 1987: 232.

30. George M.S., Belmaker R.H. Transcranial Magnetic Stimulation in Neuropsychiatry: American Psychiatric Press, 2000: 298 pages.

31. Fink M. Time-reversed acoustics. Scientific American 1999; 281: 91-97.

32. Fink M., Prada C. Ultrasonic focusing with time-reversal mirrors. Advances in Acoustic Microscopy Series. Edited by A. Briggs and W. Arnold. Plenum Press, 1996.

33. Fink M. Time-reversed acoustics. Physics Today 1997; 50: 34-40.

34. Stein L. Reciprocal action of reward and punishment mechanisms. The role of Pleasure in Behavior: Harper & Row, 1964: 113-139.

35. Stein L., Belluzzi J.D., Ritter S., Wise C.D. Self-stimulation reward pathways: norepinephrine versus dopamine. J. Psychiatr Res 1974; 11:115-124.

36. Bishop M.P., Elder S.T., Heath R.G. Attempted control of operant behavior in man with intracranial self-stimulation. The Role of Pleasure in Behavior: Harper & Row, 1964: 55-81.

37. Heath R.G. Pleasure response of human subjects to direct stimulation of the brain: physiologic and psychodynamic consideration. The Role of Pleasure in Behavior: Harper & Row, 1964: 219-243.

38. Dobelle W.H., Mladejovsky M.G., Girvin J.P. Artificial vision for the blind: electrical stimulation of visual cortex offers hope for a functional prosthesis. Science, Feb. 1, 1974; 183: 440-444.

39. Folkard C., Freshfield J. Medical phenomena: Earliest successful artificial eye (care of William H. Dobelle). Guinness (book of) World Records, 2005: 20.

40. Mowbray S., Jannot M. Best of what's next; five technologies that will transform your world: holographic TVs, spray-on space suits, bionic eyes, plastic buildings and interactive roller coasters. The bionic eye: we see the future better than 20/20; researchers have already restored some sight to the blind; why not give them super vision? Popular Science, June, 2005; 266, 6: 58-59.

41. Siegfried T. Laser spots cancer before it grows. NewScientist, April 2-8, 2005; 186, 2493: 14.

42. Weintraub A. Genentech's medicine man, CEO Arthur Levinson got the biotech pioneer off life support; will it finally deliver on its promises? Tumors need blood, and they have a devious way to get it. BusinessWeek, Oct. 6, 2003: 72-80.

43. Pearlstine N. The next big thing: the laser unclogging arteries in the operating room. Time, Sept. 8, 2003; 162, 10: 75-80.

44. Selim J. The bionic connection: will neural implants erase the boundary between the mind and computers? Are we already a lot closer to a mind-machine interface than we ever guessed? Discover, Nov., 2002; 23, 11: 48-51.

45. Kohn D. Food for thought: the most sophisticated brain implant yet brings us one giant step closer to mind-controlled machines in news and views, headlines: pitting viruses against cancer, spray-on homes, a mind-controlled robot, robot subs, ready to serve. Popular Science, May 2005; 266, 5: 29-32.

46. Carpenter M.B. Core Text of Neuroanatomy: The Williams & Wilkins Company, 1972: 180.

47. Mancini L.S. short note: A magnetic choke-saver might relieve choking. Medical Hypotheses, 1992; 38: 349.

48. Parosky M., neurologist at Erie County Medical Center, Buffalo, NY; personal communication: late 2003.

49. Andres J.C., Director, Family Practice Residency Training Program, Niagara Falls Memorial Medical Center, Niagara Falls, NY; personal communication: early 2005.

50. Cahill L., McGaugh J.L. Modulation of memory storage. Curr. Opin. Neurobiol., 1996; 6: 237-242.

51. Clark K.B. Post-training electrical stimulation of vagal afferents with concomitant vagal efferent inactivation enhances memory storage processes in the rat. Neurobiol. Learn. Mem., 1998; 70: 364-373.

52. Muir H. Hope for portable MRI. NewScientist, April 9-15, 2005; 186, 2494: 9.

53. Witchalls C. At last a scanner that can see it all. NewScientist, April 16-22, 2005; 186, 2495: 25.

54. Hogan J., Fox B. Sony patent takes first step to real-life Matrix: "A technique known as transcranial magnetic stimulation can activate nerves by using rapidly changing magnetic fields to induce currents in brain tissue. However, magnetic fields cannot be finely focused on small groups of brain cells, whereas ultrasound could be." NewScientist, April 9-15, 2005; 186, 2494: 10.

55. Vogel M. Big minds gather to think small, really small. Buffalo News 1998; Sat., Oct. 24: C-5.

56. Kurzweil R. The Age of Spiritual Machines: When Computers Exceed Human Intelligence. Penguin Books, 1999: 52, 80, 120, 124, 127-128, 205, 220, 221, 279, 300, 307-308, 313, 314.

57. Kurzweil R. Live forever. Psychology Today 2000; Feb.: 66-71.

58. Kurzweil R. The coming merging of mind and machine: the accelerating pace of technological progress means that our intelligent creations will soon eclipse us – and that their creations will eventually eclipse them. Scientific American 1999; 10: 56-60.

59. Wingert P., Brant M. Reading your baby's mind; new research on infants finally begins to answer the question : what's going on in there? Newsweek, August 15, 2005 : 32 - 39.

HOW EVERYONE COULD BE RICH, FAMOUS, PAINLESS, DEATHLESS, WELL EDUCATED, SEXUALLY LIBERATED, ETC.

FIRST: HOW EVERYONE MIGHT BE RICH AND WELL EDUCATED

First: a basic learning and work facilitative idea at a glance

The methodology about to be proposed might entail the use of (1) a stimulant modality such as ultrasound (US), electromagnetism (EM), beams of subatomic particles, ionized pharmacotherapeutic atoms, molecules and/or some other kind(s) of chemical/physical phenomena (perhaps, precisely) targeted, focused, conveyed and applied, possibly, entirely from outside of the fully intact head **together with** (2) a simple (possibly, biofeedback-based or driven) circuit, whereby a person would receive pleasurable stimulation (that would be pleasurable/rewarding by virtue of which particular neuroanatomic sites and stimulus parameter values might be used) of one or more reward-mediating pathway(s) or site(s) in the brain or elsewhere in the nervous system, **if, and only if, whenever** and only whenever, **and for as long** interval(s) of duration or period(s) of time and only for as long intervals of duration or period(s) of time **as**, that is, during or throughout any intervals of time during which the individual (stimulation recipient) were to engage in/were engaging in high-level (of complexity or intricacy) mental and/or physical processes and activity/ies, as evidenced by and driven by **specific-to-process-or-activity** physiological manifestations, that might serve as biofeedback signals (1-20). Then, consequently, that is, primarily, due to conditioning induced by the virtual or near-simultaneity of (a) these processes/activities with (b) rewarding experiences of pleasure/enjoyment, hence, by dint of instrumental chronological association, virtual synchronousness or pairing in time of stimulus (pleasurable stimulation) and response (high-level mental/physical process or activity/ies coupled with characteristic physiological emissions or manifestations), this/these activity/ies and process/es might be experienced as (being themselves, virtually intrinsically) intensely **pleasurable** and, **therefore, interesting** and likely to occur often and for long periods of time. The process or activity in question might be learning, reading, problem-solving, memorizing, remembering, skilled manual or any other type(s) of work.

Electroencephalographic (EEG), electromyographic (EMG), magnetoencephalographic (MEG), specific-brain-function-indicative or **functional** magnetic resonance imaging (fMRI) **and/or some other kind(s)** of detectable, physiologically-significant phenomena (that might serve as biofeedback), which are identifyingly characteristic of such activities/processes, would necessarily be the **turn-on** and **stay-on** signal(s) (in other words, the bio- or neuro-**feedback** signals) for the brain stimulator (BS) or (neural) pacemaker/pacesetter or prosthesis (BP or NP). A person could quickly become intensely interested in, highly motivated with respect to the associated details of any area or career-related direction and, thence, extensively knowledgeable in any area(s) of endeavor the person/stimulus-recipient were to choose. Being so **productive**, patient (defining 'patient' as: 'well enough equipped with pleasure in order to offset and undermine any frustration/'impatience'), and **versatile**, a person would be **unlikely to suffer from financial stress, poverty, hunger or other shortage or lack-of-money-related adversity.**

It is conceivable that these effects could all be produced without involving any direct contact between the stimulator and the person being stimulated. In any case, not only might there be no surgery, pain or discomfort involved, but quite possibly, there would be no tactile sensations of any kind (1-2). In view of already-accomplished research and development (3-20), it can be hypothesized that a device that would utilize the principle suggested above could probably be developed in less than **a year's time**, at a cost of (conceivably, as little as) several million U.S. dollars, which would be a minuscule investment in comparison to the billions of dollars worth of increased human productivity and new, improved and diversified work skills it might facilitate.

Next: a definition and fuller explanation

A useful definition of the word "**rich**," for this context, might be: (a) **financially able to fulfill all of one's biological needs** and (b) **able to lead one's life without experiencing financially-related anxiety or stress.**

It might be appropriate to use **biochemical** and/or **biophysical stimuli** (distinction explained below), focused and **applied** (preferably) **noninvasively** (at least, **surgically**-non-invasively; distinction explained below) by means of a relatively simple circuit, perhaps conceptually similar to one designed approximately 30 years ago (3). This device might usefully be designed in such ways that an individual would obtain A, that is, (preferably, **highly**) **pleasurable** or at least relaxing, soothing **stimulation** of one or more pathways, sites, areas, or structures in the **brain** or **elsewhere** in the **nervous system** (for example, the vagus nerve) (4).

However, the stimulation delivery system would be designed in such ways that the individual would receive A, **that is, pleasurable (or, at least, comforting, relaxing and patience-conducive) brain or other neural stimulation if and only if, for as long a duration of time and only for as long a duration of time, whenever and only whenever** the individual (stimulation recipient) were to engage in B, **that is,** high-level (of complexity or of time-pressure-related intensity) mental and/or physical activities and/or processes, as indicated by the evidence of C, that is, physiological or physiologically-related manifestations or signals (5-15) of high-level mental/physical, activities/processes that (at least consistently, intra-individually or consistently for each individual stimulation recipient) might be expected to be reliably, consistently and identifyingly manifested in the same detectable way(s) for each occurrence of the same activity or process. Any given high-level, mental/physical, activity/process might be expected to reliably, consistently and distinctively manifest itself in a detectably characteristic way, in terms of **functional magnetic resonance imaging** (fMRI), **computer-analyzed, spectral-analyzed electroencephalography** (EEG or some other modality). Each occurrence of a **different** high-level, mental/physical, activity/process might be expected to manifest itself reliably and consistently, yet distinctively differently with respect to any occurrence of a **low**-level (of complexity or of time-pressure-related intensity) mental/physical, activity/process, such as relaxing in front of a television.

The high-level, mental/physical activities/processes would be inherently (by dint of the functional nature of the brain and of the mind) coupled and concurrent with (sometimes, keenly observant, hence, highly perceptive and, at other times, deeply introspective, hence, highly intuitive) **sharply-focused attention** and virtually **uninterrupted**, amply-**sustained**, thoroughly **engrossed concentration**. Explained somewhat differently or, at least, **more generally**: each different kind of learning-related and/or work-related (generally, high-level) constructive and productive mental/physical, activity/process might reasonably be expected to have corresponding, relatively-uniquely-identifying (at least within any given stimulation recipient) activity-specific or process-specific, externally-detectable and monitorable physiological or physiologically-related manifestations (5-15).

High-level mental/physical activities/processes (Bs) might include **learning** (especially, rapid-rate or high-speed learning), whether it be of abstract or of tangibly practical information and concepts, **reading, problem-solving, memorizing, remembering** (that is, retrieving memories or already-learned and, to some degree at least, mastered items of knowledge and information that would already be fully-processed, that is, encoded and stored in the brain and/or in the mind; please note distinction below), and **working** (especially, rapid-rate or high-speed working, in particular, effective and proficient application or implementation of high-level work skills and learned task-accomplishing behavior patterns). The physiological or physiologically-related manifestations, referred to above, that might be **emitted** (as stimulation-initiating and stimulation-sustaining signals) by the stimulation-receiving individual, might be expected to be instantaneously-detectable, sustainable and recordable in real time.

For simplicity of discussion's sake, let us assume that it is physiologically unfeasible (if not impossible) to separate B **(high-level, mental/physical, activities/processes)** from C **(the measurable, quantifiable, physiological or physiologically-related manifestations** of high-level, mental/physical, activities/processes). Consequently, whenever a person might engage in B, the brain-stimulative/neural-prosthetic device would detect C-type manifestations and, therefore, begin to deliver A **(pleasurable stimulation)** to this particular person. So,

93

the person would have a reliably strong motivation (i.e., pleasurable stimulation or pleasurable activation/excitation) toward indulgence in high-level, mental/physical, activities/processes.

Thus, **because** the **pleasure** would be **actuated**, driven and **maintained by,** and also nearly, if not entirely, **simultaneous with** the sustained-by-way-of-rewarding-brain-stimulation-initiating-and-sustaining **manifestations** (emitted by the stimulation-recipient) of the **high-level** activities/processes, these **activities/processes, themselves,** by virtue of **chronological association** (entailing near- or semi-simultaneity), might be **experienced as pleasurable** and, **therefore, interesting** and likely to **occur often** and **for long periods of time**. Thus, the **physiological/physiologically-related manifestations** of these activities or processes would **instrumentally** serve as the **turn-on** and **stay-on signals** for the brain or neural stimulators. Accordingly, any person might be easily enabled to readily become intensely pleasured/ **pleasurized** or **gratified** by this person's mind/brain's attending to and processing even very minute details and very subtle conceptual nuances encompassed within any area of academic knowledge or skilled, occupational/vocational, practical-expertise-requiring, employment-related implementation.

By dint of a mechanism such as the aforementioned one, any person could quickly become intensely pleasured with respect to, hence, strongly interested in and knowledgeable about virtually any kind of **high-paying** work skills (or hobbies of any kind) that the person might choose to become interested in and knowledgeable about. For example, suppose an individual is someone whose favorite pastimes are indoor housekeeping and outdoor gardening and there are no high-paying jobs available in either of these areas. Now suppose the person realizes there are many high-paying job openings in high-technology fields, such as biomedical engineering.

So, this individual might be able to start receiving A (pleasurable brain stimulation/neural pacemaking) whenever the person were to engage in attentive reading of biomedical-engineering-based/-related printed materials or otherwise perceptually accessible media, such as might be accessible, for example, via computer screen. Then, whenever the person were to engage in B (biomedical-engineering-relevant, high-level, mental/physical or mental/behavioral, activities/processes), the brain stimulator would be sending out A (enjoyable brain stimulation) in response to its detection and monitoring of the person's emitted C (-type physiological/ physiologically-related manifestations) that might not even be directly known about (not the details, anyway), much less cared-about by the person in question. From the would-be housekeeper/gardener's viewpoint, suddenly the study of high-technology subjects (such as biomedical engineering, etc.) might, almost mysteriously, take on the attraction of great fun. And better yet, the prospect of a high-paying job might almost as unexpectedly, suddenly become a genuine possibility that might expeditiously be fulfilled.

Hence, if a person were to have access to A (pleasure-inducing brain stimulation/neural-pacesetting) and circumstances (such as a shortage of money) leading to or amounting to a rationale for becoming knowledgeable and capable with respect to high-level, mental/behavioral, activities/processes, then the person's prospects of being or becoming able to do a good job while being employed in a **high-**

level-of-practical-expertise-entailing occupation might be excellent. And regarding the pre-existing hobbies and interests (in the hypothetical example being considered here) involving housekeeping and gardening, there would be no reason to anticipate a loss of enthusiasm in relation to these areas of endeavor, although they might get relegated to the roles of recreational diversions that would, nonetheless, continue to be enthusiastically partaken in (without brain stimulation or neural pacesetting being necessary or appropriate).

Hence, almost any person, being rewarded in this **high-level**-activity-process-**manifestation-dependent** way, with **interest**-generating and **patience-** (definable here as **relatively-low-intensity-pleasure-**) generating and accommodating, gratifying brain/neural stimulation, pacemaking, might readily and easily become deeply interested in and engrossedly patient with respect to both major concepts and numerous minute details of any (preferably, well-paying) field of endeavor. Consequently, the individual might readily and quickly become well-educated about descriptive factual information, concepts and (as appropriate and financially necessary, high-speed implementation of specific) work skills, related to **any** areas of **endeavor** and modes of **practical application** that the individual might choose or that the ambient **economy** might demand or require, in accordance with whatever volumes of **supplies** of whatever **goods** and **services** might be readily **sellable** and **financially beneficial.**

The stimulation might consist in nerve cell/**neuronal activation** and/or **deactivation, excitation/arousal** and/or **inhibition/suppression**. It might be experienced by the **stimulation-recipient** as **pleasureful** by dint of a combination of

(a) **which** specific **stimulative modalities media** or **means**, (b) the magnitudes, **values**, sizes, or other quantifiable characteristics of **stimulus parameters/ variables**, and (c) **which** particular neuroanatomic **target-sites** would be **used** (4, 16-36).

Also, **depending** on **which** particular **stimulation modalities,** stimulus **parameter values** and **target sites were** to be **used, possibly, no pain, tactile sensations,** other **perceptions** (1, 2, 30)**, nor even** appreciable **effort** (as explained below) would **need** to **be involved or** be **unavoidable.**

The **effort**, which **generally** (for most people, at least, seems to accompany or) **accompanies learning** and (what we think of as) **work(ing)**, may be thought of as **goal-directed** pain. The pleasurable facilitation of learning and work, as suggested herein, might be expected to minimize or even effectively eliminate the **need for** (this pain, which is the essence of) **effort,** perhaps by the mechanism of (a) **reciprocal inhibition** (37).

Reciprocal inhibition can be understood as follows: **excitatory stimulation** of **pleasure**-subserving or, in other words, pleasure-**mediating** anatomic sites **might entail indirect inhibition of pain**-subserving sites, by means of naturally-occurring inhibitory projections or pathways, extending from pleasure-subserving to pain-subserving sites. Analogously, pain-mediating sites might have naturally-occurring (reciprocally) inhibitory pathways that extend to pleasure-subserving sites.

Another way or mechanism by which learning and working might be virtually divested of their painful/**effortful aspects** might be by (b) **simultaneous** excitatory **stimulation** of **pleasure** pathways or sites **and** (together or chronologically-coupled with) **direct inhibitory stimulation** of **pain**-subserving pathways or sites.

Regardless of the **mechanism(s)** by which **inhibition of** learning-/work-associated (pain of) **effort** might be achieved, **the phenomenon** of such inhibition, entailing minimization or even virtual elimination of the need for expenditure of effort, might be referred to as the **de-effortization, deeffortization, deffortization, deffortation** or **defortation** of learning and work(ing).

Analogously, the **phenomenon** of learning and work being perfused with brain/neural-stimulation-mediated pleasure and being rendered reliably, highly enjoyable might be referred to as the **enjoyitization, enjoyitation** or **pleasurization** of **learning** and **work.**

By means of the pleasurization and relative defortation of learning and work, the **human condition** as we (most of us, anyway, seem to) know it, that is:

a)   we (each of us, individually) tend to **experience much pleasure** when we (ourselves) **succeed** at a learning or work-related task and

b)   we tend to experience **much pain** or **displeasure** when we **fail** at a learning- or work-related task

might be changed so that:

c)   we would still experience much pleasure (maybe more than we do already/currently) when we would succeed but, **most significantly,**

d)   we would, due to brain-stimulation-mediated inhibition of pain and suffering, experience virtually **no pain or displeasure** when we would fail.

Consequently, we (each of us, individually, and all of us, collectively) might tend to be elated by our successes without being dejected or demoralized by our failures. Since (c) and (together with) (d) correspond to a relatively optimistic outlook, it can be inferred that the human mental condition, as a whole, might be improved. Moreover, as can readily be surmised or inferred by comparing one's observations and impressions of the learning and work performance of optimists with that of pessimists, the **likelihood** (and frequency) of success and **quality** of performance might, comprehensibly, be expected to, respectively, **increase** and **improve**.

Depending on each (that is: any given) stimulation-recipient's own choice and exercise of free will, (**pleasurization** and **defortation,** hence) **facilitation** of mental/physical processes might be such as to only be of value to the stimulation-recipient as amusing recreational phenomena of the pastime or hobby type. However, **more valuably**, from a financial/economic standpoint, each recipient might better be persuaded that the facilitated mental/physical processes might more wisely be highly relevant to the realm of gainful employment.

Summarizing some points made above, an important point to keep in mind is that high-level mental/physical activities/processes might be determined to have (as their **characteristically-associated** and **each-individual-stimulation-recipient-identifying**) physiological/physiologically-related **manifestations**, **some,** possibly, more-or-less unique-to-each-recipient, **consistently-recurring patterns** of data-points (**signals**) of any of a number of different kinds of detectable, measurable and recordable **modalities** that might be used as stimulation-triggering and stimulation-maintaining/sustaining signals (5-15).

A list of these modalities might include electroencephalography (EEG), quantitative, **computerized** or computer-frequency/spectral-analyzed EEG (CEEG), magnetoencephalography (MEG) (38), functional magnetic resonance scanning and imaging (fMRI), optical imaging (39), electromyography (EMG), thermography or thermographic radiant-heat-quantity-related infrared (IR) transducer-mediated imaging, (perhaps, three-dimensional) ultrasonography (US or 3DUS), Doppler ultrasonography, positron emission tomography (PET) scanning, single photon emission computed tomography (SPECT) scanning, and others.

As learning-facilitative (LF), **work-skills'-acquisition-facilitative** or **work-skills'-performance-facilitative (WF)** brain/neural-stimulation/pacemaking/ prosthetically-mediated **turn-on** and **stay-on** signals, these mental/physical, activity/process-**identifyingly-associated/identifyingly-linked** manifestations/ characteristics/signals might be referred to as Learning/Work-Associated/-Linked **Manifestations** (LWAMs or LWLMs), Learning/Work-Associated/-Linked **Characteristics** (LWACs or LWLCs) or Learning/Working-Associated/-Linked **Signals** (LWASes or LWLSes) (5-15).

The following two quotations might **seem** to convincingly/plausibly validate the notions that such **signals** both exist and are medical-technologically accessible: on page 116, (a) "A close correspondence exists between the appearance of a mental state or behavior and the activity of selected brain regions" and, on page 115, (b) "Neuroscience continues to associate specific brain structures with specific tasks" (40).

For this context, **biochemical stimuli** might be thought of as any stimuli that predominantly entail particles or particulate matter, such as one or more biological- or medical-effect-mediating, pharmacotherapeutic molecules, whole atoms, ions etc.

Whereas, **biophysical stimuli** might be thought of as any biological- or medical-effect-mediating stimuli that predominantly entail subatomic particles (e.g., electrons) or biological- or medical-effective-mediating wave(form)s of virtually any kind, such as sound, electromagnetic waves or quantum wavefunctions, such as can or might be retroreflected from a boundary/interface between a normal conductor and a superconductor (41).

However, in view of the quantum mechanical phenomenon of wave/particle duality of energy and matter, it is clear that biochemical and biophysical stimuli cannot validly be considered strictly, mutually exclusive or categorically distinct from each other.

The terms '**noninvasive**' and '**surgically-noninvasive**' are **not**, in this context anyway, **interchangeable**. For example, in proceeding toward the goal of explaining the appropriate distinction, let us consider transdermal **permeation** or percutaneous transmission of microminiature (42) robotic, electronic and/or pharmacologic/medicinal agents or "**nanobots**," (a term used by R. Kurzweil defined, in essence, **paraphrastically**, adaptedly herein) as explained in detail on pages 307 and 68, respectively, in the next-cited two references (39, 43) as "self-replicating" entities (robots built by means of nanotechnology) that are tiny enough for billions (or even trillions) of them to smoothly travel through a nanobot-recipient's circulatory system. Within such a recipient, the volumetrically-minuscule anatomic environments affected might, as a consequence of being circulated-through (by swarms of nanobots), undergo therapeutic (or otherwise adaptive-to-reference-frame-in-question) functional modification(s).

Thus, there might (at least, potentially) occur the phenomenon of **permeation** of any therapeutic or quality-of-life-enhancing entities, perhaps encompassing the full extent of traversing all the way from the periphery of an organism, through all intervening body-tissue types and from there proceeding deeply into all portions and ramifications of the circulatory system. Such an infiltrative phenomenon would **surely** qualify as an **invasive process**. However, because it would not rely on/or necessarily entail surgery of any type, it would **not** qualify as **surgically-invasive**. On the contrary, it would validly be considered **surgically-non-invasive, despite** being, in an **overall**, definitive sense, effectively **invasive**. More generally speaking, swallowing pills is an invasive treatment, but is clearly not surgically invasive.

In addition to **permeation** (44), a partial/non-comprehensive list of some other examples of **invasive**, yet **surgically-noninvasive** means of potentially, possibly therapeutic/life-quality-improving means of conveyance might include **ingestion, inhalation**, and **injection via intermolecular, interatomic and/or even intra-atomic or subatomic interstices** so small that the injection-recipient would not be aware of any skin being broken or any other disruption of the integrity or wholly intact condition of the tissue(s), anatomical structures or (components of) organs located between the therapeutic entry-points on or in the recipient's body and the site(s) within the recipient that would appropriately be treated with the therapy.

The **brain** or **neural stimuli** and **stimulation might** consist in or **be conveyed by** means of (possibly, sharply-focused) (a) **electromagnetic modalities**, such as, for example, **transcranial magnetic** (brain) **stimulation** (TMS) (4), (b) **acoustic phenomena**, such as **infrasound** and **ultrasound**, (c) beam(s) or stream(s) of one or more individual (or kinds of) medicinal/pharmacologic molecules, atoms, ions or subatomic particles that might be forcefully-powered, aimed-at and precisely-directed toward and into **pleasure**- (i.e., **reward-**) -subserving sites in the brain or, conceivably, elsewhere in the nervous system, or (d) other type(s) of (anatomic-/neuroanatomic) **target-location-specific** therapeutic delivery system(s).

These systems might be readily capable of accessing precisely-focused-on, specifically-aimed-at target locations anywhere within the treatment-seeking subject or stimulation-recipient. Such **high degrees** of **localization** or (high) resolution would possibly be, by current standards, highly **nanotechnologized** (43, 45) or microminiaturized. They might be circumscribed within very small areas, contained in minute volumes, measuring perhaps a tenth of a cubic millimeter or even some (tiny) fraction thereof (46).

The stimulus-focusing and stimulus-conveying/delivering apparatus might utilize waveform superposition principles (constructive and/or destructive interference) and/or mechanisms adapted and derivative from, or even actually entailing lasers, masers, phased arrays, tomography, holography, nuclear magnetic resonance, NMR (or, in terms of its medical applications, **magnetic resonance imaging**, MRI), superconductors, fiber optics, analog or digital circuits and waveform/signal-processing or other (perhaps, yet-to-be-conceived-and-devised) technologies.

The stimulation-mediating device would actually be a brain-, neural- or neurophysiological stimulator, pacemaker, pacesetter, or other kind of nervous-system-activity-or-function-modulator, -modifier or prosthesis, as explained presently.

Neural **pacemakers**, may be construed, mechanismically, as conveyors and deliverers of brain or neural stimulation, which is generated and applied in such ways as to engender some sort of pace, rhythm or pattern of response or responsiveness within or among cells (or their components) that can be maintained at some level(s) of balance, **equilibrium** or regulated interplay **between activation** and **deactivation**.

In view of many conceivable applications fitting the criteria of both brain/neural **stimulation** and brain/neural **pacemaking/pacesetting**, all four abbreviated terms: (1) **BS**, (2) **NS**, (3) **BP** and (4) **NP**, may be considered practically equivalent and used interchangeably. And these four categories might, collectively, be designated as **neural prostheses** or **neuroprostheses** (NPs). The acronym **BSNP** can be used to signify any one, more than one, or even all four categories. The **NP** part of **BSNP** may be interpreted as signifying (a) **neural** prostheses in general or (b) **neural** pacemaker-type, neural prostheses in particular, depending on which interpretation would seem more appropriate for any context being considered.

Consistent with an emphasis on how to improve and diversify learning abilities and work skills, **neuroprostheses**, might (most readily and appropriately for this particular context) be construed as being primarily intended to **alleviate** or **minimize** various learning disabilities, attention deficits or deficit disorders, depressive, anxiety and other psychiatric disorders or illnesses, as well as neurological or neuropsychiatric limitations and deficiencies or mere circumstantial, educational shortfalls in relation to actual or potential high levels of technological prowess, as might be prerequisitely associated with high-level/high-paying employment opportunities.

A reason why a combination of (a) acoustic/sonic and (b) electromagnetic stimulation **might** be found to be adequate for many herein-suggested applications might be a mutually complementary (additive, potentiating or synergistic) interaction between the relatively high-level **focusing** ability of **ultrasound** (47-49) and the relatively high-level **penetrating power** of magnetic stimulation (4, 48, 49). The high level of magnetic penetratingness is consistent with the finding that magnetic fields are not impeded in their passage through (the skull) bone, **or** through soft tissues.

Ultrasound (when appropriate and adequate magnitudes or values of stimulus parameters are used) might exert its stimulative effect(s) primarily by mechanically stretching, deforming and pulling open **channels, pores** or passageways in the neuronal/nerve-cell membranes and thereby increasing neuronal **permeability** and facilitating neural-activity-mediating ionic, molecular, or, in any case, particle-transporting and neurophysiological-activity-modulating **currents**, flowing inward toward, actually **into** and outward from/**out of** the neuron(s) (49).

And magnetic stimulation (when appropriate and adequate values of stimulus parameters are used) might exert its stimulative effect(s) primarily by **creating** or **engendering** (generally, ionic) current(s), flowing into and out from the neuron(s) (49). Thus, the ultrasonically-mediated stretching-widely-open of channels in the neuronal membrane(s) might facilitate and catalytically augment the magnetically-induced ionic currents that would increase neuronal activity, excitability and responsiveness in such ways as to facilitate brain, neural and neuronal stimulation and, thereby, readily implement the proposed mechanisms of learning-abilities' and work-skills' enhancement.

Consistent with the idea of using dual-modality, electromagnetic/ultrasonic stimulation would be the use of simultaneous, hence, **superimposed electromagnetic and ultrasonic fields, perhaps** with both being of the **same frequency** (46). Then, "the ultrasound field could be used to define the region to be stimulated, with the electromagnetic field providing a mechanism for stimulation, at reasonable field strength of each" as expressed by Robert A Spangler (49).

One way (undoubtedly, **not the only way**) of bringing about precisely-focused, high-resolution, reversible, noninjurious, functionally-modifying BSNP, might be achieved by **combining** (a) the basic approach delineated by the late William J. Fry in his 1968 paper (46) with (b) the basic approach entailed in "time-reversed acoustics" (41), including, perhaps, the use of **"time reversal"** (i.e., **sequence-reversal,** stimuli-absorbing, stimuli-reflecting) **mirrors** (TRMs), as noted by Mathias Fink (41, 50-53).

Acoustic time-reversal mirrors are explained on page 92 (41), essentially as follows: "...a source emits sound waves.... Each transducer in a mirror array detects the sound arriving at its location and feeds the signal to a computer....each transducer plays back its sound signal in reverse in synchrony with the other transducers. The original wave is re-created, but traveling backward, retracing its passage back through the medium,...refocusing on the original source point."

An observation that might be of particular relevance, as expressed by Fink on page 97 (41) is the following: "Porous bone in the skull presents an energy-sapping challenge to focusing ultrasound waves on a brain tumor to heat and destroy it. A

106

time-reversal mirror with a modified playback algorithm can nonetheless focus ultrasound through skull bone onto a small target."

It might be valid to infer from this observation that if one were to use **somewhat different** values of ultrasonic **stimulation parameters/variables** than those that might be useful in destroying a tumor, one might be able to (**nondestructively, noninjuriously,** and reversibly) **functionally** stimulate **a small target area or volume** in the living **brain**, inside of the fully intact head (meninges, skull, scalp, etc.).

Moreover, since time-reversal techniques may also be useful with **electromagnetic waves** (and quantum electron wavefunctions), they (T-R techniques) might offer a feasible way to implement W. J. Fry's idea of **combining ultrasonic** and **electromagnetic** phenomena to bring about "electrical stimulation of brain localized without probes." The crux of the combinative idea is expressed in the 1968 paper on page 919 (46) in this way: "The basic principle is partial **rectification** (in the focal region of an ultrasonic field) **of** the **alternating current** that flows **in response to** an externally applied **electric field** (of the same frequency). Since the magnitude of the electrical conductivity of the tissue varies with temperature, adiabatic **temperature changes** (produced by the acoustic disturbance) cause a **periodic variation** in **conductivity** that **results** in a **net unidirectional transfer of charge**."

It is conceivable that some adaptation of a combination of the insights of Fink with those of Fry might possibly lead to an acoustic/electromagnetic method capable of (a) detecting, monitoring and effectively **utilizing learning-work(ing)-associated-**neurophysiological manifestations/neurophysiologically-related **signals**

(LWAMs/LWASes) and (b) noninvasively stimulating reward- (i.e., pleasure-) mediating structures/pathways (16-36, 53-54) in the brain in notably effective, learning- and work-facilitative (LWF) ways.

A "saser" (acoustically **analogous** to a **laser**) might be characterized as "bright sound" or "a laser that's made from sound," expressed here in an acronym form that abbreviatedly represents the analogous-to-laser concept of "**sound** amplification by stimulated emission of (sonic) radiation" (55). Sasers are currently in early experimental and developmental stages. A diverse assortment of designs are in the process of being conceived and implemented in preliminary ways.

Component parts, media, and operative phenomena include sound-transmissible crystals, tiny blocks of glass or ruby (aluminum oxide containing sparsely distributed chromium ions), laser-beam-induced initiation of sound amplification, piezoelectric transducers that convert fluctuating voltages into high-frequency vibrations, semiconductors such as gallium arsenide consisting in laminated structural designs, high-energy-particle-bombarded pieces of silicon, water-filled vessels containing billions of tiny, electrolysis-engendered gas bubbles that are squeezed by being subjected to electric fields or having their containers' sides squashed, **phonons** (high-frequency sound waves) or resonating lower acoustic frequencies. The goal of **amplified** (already accomplished to the extent of a factor of at least 30 "or so"), highly directional beams of sound waves is construed in terms of potential practical applications, as exemplified forthwith.

A list of intended and anticipated implementations of sasers might validly include powerful **acoustic** microscopes, defect-detecting, thickness-measuring and quality-assessing **probes** and **sensors** designed for use with respect to various composite materials, microprocessors/computer processing units (CPUs), devices that might increase signal-to-noise ratios (SNRs) in diversely-constituted circuits by means of quietening the noise inherent in virtually all electrical circuits and, **possibly**, relevantly to the prospects of **detecting** and elucidating characteristics of **mind particles** (explained below), sasers that might be used in the capacity of ultra-sensitive particle detectors that would be analogous to photomultipliers.

Conceivable adaptations of **sasers** might **also** be **useful** when applied **together with lasers** as the respective **acoustical/sonic** and **electromagnetic** components of the aforementioned combinative paradigm entailing time-reversal (most relevantly in this context, **stimulus/response pattern** or **sequence**-reversal) (41) and probe-free, electrical brain stimulation/neural-function-modulating/pacemaking (46) technologies.

However, whether or not this or any other particular kind of approach should prove workable, it stands to reason that there probably, if not **undoubtedly**, could be many **more than** just **one** way of effectively accomplishing this potentially financially/economically valuable goal.

For example, a purely electromagnetic methodology or a purely acoustic/sonic approach might be adequately effective to accomplish significant or substantial learning/educational and work skills' improvement and facilitation if suitable and adequate values of stimulus parameters are focused-on/aimed-at/targeted-to pleasure (or 'reward') centers possibly located in one or more of the following neuroanatomic areas, regions, pathways, sites, or structures (16): the medial forebrain bundle, some lateral hypothalamic and some limbic sites/structures, the cingulate cortex, anterior thalamus, hippocampus, amygdala, caudate, septal area, nucleus accumbens septi, forebrain/prosencephalon, midbrain/mesencephalon, medulla, entorhinal, retrosplenial and/or cingulate jutallocortex, or cerebellum (17, 18).

In particular, vagal nerve stimulation (19), septal stimulation (20), (whereby "patients brightened, looked more alert, seemed more attentive to their environment,...could calculate more rapidly and, generally, more accurately (with) memory and recall **enhanced** or unchanged"), brain sites involved in the perception of speech (whereby auditory/vocal hallucinations, in a majority of schizophrenics tested, were diminished or alleviated (21, 22) and functional-MRI-indicated, simultaneous activation of sites in the prefrontal lobes together with sites in the parahippocampal cortex (11) might seem promising as potential memory, learning, and work-skills' improvement/facilitation, neuroanatomic-subserving foci (i.e., focuses)/loci (i.e., locus-es).

Some other approaches/methodologies that **might** also prove useful/helpful in terms of brain stimulation/neural modulation/pacemaking **might** include some adaptations and applications of one or more of the following potential or already-existing technologies: (a) contact-lens-size (56) or, conceivably, even (much) **smaller** (57-59) **electrodes**, merely **placed** in **appropriate**-for-specific-application **position(s) on** (the outsides of) patients', students' or workers' **heads**, in order to serve as brain-signal (56) and/or brain-stimulation mediators, (b) neural implants (39, 43, 60), such as nanobot-based implants that might circulate throughout the **recipient's body** (**including** the body's associated and **component brain**), **brain-computer-interfacing (BCI)** with **functional electrical**/electromagnetically-induced, physiological **stimulation, FES** (61) being engendered thereby, (c) "neuron transistors" (such as adaptations of field effect transistors, FETs) (39, 43, 62-67) that "noninvasively allow communication between electronics and biological neurons" (43) (d) non-contact-requiring ultrasound (or other acoustic phenomena) possibly entailing "layers of material," added on to a sound emitter, "thereby matching (the emitter's) impedance to that of air" (68), (e) ultraviolet, visible or infrared laser-based or otherwise electromagnetically-mediated electrical current or electron beams, possibly entailing one-molecule transistors (69), small-number-of-atoms- (e.g., 58 atoms) nanotechnologically-comprised, ratchet-like motors (68) conceivably coupled with quantum tunneling, defined on page 313 (39) and electron-based quantum ratchets (70) that might constitute a basis whereby to eliminate the need for "a nightmare of connecting wires" and thereby implement a far-reaching realm of "wireless electronics."

What about situations in which rewarding brain/neural stimulation might actually be **distracting**, hence, **obstructive** to learning and working? Depending on (a) values of stimulus parameters, (b) the **stimulation** modality/ies, and (c) which particular **neuroanatomic** "reward" or pleasure-subserving pathways, "centers" or sites might be **used, pleasurable** brain/neural **stimulation might** actually **distract** or **pull** the **attention** of the patient, recipient or aspiring student/worker/-worker-in-training **away** from the subject matter to be learned and mastered, thereby **impairing** rather than **facilitating** learning, **working** and other kinds of constructive performance and processes, such as hobby-related endeavors.

111

Two (but **not** necessarily **the only**) possibly effective solutions to this distraction/attention-undermining problem might be 1) to use some **other**, **different** stimulus characteristics or parameter values, some different stimulus modality/ies or means, and/or different neuroanatomic target sites and (2) to stagger, straddle or **alternate** (relatively brief) pleasure- stimulation periods with (relatively brief) learning/work-skills' acquisition or application/performance periods.

By chronologically **alternating (a)** relatively brief (for **example**, five-minute-long) learning/work/performance periods, while their constructive, high-quality occurrence would be virtually simultaneously substantiated and signaled by mental/physical-process-indicative manifestations **with (b)** relatively brief (for example, one-minute-long) pleasureful brain stimulation-delivery-reception periods, then, even if the stimulation were somehow or in some way(s) intrinsically **distracting** to learning, working or other modes of constructive activities (e.g., sports, hobbies), nonetheless, **due to** (the learning/working-performance-facilitation-stimulation system's entailing the conflict avoidance feature of the separation in time of the (a) learning/work/skills'-performance period(s) from (b) the gratifying stimulation periods, the pleasure or "reward" periods might, nevertheless, be expected to motivatingly facilitate and improve learning, working and skills' performance.

Conceivably, there might be a potentially feasible prospect of **instantaneously fast, effort-free, pleasure-free**, and **even conscious-awareness-free** learning, working and other kinds of performance facilitation. Moreover, sooner or later, any feasible **instantaneous**/ultra-fast, altogether pleasure-free, pain-free, effort-free and subconscious or unconscious methods of **transferring**, **encoding** and **storing** enormous quantities of knowledge and information in virtually any brain or mind (possible nature of distinction explained below) might be discovered and implemented. But in the meantime, relatively defortized, pleasurized, rapid (but not necessarily instantaneous) and conscious-awareness-**entailing** or -**necessitating** (as opposed to consciousness-bypassing) learning/working/skills-performance-enhancing and facilitative methods might be significantly valuable.

Even without the discoveries or inventions of **(a) instantaneously-effectible**, conceivably (neurophysiologically) encodable/decodable **learning, work**-skills' acquisition and skills' **performance**-enhancement **facilitation** (IELWPF) **and** possibly **even without** (b) conscious-awareness-/conscious-mind-/**consciousness-bypassing learning, work** and **performance facilitation** (CBLWPF), but **merely with** (c) **enjoyitizing/pleasurizing, learning/work/performance-enhancing-facilitation** (EPLWPF) and (d) **de-effortizing learning-working-performance-enhancing facilitation** (DELWPF), the following scenario might be possible.

By means of EPLWPF and DELWPF (together specifiable as EPDE-LWPF), we might be enabled to be/become virtually **instantly** strongly **interested in** and **quickly, broadly,** maybe even **comprehensively knowledgeable about** and **proficient** at the application of skills **associated with** or **with respect to whichever areas of endeavor** we might **choose** (with each of us **making our own** choices and **decisions) to be** gratifyingly, prosperously and capably **employed** in terms of.

If and when we might ever have the benefits of all four kinds of LWPF (a-d, above), then, as **one** aggregate, fourfold kind of LWPF, it could be designated as **instantaneous, consciousness-bypassing, enjoyitizing/pleasurizing, de-effortizing**

113

learning, **working** and other kinds of **performance** enhancement and **facilitation** (ICBEPDE-LWPF).

However, if the relatively **readily implementable** basic methodology of (enjoyitizing, pleasurizing, and **de-effortizing**) EPDE-LWPF, essentially as explained herein (above), were to be taken to fruition (under optimal research and development-associated circumstances, this goal might be accomplishable in as little as a year or two) (1-148), then any EPDE-LWPF recipient might readily be enabled to expeditiously become not only (conceivably) very **well-educated** (maybe, in some cases, at least, encyclopedically so), but, also (in connection with readily becoming sustainedly and reliably, employment-relevantly **productive** and **versatile**) **unlikely** to suffer from deprivation of material necessities or from financial stress, poverty, chronic hunger or any other shortage- or lack-of-money related adversity. Hence, any such EPDE-LWPF recipient/beneficiary might be expected to be **rich**, according to the definition given above. A noninvasive learning/working-facilitative, brain-stimulation-neuroprosthetic-pacemaker/pacesetter system could, conceivably, come into practically useful being in as little as one to five years, in connection with and as a consequence of well-conceived and well-carried-out research and development, at a relatively inexpensive cost of several million dollars (1-148).

HOW EVERYONE MIGHT BE FAMOUS

Rene Descartes's renowned expression, "I think, therefore, I am," considered together with the realization that some diseases, such as Alzheimer's, etc., might

deprive us of our **ability to think**, might engender a modified version of his observation that might be expressible as: **I experience**, therefore, I am.

There is **something** about (or some aspect of) you, me and every other sentient, conscious individual which, on a lifelong basis, stays the **same** and **maintains** each of us as the selfsame individual throughout our entire respective lifetime. Is it (a) our genes?, (b) our (cumulative) memories?, (c) our personality/ies?, or (d) some part of our physical composition or makeup, such as some irreplaceable cell(s), molecule(s), atom(s), subatomic particles, etc.? Is it one or more of (a) through (d) that maintain(s) each of us as our respective identities?

Although identical twins (and clones of any individual organism) are understood and considered to have the same genes, it is clear they are not one and the same individual or consciousness. So, this realization would seem to rule out genes as the lifelong identity-defining and identity-maintaining essence of each conscious individual.

It can be contended that "identical twins or biological clones are not 'the same person or people,' **because they have different memories**." (71). A thought experiment might elucidate the role (if there is one) of memories with respect to the identity of any given individual.

Suppose we have, as volunteer experimental subjects, two identical twin siblings, who can be designated as person A and person B or, simply, A and B, respectively. Now, suppose we, as a species, at some point in the future, have access to memory-erasing and memory-decoding, -encoding and memory-implanting equipment or devices. Suppose we were to erase each and every one of twin A's memories and implant in A's brain each and every one of twin B's memories (after having deciphered or decoded them carefully, noninjuriously and non-disruptively to B and then re-encoded and implanted all of them into A's brain).

Consequently, twins A and B would have **all** of the **same memories** (and no different ones). At this point, would A and B become one and the same person, mind or consciousness? No, of course not. A and B, at this point, would **effectively** have had all of the **same experiences** (that is, they would have all of the same records of experiences or memory traces, "engrams" (72) or encoded histories of experiences) in their respective brains/minds. But would having (records of) all the same **experiences** render these two **experiencers** one and the **same experiencer** (i.e., experienceER)?

A distinction might appropriately be made here between (a) **what** gets **experienced** (i.e., experienceD) and (b) **who** does the experiencing (i.e., experiencING). So, despite having all the same experiences (records of experience), that is, all of the same memories (memory traces), **A and B remain two** separate and distinct **experiencers**. Hence, a **difference of experiences** (or memory contents) **would not** seem capable of **explaining** a **difference** of **experiencers**, that is, a difference of their identities. In other words, **what** gets experienced **does not**, in any way, **specify who** experienced it.

Twins A and B might be expected to have similar, but not identical, personality traits or features. Next, suppose we, as a species, at some point in the future, have access to personality-trait-modifying or personality-feature-erasing, -decoding, -encoding and -activating equipment. Suppose we were to modify and/or erase each of

A's personality features and put in their places or substitute each of B's corresponding features.

Consequently, twins A and B might have so perfectly identical personality profiles that the behavior of the two would be virtually indistinguishable from the standpoint(s) of any observer(s). Would two individuals' being characterizable as having identical or indistinguishably-similar personality profiles render them one and the **same** consciousness, mind or identity of experiencer? Or would they simply remain as **two separate consciousnesses** that would merely **behave** virtually identically in all observable situational contexts? The latter possibility would, intuitively, seem far more probable and credible than the former.

Thus, two individuals, even if (a) they are genetically the same (as in cases of identical twins), (b) even if they were to have identical records of experience, that is, identical cumulative memory contents and (c) identical personality traits and profiles, would still exist as two separate and distinct minds, conscious entities and experiencers. Hence, neither genetics nor memories nor personality features/profiles would seem capable of uniquely describing, specifying and constituting any given mind or consciousness.

The proposed answer to the question of what it is that constitutes the **unchanging essence of** each individual's **identity** might be that **what maintains you, me** and **every** other **individual** as the **same individual** throughout our entire, respective lifetime(s) is that the **very same experiencing entity**, that is, the **same** biochemically-/biophysically-based, discrete **consciousness** or, equivalently, but expressed slightly differently, the potentially tangible, detectable, isolatable and

117

implantable **same experiencer** (a thing or an object) will/would/does **experience** your, my or any other individual's respective life at age 110 (assuming, for discussion's sake, such prodigious longevity) **as did experience it** at age three (as well as at any other age, within or outside of the three to 110 year age range).

You, I and any/every other individual might encounter some difficulty or doubts in responding affirmatively to the question, "Is the way **I** experience the world around me the way it **actually, really** is?" One might readily respond, essentially as follows: "Regardless of the **accuracy**/validity **or inaccuracy**/invalidity of how I perceive and interpret the 'world'/environment around me, which could, conceivably, be merely an exercise in **virtual reality** (73-76), one that entirely conceals from my perception an underlying **real** reality, in which I am merely a lifelong experimental subject, nevertheless, there are two things that I do feel relatively, confidently affirmative about and feel I do know, virtually for **sure,** are: (1) I am experiencing **something**; this life is **something** and (2) I am **experiencing** this something as a single, essentially separate, even solitary, **individual, unitary entity**, that is, **a consciousness**, who is aware of everything I experience. Or viewed and expressed somewhat differently, I am **experiencing this**, my life, as an **individuated, undividable experiencer** or **indivisible consciousness.**"

But if you, I and anyone/everyone else is an indivisible **experiencer,** biomedically (i.e., biochemically/biophysically) bonded to or otherwise confined within a **brain** and **its** associated or corresponding **body** (abbreviatable as a **BB** or **BBP**, intended to signify a **brain-body pair**), **what** then is the **biological** or **physiological basis** of this **undividable** experiencer which **is** (the unitary) you?

Using the most powerful microscopes and medical imaging equipment and methods currently available to the human race, even if coupled with the most painstaking analyses and the most perceptive observations, it might (or might **not**) be readily possible to detect and discern a **singular, discrete, unitary** biological, physiological **entity** which is your, my or anyone else's **indivisible experiencer** or **undividable consciousness**.

One **possible** reason why we might **not** be able to visualize or isolate any single, unitary, undividable experiencer-consciousness (which **is** you, me or any other **specific** individual) might be that the biological, physiological entity in question **might** simply be **too small** to be visualized and isolated at this point in time, even when the best currently existing equipment is used.

So, let us suppose that, at some point in the future, perhaps by dint of more powerful microscopes and imaging modalities than any currently available, it will become possible to actually **see** and, then, isolate each individual's indivisible experiencer-consciousness or, same-meaningly, **mind**, which, conceivably, may travel to any point(s) in the individual's body, but may spend the majority of its time, in accordance with what we seem to feel, in the **brain**. Such a visible, isolatable chemical/physical entity might be designated as a **mind-particle-experiencer-consciousness** or, alternatively, a **mind-particle-consciousness-experiencer**, abbreviatable as an MP, MPEC or MPEX.

In essence, you **are** your MPEC. The person you see in the mirror (any time you look) is merely the brain-body pair (BBP or, simply, BB) within which your MPEC, hence, your mind, is bonded, bound and confined by dint of implantation therein during gestation. A brain-body pair might, alternatively and equally validly, be designated as a **body-brain pair** (a body, including its component brain). The choice of the former designation (brain-body pair) rather than the latter is purely arbitrary.

Daniel C. Dennett, in his book, **Consciousness Explained** (77), on pages 101 and 102, comes very close to conceptualizing this notion of an actual, discrete **particle** constituting the **biological basis**, the necessary and sufficient essence of each one of our respective, unique consciousnesses, each of which **is** a person's respective **mind** or **consciousness**, in his statement, "For most **practical** purposes, we can consider the **point** of view of a particular conscious subject to be just that: a **point** moving through space...." The concept he suggests most clearly coincides with the herein-proposed hypothesis of a discrete **mind-particle-experiencer-consciousness** or, alternatively, a mind-particle, consciousness-experiencer (MP, MPEC, MPEX, or **MP-CONEX**) if the MP is construed to be a **point-particle** or point-sized, point-shaped (**perhaps,** spherical) particle.

Also consistent with the hypothesis of a single, indivisible (mind) particle being the biochemical/biophysical basis of **each person's** individual, **unique mind** (or consciousness) is this quoted observation:

"...there is room for **only one thing** in the **spotlight of attention** at **any one moment**," which appears on page 32 in "States of mind,..." (14).

Such a mind or consciousness-particle might routinely, pervasively, and information-gatheringly/-sharingly/-disseminatingly/and -integratingly interact (by instantaneously making and then breaking huge numbers of chemical/physical bonds), directly or indirectly, with any and all chemicals constituting or otherwise contained within or passing through the human body, including, probably predominantly, chemicals within the body's component brain.

Subsequently, on page 430 in Dennett's book (77), reference is made to a material substance consisting in "some...special **group** of atoms in your brain" as the hypothetical essence of any given person's consciousness, mind or identity. A reasoned response to this hypothesis might be that no one's individual/individuated consciousness, identity or mind could possibly consist in a **group** (?!) of **any** thing or of any substance or kind. Since each person's identity, consciousness or mind seems to be **just one entity,** the biomedical, physical/chemical basis of individual identity (each individual's) can **correspondingly, accordingly** and **rationally** be expected to be **just one physical thing/chemical thing** and cannot plausibly consist in any kind of **group** (of anything). This one physical thing (or one chemical thing) cannot be, for example, a **single atom**, because even **one** atom is made up of a number, greater than one, of discrete, separate (subatomic) **component** parts or particles.

Regardless of whether or not the adult brain engages in the process of more-or-less continuously making new cells to replace older, dying ones (78-81), it stands to reason that if a **group** (of atoms or a **group** of any other kind/s of entities) is precluded from being the biophysical/biochemical basis of each or of any individual person's indivisible, **unitary** consciousness, then it **also** stands to reason that **any group** of brain cells (whether periodically-replaced or permanent on a life-long basis) would **also** be **precluded** as the chemical/physical basis, that is, the necessary and sufficient, defining essence of each or any individual's singular, undividable consciousness, by dint of the same fundamental reason.

In particular, it does **not** seem **logical** or **plausible** that a **group** (!) of **any** thing(s) (for example, a **group** of subatomic particles, such as collectively constitute a single atom, a **group** of atoms, a group of molecules, of brain cells or a group of any other discrete entities) could possibly be the definitive physical-chemical essence/ basis of any unitary, indivisible, singular phenomenon, such as each person's **separate, unique, undividable** and **unitary mind** (mind-particle-experiencer, MPEX) or **consciousness** (mind-particle-experiencer-consciousness, MPEC). This would seem to be true notwithstanding some very interesting and possibly correct (but outside the scope of this particular context) split-brain studies-derived suggestions of there being at least **two** (separable) minds per BBP (82-84).

However, any given person's mind, or, definitively, any particular person's mental and physical/chemical identity **could plausibly** consist in any **one** specific, single, **indivisible, subatomic particle** contained **in** any **one specific atom**. But if this were true, then there might plausibly be trillions of trillions of minds (i.e., subatomic particles = consciousnesses) contained within each individual brain or brain-body (pair).

Considering the possibility that this idea (of trillions of individual, undividable subatomic particulate conscious minds inhabiting each living BBP) **might** be correct, let us conjecture that each one of the **subatomic-particulate-consciousnesses** (SPCs) might have **some** amount of free will and **some** amount of implementable power with respect to what the host brain-body pair as a whole **says** and **does**.

However, without having any particular reason to think otherwise, let us assume that **each** one of the trillions of SPCs has the **same** amount of free will and enforceable power over the BB (as a whole) as every other SPC does. And even though each SPC might (erroneously) believe itself to be the sole occupant/inhabitant of the BB in question, the fact would remain that **it** (any given SPC) would have no more (or less) power over the BB's speech and behavior than any other SPC residing therein.

Let us assume, for discussion's sake, that the amount of free will and enforceable power of each individual SPC with respect to the multi-trillion-mind-population-widely **shared** BBP would be analogous and effectively proportional to the power of the one vote that each citizen in a democracy has the recognized right and ability to implement or cast in an election.

Under such analogous circumstances, each SPC would have no more ability to control or predict what the host BB would do or say (in relation to itself, in relation to other animated, apparently living BBs, or in relation to apparently inanimate, non-living objects) than an averagely empowered, individual citizen living in a democratic nation would have any ability to effectively dictate, control or predict events or news of an intra-national or international nature. Hence, each SPC would be continuously, somewhat surprised by the things its native BB would say and do, similarly as each of us forward-looking citizens is, perhaps regularly, somewhat surprised by what we read in each consecutive day's newspapers.

I will readily admit that I am **occasionally** surprised by the (sometimes embarrassing) things I say and do. But if I were merely one of trillions of conscious, one-vote-apiece-wielding occupants of what I consider to be "my" brain-body, with **each** of us (trillions of residents) contained herein (in this "my" BBP), **mistakenly**, feeling we are the **sole** inhabitant, then, I would expect to be **regularly** surprised by what my (host) BB says and does, **continually** rather than only occasionally.

By reason of the observation that I am **only occasionally** (rather than regularly) astonished by my words and/or actions, there would seem to be a strong suggestion that I (my mind or MP) truly am or is alone as the **sole conscious determinant** and, consistently (or, at least, not inconsistently) the **sole conscious occupant** of this brain-body pair wherein I reside. So, it may seem **logical** and (by dint of entailing a simplifying assumption or premise) **sensible** to return to the notion that each BBP is occupied by **only** one **mind/consciousness**, despite the (**possibly correct**) split-brain studies-based suggestions of at least two minds/conscious entities per BB. So, let us proceed with this one MPEX per BBP assumption.

Explaining the situation somewhat differently, despite the often **convincing**, or **at least** strongly **persuasive** split-brain-study-derived notions of two conscious entities residing in each brain, if only **for simplicity** of discussion's **sake**, let us, in this context at least, embrace a **one** conscious entity (MP) per BBP assumption.

As delineated above, it would seem somewhat implausible to suppose that the chemical/physical basis of **anyone's mind** is merely **one** particular **specimen** of the tiniest undividably-elemental category of subatomic particles of one particular atom contained within the BBP in which any particular mind happens to dwell or be bonded within.

It would seem more plausible to postulate that the biological-physiological, chemical-physical (hypothetically, **perhaps**, too-small-to-be-seen-or-imaged-with-existing-equipment) basis of the conscious mind is or might be an extremely tiny particle of a possibly as-yet-undetected and undiscovered **kind** of matter, that is, a **conscious**, **experiencing** kind of matter, in particular, a **mind particle (experiencer-consciousness** or **consciousness-experiencer, MP-CONEX**), as opposed to and different from possibly, relatively much more plentiful, presumably (but not unequivocally) **non-conscious**, non-aware, non-experiencing particulate **matter**, that is composed of one or more particles, such as, electrons, protons, atoms, ions, molecules etc. Such seemingly non-experiencing, non-aware, non-conscious matter seems to be the mainstay of contemplation, theorization, experimentation and practical application as undertaken and implemented by an apparently vast majority of all kinds of scientists. It would seem readily conceivable that **conscious matter**, such as indivisible mind **particles**, might have properties that are significantly **different from** particles of presumably (outwardly, at least) **non-conscious**, non-self-aware, non-environmentally-aware matter, such as (presumably, that is, inferentially based on the preceding thought experiment entailing the **somewhat** implausible possibility of trillions of conscious, experiencing, self-aware, subatomic particles within each living brain/BBP) neutrons, protons, etc.

WOULD A CLONE OF YOU BE ANOTHER YOU?

If the undividable experiencer-consciousness or MPEC bonded within or inhabiting any particular clone of your BB were **not your** MPEC or MP-CONEX, then the clone would **not** be you. Instead, it would merely be a younger, virtual twin of you. If, on the other hand, we were to extricate you (i.e., your MPEC) from the brain-body in which you currently reside and implant it into a clone of you, then the clone would **indeed** be (a younger version of, but nonetheless) you.

However, if one were to bond your MPEC (i.e., **you**) to a clone of the brain and associated body within which another individual, for example, I (that is, my MPEC) currently resides, then **that** clone (of **my** brain-body pair) would be **you** and would **not** be me, by virtue of your MPEC's presence in the clone and my MPEC's absence from the clone in question. So, you, that is, at least for discussion's sake, let us hypothesize that you **are** your MPEC and you are **not your** brain-body pair (the one into which you were born).

Thus, you are **not** your brain **or** any other part(s) of the rest of your body. I am **not** my brain or body. I am my MPEC, MPEX MP or MP-CONEX. And any other person is **that** person's MP, **not** the brain-body, BB, in which it finds itself. And **any** brain-body pair your MPEX inhabits/gets bonded to **becomes** you. Any BBP or BB my MPEX gets implanted into becomes me. And any BB that **any** other specific one else's MPEC gets bound to, accordingly, becomes **that** specific (any) one.

DOES ONE'S MPEC AGE?

Understanding the aging process as, essentially, one whereby a living organism gradually falls apart into its (previously more-or-less effectively, structurally/ functionally interactive) component parts, it would seem **unlikely** that a mind-particle-

126

experiencer-consciousness (MPEC) would or could age, because, being a unitary, indivisible entity, an MPEC would have no component parts to fall apart **into**.

BY CIRCULATING EVERYONE'S MPEC THROUGH POSITIONS OF CLOSE PROXIMITY WITH EVERY OTHER MPEC AND LITERALLY THROUGH EVERY LIVING BBP, EVERYONE WOULD BE FAMOUS AND BETTER ABLE TO LIVE IN PEACE

By circulating (perhaps over and over again, unceasingly) every MP through positions of close (enough for mutual exploratory, edifying, interaction-permissive and -facilitative) proximity with respect to every other MP and also through (temporary and brief periods of bondedness within) every living BB on the planet, every MP would thereby come to know and appreciate the unique knowledge collection and special immutable, unique qualities of every other MP and the knowledge contained in and **characteristics** (though not necessarily immutable, by dint of always- and ever-possible genetic and other kinds of modifications) of **or associated with** every BB on earth. Hence, Everyone would be famous, because **Everyone**, i.e., every MPEC, would be well-informed and close-contactedly knowledgeable about every **other** MPEC as well as in relation to every living, human BBP on the planet.

Consequently, worldwide fame would be one of the byproducts (even if not deemed a worthy goal in and of itself) that would accrue to every MP who would (want to and/or be willing to) partake of **global MPEC/BBP circulation.**

Due to the potentially (world-) widely-spread circulation not only of vast knowledge, but also, potentially, of each and every participant's **feelings** and deepest, heartfelt concerns, desires and aspirations, sincere cooperative motives leading to the formation of stronger than ever-yet enjoyed bases for global harmony and peace might come into existence.

WOULD THERE BE ANY PRIVACY POSSIBLE FOR MPECS OPTING TO PARTICIPATE IN GLOBAL MPEC/BBP CIRCULATION?

Yes, there might still be the possibility of privacy. Each consciousness (MPEC), **although** a **unitary entity**, might, nonetheless, have internal differentiation into **various structural** and **functional areas** or inseparable **parts**, in much the same way as a statue representing a human figure, even if it is carved from a **single piece of marble**, might be differentiated into various **structural** regions or parts (e.g., head, arms, torso, legs, hands, feet, etc.), which respectively, perform the various, different-from-each-other, **functional** roles of representing and depicting the various and different parts of an actual human body.

For simplicity's sake, let us, hypothetically, visualize an MPEC, for example, as a unitary, **hollow sphere**, the topography of the internal and external surfaces of which may be differentiated into variously-functioning, hill- and valley-like features, ridges, grooves, tunnels, helical structures, hammerlike appendages or extensions, stairway-like gradations, wheel-like or rotary areas, diaphragm-like regions, pulley, ratchet and conveyor-belt-like substructures, enclosures of various shapes, alternately expanding and contracting zones, etc. Let us suppose these diverse structural features, in their mutually cooperative and helpful roles, are capable of processing, sorting, according to criteria of style and substance, and storing (**both** within the MPEC itself and, possibly, also within the particular brain-body pair in which the MPEC under consideration is bonded) **various kinds of experiences**, such as perceptions, information, memories, thoughts, emotional responses and other kinds of ostensibly subjective or experiential phenomena.

The kind of **cubicles** within the structure of each MPEC that might be **used for** (a) **processing** and **storing** encoded, perhaps encrypted, representations of highly **personal, possibly appropriately**-maintained-as-private, educationally-irrelevant, work-skills-irrelevant, generally intensely **emotional experiences**, perceptions, information, thoughts, memories, etc. might be expected to be structurally **different** from the kind of **cubicles**, also within the structure of each MPEC, used **for** (b) processing and storing encoded, but probably **not** encrypted forms of relatively **impersonal**, perhaps businesslike, business-type or professional, mostly unemotional but **educationally-relevant** and **marketably-valuable** experiences, perceptions, information, thoughts, memories, concepts, skills, and other objectively valuable phenomena.

Consequently, **privacy** could perhaps be **preserved by and for** all MPECs, participating in MPEC/BBP (possibly worldwide) circulation, by dint of each, individual consciousness (MPEC)'s modifying its internal and external topographic features, shapes or structures, so as to create virtual, functional, **locked lids** or **locked doors** over the cubicles used to contain (a) -type phenomena (as denoted directly above), while leaving fully **open** and **accessible** (to and for all circulation-participant MPECs) all of the cubicles used to contain (b) -type phenomena (as, also, denoted directly above).

Similarly, each brain (part of each brain-body pair) might have (c) emotionally-loaded, highly-personal, educationally- and employment- skills-unrelated phenomena, that is, the memory traces of such phenomena contained in functional, virtual or structural compartments **of one kind** which could, effectively, have **locked lids** or **locked doors** in relation to/from the standpoint of every MPEC (except the one originally **born** into the particular BBP). And (d) emotionally-relatively-neutral, educationally- and employment-skills-related knowledge and information might be stored **in another kind** of functional, virtual or structural compartments that would be **fully open and accessible to** every MPEC passing through **each** particular BBP.

Hence, privacy might remain as a durably reliable possibility. And since each MPEC and each BBP might be expected to contain a unique collection of knowledge, memories and skills (with, at least, some of them being **highly marketable** or directly beneficial to oneself, i.e., to each one of us, individually), most (of us) MPECs might be expected to **choose** the quality-of-life- (in particular, education- and wealth-related-) -improving effects that would be associated with worldwide MPEC/BBP circulation.

Nonetheless, it would seem reasonable, or even necessary, in view of notions of ethical rectitude, to acknowledge and facilitate each MPEC'S right to make **its own decision** as to whether or not to (a) remain exclusively bonded to the brain-body into which it were (was originally) **born** or (b) participate in world-wide MPEC/BBP circulation. If and when such circulation might prove feasible, then the marketable employment-relatable and directly self-benefitable knowledge and skills accessible to self-excluded, **non-circulating MPEC's** would be so minuscule, **compared to** the quantities and qualities of these educational/vocational phenomena available to **circulating MPECs**, that non-circulators would, in effect, be relegating themselves to lives of (at best, **relative**) under-educatedness and poverty.

EVERY MPEC IS INHERENTLY, INTRINSICALLY AND IMMUTABLY UNIQUE

Some people (i.e., some MPECs) might worry that by their circulating through spatial positions of observationally-facilitative, relatively close proximity with every other MPEC and circulating, **literally, through** every BBP, there would result a homogenizing, unique-identity-depriving effect on all circulation-participant MPECs.

For simplicity-of-discussion's sake, let us assume that **each MPEC in the** universe is intrinsically **different** from every other MPEC **and unique**, with respect to the entire universe, **both subjectively**, in terms of **who** it is and, **correspondingly, objectively**, in terms of **what** it is, from the standpoint of potentially-observable characteristics. This assumption would seem to emerge readily from the realization that among all of the conscious entities (MPECs) in the universe, **only one** of them is **you**, i.e., **your unique MPEC**. Therefore, no appreciable reason would seem discernible as to how or why anyone's MPEC's uniqueness could be undermined in connection with its gathering any amount(s) or diversity/kind(s) of knowledge from any, many or all (other) MPECs and/or BBPs in the world or in the MP-BB-circulation-participant-system.

In summary, by means of planet-wide circulation of each (circulation-participating) MPEC through (positions of knowledge-and-information-sharingly-

131

close proximity with respect to) every other participating MPEC and through every (MPEC-participant-corresponding) BBP, all of the participating (circulating), undividable consciousnesses (MPECs) and all of their associated brain-bodies (BBPs) would be known to each and every circulation-participating MPEC, hence, would be world-famous, according as the number of participating MPECs might draw near, become close to or approximate the total, global MPEC population number.

The following quoted observations (a-c) seem to support and strengthen the idea of a unitary, discrete particle of some kind of actual matter being the chemical/physical/medical-scientific basis of each person's unique, unitary mind (consciousness-experiencer).

(a)   "The brain and body are built by DNA, and everyone's DNA is pretty much the same. We all have 99.9 percent the same DNA as Michael Jordan, Albert Einstein, Elizabeth Taylor, Charles Manson, Julius Caesar, Julia Child, and Jules Verne. All of them and everyone who has ever lived have the same 100,000 or so genes, which are organized into the same 23 chromosomes. But 'pretty much the same' is not exactly the same. There are differences in DNA - about 0.1 percent, or one bit out of every 1,000" (85). According to another source (86), "there are thousands of tiny variations among individuals, but the overall variation is no more than 0.2 percent."

(b)   "Human DNA is 98.4 percent identical with the DNA of chimpanzees and bonobos, a lesser-known chimpanzee-like ape. What is it in that other 1.6 percent that makes us different from them?" (87).

(c)   "Which species is closer to chimpanzees: humans or gorillas? Obviously, chimpanzees and gorillas look very much alike. And humans look very different from both. So, naturally, everyone expected that chimpanzees and gorillas would be each other's closest relatives. But Sibley and Ahlquist took the two strands of DNA, zipped, heated...and found that chimpanzees were more closely related to humans than they were to gorillas.... For anyone who still doesn't like the idea that we humans are more closely related to chimpanzees than gorillas are, what can be done?" (88).

These observations would seem to tend to or might possibly support a mind particle theory of each person's mental identity, because it seems virtually inconceivable or implausible that all of the constitutional differences between any two randomly selected people or among the entire, apparently enormously-variable human race **or** the much greater apparent differences between humans as a group and the "great" anthropoid apes (e.g., chimpanzees, bonobos and gorillas) as a group **could be fully accounted for** by genetic differences of only 0.1-0.2 or 1.6 percent, respectively.

Perhaps, the seemingly **unaccounted for** inter-personal (inter-human) variability and seemingly unaccounted for inter-species (humans as compared with other, anthropoid primates) differences **might** possibly, potentially **be accounted for**, at least in part, **by** potentially observable and measurable high degrees of variability of characteristics or properties of MPEXes (mind-particle/consciousness-experiencers) between and among different individual humans and **by** major differences between the MPEXes of humans (as a group) and the MPEXes or MPEX-counterparts (if there are any) in the other species (as a group). And **if the other** anthropoid primate **species'**

members do not each **have** any kind of **unitary mind-particle**/consciousness-experiencer, then the large human-as-compared-with-"great"-apes differences could possibly be, at least in part, accounted for in terms of the presence as compared with the absence of highly-variable minds (MPEXes).

So, it is possible that from the moment when a (human) mind (an MPEX) gets implanted into a human fetal brain-body pair, BBP, to the moment of arrival at the point of full adulthood, the (perhaps highly **inter-MPEX-variable**) characteristics of this MPEX may exert or have exerted some powerful guiding influences on any, some or every aspect of the differentiation, growth, development and maturation of every cell in every human brain-body pair. These powerful MP-intrinsic guiding influences might also explain **at least some** or **part** of the reason(s) why genetically identical twins have biometric differences from each other, such as differences in their fingerprints, faces, and in the irises or irides (89) of their respective eyes, despite having identical genes (90).

A pair of conjoined twins (joined at the head), Laurie and Reeba Shappell, on whom a segment of a recent documentary television program (90) is based, seem to have **two** fully **separate minds**. They have significantly different personalities and do not directly or simultaneously experience the same or each other's emotions or feelings. For example, one twin said, in reference to the other, "When she has pain, I don't feel it. And when one of us is angry, the other one does not feel the anger; unless we're angry about the **same thing**." This is the case **despite** the brain-imaging-deduced fact that **in many ways** (neuroanatomically-speaking) **they share** (apparently one, that is) the same **brain**. Or perhaps they have intricately-interwoven, but,

134

nonetheless (at least, according to brain-imaging equipment providing the highest currently possible resolution or power of visual discernment, under the twins' circumstances) **extensively overlapping brain pathways, areas** and volumes, especially in the frontal, temporal and parietal regions.

The (readily apparent, though, not necessarily genuine or true) incongruousness of two minds in, essentially, one brain might seem to further support and strengthen the idea that each person's mind (-particle-consciousness-experiencer) might be a separate and distinct chemical/physical entity. This entity or object might be bonded to and might spend most of its time traveling **within** the brain, but perhaps cannot accurately be equated with or conceived of as being the same object as the brain is.

ANOTHER WAY OF EVERY MPEC AND EVERY BBP BEING FAMOUS (AND PEACEFUL) WOULD BE VIA MPEC-INTERNET

Although MPEC circulation (the process of circulating each participating MPEC) through every living BBP and (through positions of close proximity to) every other (participating-in-circulation) MPEC might render all participating MPECs both **highly** knowledgeable as well as famous, a possibly **less-energy-demanding** (with respect to anticipatably high amounts of energy associated with rapidly and repeatedly making and breaking MPEC-to-MPEC-juxtapositional interactions and MPEC-to-BBP bonds of implantation) and a more **energy-efficient** method of **virtual** MPEC-BBP circulation, which might achieve the same results (gigantic knowledge and world-wide fame for all participating MPECs) might operate as follows.

Conceivably, every MPEC **naturally** forms a circuit with every (other) MPEC **and also** with every BBP on earth, by means of (a) perhaps a virtually, infinitesimally slender **outgoing** (knowledge-seeking) appendage and (b) a similar, also-virtually-infintesimally slender **in-coming** (potentially knowledge-loaded and -conveying) string-like or thread-like process, branch, arm-like appendage or interconnection, with (a) and (b) together constituting a loop or circuit between every two MPECs and between every MPEC and every BBP.

If this is true, then the reason why we do not seem to perceive these interconnections might be inferable from the explanation about to be presented. Each MPEC-to-MPEC, MPEC-to-BBP and BBP-to-MPEC (almost **infinitesimally slender**) interconnection might contain a mechanical (on-off, close-open) switch. Most of these interconnections currently are (and in the recorded history of our planet apparently always have been) firmly fixed into the information-**no-flow**, **off** or **open circuit** condition. Hence, knowledge, pleasure (and displeasure) are **not** automatically shared among all MPECs. On the contrary, when any one of us experiences, feels or appreciates any of these phenomena, we generally, very often or usually perceive ourselves as experiencing them in an **individuated** if not in a solitary way, relatively disjointed from the knowledge, pleasure (and displeasure) of others.

Nevertheless, according as the switches might infrequently, intermittently and spatially-sparsely **close** into an information-**pro**-flow, **ON** (as opposed to **OFF**), or closed-circuit condition or configuration, then, there might be, by this means, a genuine structural, biomedical, physiological basis for the **Collective Unconscious**, perhaps as postulated by Carl Jung (91,92). This sporadic closed-circuit condition

136

may also be the basis of the hypothesized interconnectedness of all particles in the universe, as suggested by experimental findings (93-95). **Relatively infrequently-occurring** and, sometimes, brief **instances** of these **switches** being **closed** and, therefore, **permissive** of all kinds of **informational** and emotional **inter-flow** might be at least the initial bases or catalysts of love, friendship, mutual empathy and intuitive knowledge.

However, considering the possibility that such MPEC-to-MPEC, MPEC-to-BBP and BBP-to-MPEC interconnections might **not** naturally exist, a question arises: is it conceivable that it might behoove us to muster and implement the motivational wherewithal and technological expertise (culled from within the altruistic and mechanically-inclined resources of our wisdom and knowledge) that would be necessary to construct and activate such interconnections among all of us who might be willing and wanting to live in highly harmonious, mutually informative and educational, sharing and caring ways? The answer might conceivably, sooner or later, and arguably auspiciously, be **yes**!

It would seem reasonable to infer this affirmative answer regardless of whether the universal-harmony-conducive task be one of (a) discovering MPECs and (subsequently **discovering**) naturally-existing, interconnecting one-MPEC-to-another-MPEC-then-back-to-the-first-MPEC and MPEC-to-BBP-then-back-to-the-same-MPEC circuits and then determining and implementing means whereby to close the circuits and thereby actuate and sustain flow of harmony-facilitative phenomena or a task of (b) discovering MPECs and subsequently constructing - out of some, possibly, human-made material or other kinds of interlinking substance(s) - the requisite interconnections, which would be designed and implemented in such ways as to permit many kinds of harmonizing inter-flow. In either case (a or b), the prospects of inducing numerous kinds of constructive developments might be reassuringly boundless! Let us refer to a/any one-MPEC-to-another-MPEC-then-back-to-the-first-MPEC circuit as an MPEC-through-MPEC circuit. And let us refer to a/any MPEC-to-BBP-then-back-to-the-same-MPEC circuit as an MPEC-through-BBP circuit.

If it were possible to manufacture and put in place virtually **infinitesimally slender**, ON/OFF-switch-containing interconnections (a) between each MPEC and every other MPEC, (b) between every MPEC and every BBP and (c) between every BBP and every MPEC, then by the simple action of opening and closing the ON/OFF switches contained in the interconnections, it would be possible to achieve **virtual**, as opposed to actual, **circulation** which would be analogous to the Internet of computer-associated renown.

Let us suppose the world's human population were ten billion people (i.e., ten billion MPECs, with each of us MPECs bound within our own corresponding BBP into which we were, respectively, born). Then, assuming all of them (us/we) were to want to participate in the MPEC-BBP internet, that is, participate in **virtual** MPEC-BBP circulation, then **each of** us, that is, each of our MPECs would have twenty billion **connections** or, synonymously, **segments** (with each full **circuit** being composed of two segments - one for (a) seeking and locating information/knowledge and another for (b) receiving, securing and consolidating information/knowledge, thereby, together (a and b) constituting a complete, functionally or effectively, **(loosely speaking:) circular** pathway for each MPEC-through-MPEC circuit) to and from the other ten billion (actually, ten billion-**negligibly-minus** one, with this **one** representing an **unnecessary** circuit **with itself**) MPECs and twenty (additional) billion connections (or segments) to and from the ten billion living human BBPs.

So, the total number of **interconnections** or, equivalently, **segments** would be: 10^{10} x $(2$ x $10^{10}) + 10^{10}$ x $(2$ x $10^{10}) = (2$ x $10^{20}) + (2$ x $10^{20}) = 4$ x 10^{20} interconnections or segments, with each containing an ON/OFF or CLOSED-/OPEN-circuit switch. Hence, there would be **half** of **this number** of **complete** two-interconnection- or two-segment-containing circuits or 2 x 10^{20} **complete circuits**, within or among the participant population as a whole, with this number comprising 10^{20} MPEC-through-MPEC circuits and 10^{20} MPEC-through-BBP circuits.

During any finite duration or interval of time (the specific length of which might be determined as the resulting average value of a one-vote-apiece- or one-vote-per-participating-MPEC selection process, but for illustrative purposes, let us consider for example, during each full **one second** of time (i.e., one-sixtieth of a minute)), each MPEC might have each one of its **ten billion MPEC-through-MPEC circuits** and each one of its **ten billion MPEC-through-BBP circuits, sequentially, turned on** and **then off**, in series, i.e., only **one-ON-at-a-time** (that is, switched to the **closed** position) once, for a **turned-on** duration of one twenty-billionth of a second (and a **turned-off** duration of one second minus this one twenty-billionth of a second) for **each** one of **every** MPEC's twenty billion circuits. Hence, during each twenty-billionth of a second of time, **each MPEC** would be **gaining** knowledge and other information **from** and, **simultaneously**, **imparting** knowledge and information **to** another entity or object (i.e., one of the other conscious MPEC(s) or the knowledge/information storage facilities-compartments or other kind(s) of receptacles of one of the BBP(s)).

And within each one-second-long interval, each of the ten billion MPECs (i.e., each of us human minds) would have gained knowledge and other information from and imparted these valuable phenomena to **all** of the other ten billion (minus one) MPECs and all of the ten billion BBPs. Such a system would constitute an **MPEC-BBP internet** or, synonymously, a process of **virtual** MPEC-BBP circulation (abbreviatedly designatable as **MPEC-internet** or **virtual-MPEC-circulation**) that might be expected to entail **less** necessary **consumption** or **expenditure** of **energy** than **actual** MPEC circulation, while **sharing** (obtaining from and imparting to BBPs and **other** MPECs, i.e., MPECs other than oneself) the **same amount** of **knowledge** and **information** as in the case of **actual** MPEC circulation.

This kind of virtual MPEC circulation (or MPEC-internet) might appropriately, alternatively, be dubbed (MP-CONEX-, MPEX-, MPEC- or) MP-internetus, MPEX-internet-**us**, MPEC-**inter-connect-us**, MPEC-inter-**connect**us, MPEC-inter**join**us, MPEC-inter**joyn**us, MPEC-inter**link**us, MPEC-**internet**us, MPEC-inter**nexus**, MPEX-interconnectus, simply, MP-interconnectus, etc. Analagously, **actual** MP circulation might be referred to as: MP-intercirculatus, MP-CONEX-intercirculate-us, MP-inter-perfuse-us, etc.

HOW EVERYONE MIGHT BE PAIN FREE

The seemingly widely-held view that pain is as necessary a part of conscious experience as pleasure is, may prove incorrect. The question, heard more than once by this author, "How would you know pleasure if you did not know pain?" seems **only** as rational (which is to say, **not very** rational) as the question, "How would you know love if you didn't know hate?"

All of the adaptive value of pain could possibly be achieved with, and functionally replaced by, gradations of intensity (and various qualities or kinds) of pleasure. For example, suppose a person's body becomes diseased in some way. The disease (currently) produces pain. At times, this pain might become so intense as to be intolerable and, therefore, constitute uncontrollable pain: i.e., **suffering**, that is, pain so intense that the afflicted individual cannot control impulses leading toward suicidal ideation. The diseased person, in response to the pain, visits a physician, or other health-care professional/practitioner, who prescribes medication which cures or effectively treats the disease and fully relieves the pain (suffering and suicidal ideation).

However, the same fortunate result could conceivably occur without pain (or suffering) necessarily being involved, as follows. A person's body becomes diseased. The disease produces **no pain** (or suffering), but **does** put a **stop** to any experience of **pleasure**. In this case, the diseased person, alerted **by** and in response **to the cessation or**, at least, marked **diminution of pleasure**, might be expected to visit a physician or other treatment provider who might prescribe a medication that might cure or effectively treat the illness, and, consequently, restore the patient's pleasure and enjoyment of life to their usual, amply high levels.

So the same curative or adaptively treatment-effective results might be expected to occur in connection with varying, **but completely painless**, (and completely **without** and free of suffering) intensities or **degrees** of **absence** or **presence** of **pleasure**, which could serve as varying intensities of **signals** for **proportionately** (to-a-relative-**absence**-or-**inversely-proportionally**-to-a-relative-**presence**-of-spontaneously/**naturally**-occurring, **good-health-associated pleasure**) **appropriate** degrees of alertness, sustained vigilance and medical intervention, just as might occur with a hedonic spectrum including pain or actual discomfort of some/any kind(s).

While serving as an analogy in relation to the not-necessarily-valid notion of pleasure being appreciable only through the contrasting experience of pain (or suffering), the following example may also serve to rebut any notion of love being appreciable only through a contrasting experience of hate. Suppose a person A receives an invitation to a party from person B (whom A hates) and another invitation from person C (whom A loves). Understandably, A will probably decline B's invitation and accept C's invitation.

The very same result (acceptance of C's invitation and rejection of B's) could be expected if A were to love C and feel merely **neutral** (but, **not** at all **hateful**) toward B. These examples, hopefully, may be convincing of the ideas that pain is not a prerequisite for the appreciation of the goodness (enjoyableness) of pleasure or a prerequisite for an individual (an MPEC) to function adaptively (with respect to danger, risk or threat). And hatred is not a prerequisite for the goodness of love to be appreciated or for an individual to function appropriately in relation to both loved and not-especially-loved other individuals.

WE MIGHT CURRENTLY OR EVENTUALLY RENDER OURSELVES INCAPABLE OF EXPERIENCING PAIN OR SUFFERING BY MEANS OF BSNP OR (INSTANTANEOUS) GENETIC SELF-RE-ENGINEERING (IGSRE)

For example, by extrapolating suggestive if not definitive evidence (20, 96-102), it might be possible to validly infer that (BSNP:) brain stimulation/neural pacemakers/prostheses might be implemented in such ways as to pervasively eliminate virtually all kinds of pain and suffering (with 'suffering' being defined, for this context, as uncontrollably intense pain). This goal might be accomplished by means of a) surgically-implanted electrodes or, **preferably**, b) surgically-**noninvasive** (e.g., electromagnetic, ultrasonic, waveform-mediated or other kinds of chemical-physical modalities or means, perhaps targeted-to-specific-neuroanatomic-sites/receptors, etc.). Of course, we would want to include in our repertories of pain/suffering-alleviative-BSNP, effective devices/mechanisms whereby to bring about patterns of pleasure-intensity-variability that might enable us to take appropriate "fight-or-flight" action whenever the continuity of our pleasure might be threatened or endangered, as explained above.

Alternatively to BSNP (or used together with it, in ways that might increase the overall therapeutic, pain/suffering-alleviative efficacy), one or more genetic engineering approaches, such a the one suggested presently, might be effectively implemented.

By extrapolating the genetic common denominators (of individuals with high thresholds of pain and suffering of all kinds) upwards into ranges where no perceptions of pain or suffering are possible and then inserting the necessary

143

modifications into the genes and chromosomes of all the cells in our brain-bodies (103), we might instantaneously render ourselves incapable of experiencing any kind of pain or suffering. Of course, we would also want to insert, into our genotypes, effective programs of pleasure-intensity-variability, which would enable us to take appropriate protective "fight-or-flight" action whenever the continuity of our pleasure might be threatened or endangered. The notions of using brain stimulation/neural prostheses and/or of genetically engineering ourselves in such ways as to preclude any experience/-ing of pain or suffering are explored in some detail in an earlier paper (104).

A BSNP-based approach, by which the entire human race might readily and markedly benefit in terms of relief of pain and suffering, seems to be currently feasible (1-70, 96-102), as might also be true in the case of learning- and work-skills-facilitative (LWF-)BSNP. In view of existing knowledge and already-accomplished research and development (1-70, 96-102), it seems probable that both pain/suffering-alleviative and learning/work-skills facilitative BSNP could be brought about in a mere few or several years' time, at a cost that would probably be in the multi-million dollar (but not the billion-dollar) range (references: the same as directly above). Alternatively, genetic-engineering or gene(tic)-therapy-based approaches to pain/suffering relief and learning- and work-skills' facilitation (103) seem to be potentially (or, perhaps, even only-eventually) but probably not currently **readily** altogether feasible, at least not in immediately or currently producible, dramatically **pain-and-poverty-alleviating** ways.

HOW WE MIGHT BECOME DEATH FREE OR IMMORTAL

In view of each of our MPEX's possibly being ageless, as hypothesized above, one way in which we could conceivably become deathless or immortal would be by transferring to a new clone of the original brain-body into which we, respectively, were born, whenever the most-recently-issued BBP-clone might become too aged or otherwise unfit to continue living.

Another way of freeing ourselves from the prospect of death, one that would be educationally and informationally far more interesting than the way noted in the directly preceding paragraph, would be by means of MPEX (mind particle or experiencer-) circulation or **virtual** mind particle circulation (MPEX-internet) as explained above. Nonetheless, even with MP circulation or MP internet, too-aged-to-continue-to-function or otherwise unfit-for-continuing-to-live BBPs would need to be replaced by cloning, genetic engineering, (neural-) stem-cell-entailing or some other kind(s) of reproductive or regenerative methods (105-110). Via MPEC circulation or internet, one would be continually and unendingly gathering the educational and informational benefits of billions of different MPEXes and billions of different BBPs, instead of being limited to the relatively meager range of possibilities that would be associated with the same BB's being cloned over and over again.

HOW EVERYONE MIGHT BE VERY WELL EDUCATED

Relative to current educational levels and occupational standards, substantial augmentation and enhancement of individual **per-person** (i.e., per-**MP**) knowledge accumulations and work-skills-related repertories might be brought about or catalyzed by **methods** that could be (a) **probably** de-effortized, (b) **possibly** pleasure-enjoyitized, and (c) **conceivably**, potentially, engendered in such ways as to occur seemingly automatically, instantaneously and below the threshold of conscious awareness. These methods would preferably consist in or entail (at least, **macroscopically**-speaking) surgically-**noninvasive**, deep or superficial brain-/neural-process-facilitative, **computerized**, (preferably, micro-miniaturized, nanotechnologized) neural-function-modifying or -modulating **implants or non-implanted**/non-implantation-requiring devices, mechanisms, modalities, or means.

They might all be considered appropriately placed within a category of BSNP (brain stimulation/neural prostheses) together **with** (or, perhaps, **without**) **pharmacologic** performance-improving agents and/or pharmacotherapeutic/medicinal substances. These methods/treatments **might be**, collectively, mutually-potentiatingly/**synergistically** helpful, simply **additively**-beneficial, or perhaps even **singly**, individually-adequately effective, so as to qualify most of us as **very well educated**.

Further improvement of educational and vocational potential and achievement might be brought about by methods whereby **any consciousness** or conscious entity (MPEC) **bonded** to **any** brain-body pair, **BB, could** (at any point(s) in time during its period of occupancy, inhabitation or bondedness within that particular BB, whether that period be 100 years, one twenty-billionth of a second or any other duration) **very rapidly or instantaneously** (as direct consequences of the conscious entity's, i.e., the MP's making selections and implementations entirely in accordance with its own free will and choice) **either add** (insert into the BBP's genotype) or **delete** (eject from the genotype) and virtually-simultaneously **activate** or **deactivate genes** of any quality-of-performance-related or of any other quality-of-structure-or-function-related kinds(s) (103).

Hence, any consciousness (i.e., MP or MP-CONEX), bonded within any brain-body pair **could** at any chronological point(s) during and throughout its period of bondedness therein, in accordance with its exercise of its own intrinsic free will **improve** (according to its own criteria of what constitutes improvement) the effective intelligence, educational and vocational wherewithal of the BB in question by instantaneously changing any, many or even all of its (the BB's) characteristics by instantaneously making genetic alterations within any, many or all of the BB's cells. This freedom and capability would constitute **instantaneously-implementable genetic self-re-engineering**. It would perhaps be accomplishable via (a) gene pills, possibly entailing the use of modified, specially-adapted bacteria, viruses, transposons (76), plasmids (73, 76), etc., (b) aimed-to-precisely-predetermined-location particle beams or (c) other means.

This kind of spontaneous, ongoing, never-immutable **genetic engineering** might be a substantial boon to the prospect of **self-improvement**, as part of an overall panorama of pursuit and possibility, and especially a boon to the prospect of educational/vocational self-actualization and fulfillment. Ramifications of this boon might include **all** aspects of the **state of being** and **process of doing** or **becoming** something and **someone** better than ever before, according to one's **own** standards and criteria, including even aspects pertaining to purely cosmetic properties, physical appearances of any BBP and related phenomena, such as height, weight, sexual attractiveness, as might be associated with the nature or degree of development of primary or secondary sex characteristics, etc.

HOW EVERYONE MIGHT BE **EXTREMELY** WELL EDUCATED

In order for us to better keep pace with **computers**, which apparently are becoming "smarter by the minute" (111), it might behoove us to consider **option A:** perpetually-recycling MPEC circulation or MPEC internet (virtual MPEC circulation) of each and every one of us (MPECs) who choose to participate in being repeatedly cycled through, that is, throughout the full gamut of all of the **ever-changing, ever-increasing knowledge** and **information accumulations**, aggregates or **collections** contained within each of the billions of individual mind particles (MPECs) and each of the individual brain-body pairs, BBPs, because option A **might serve us better than option B:** brain stimulation/neural prostheses, pacemaking, even when/if used together with instantaneously-effectible genetic self-re-engineering.

However, it may be reasonable to expect that the relatively biggest and best advantages might be enjoyed by combining the use of **both options A and B.** Additional educational enhancement and knowledge-augmentation within each (consciousness, mind or experiencer, that is) MPEC might be brought about/facilitated by repeatedly **cycling/circulating** or interconnecting **each** (circulation/MP-internet-virtual-circulation-participating) MPEC or **MP not only through** the knowledge collections/aggregates contained in **BBPs and** those contained in **other MPs**, but **also through** (the data, especially potential or actual **employment-relatably valuable material**/information that might be **contained** in enormous quantities within the fundamental underpinnings of the information-explosion, in particular, **within** and available by means of traversing through) **computers**, themselves.

If we were to pose the question, '**How highly** or **how well educated might all of us** (MP circulators or MP-virtual circulators, that is, mind-particle internet participants) **be if** the **MP-circulation cycle** or **MP internet** were to **merge** a portion of itself, that is, a **portion** of **its cycle** were to be spent **within** the information-loaded realms of actual computers and especially within the realms of the actual **computer internet**/global information superhighway/world wide web?', a possibly valid answer might be: 'stratospherically highly, encyclopedically or **comprehensively well educated**.'

HOW EVERYONE MIGHT BE SEXUALLY LIBERATED

Brain stimulation/neural (possibly pacesetter or pacemaker) prosthetics (BSNP), whether involving excitatory or inhibitory neuroprostheses, depending on the choice of the individual, might be helpful, as follows. Its value might be appreciable when applied to sexual-impulse-subserving/-mediating pathways in the brain, while using appropriate, effective stimulus parameter values. BSNP might be used to **enhance** erotic or sexual impulses one wishes and chooses to feel and act on (with enhancement designatable as a **libiditron** mode of BSNP therapy), possibly even to the point(s) of full gratification or orgasm(s), single or multiple in occurrence, with an orgasmic mode designatable as an **orgasmatron** (111, 112) mode of BSNP. Or it might be used to **suppress** sexual impulses one would prefer not to be compelled by, with appropriate, adequately effective inhibition being designatable as a **sublimitron** mode of BSNP therapy. This mode of application might be helpful whenever one feels sexual behavior would be inappropriate-to-context or whenever one would prefer to divert or sublimate arousal into some non-sexual cognitive process and its associated behavioral expression.

Instantaneous genetic self-re-engineering might add on another more powerful dimension of capability in relation to erotic/sexual self-determinism, again, in accordance with individual choice and MPEC-intrinsic free will.

HOW EVERYONE MIGHT BE HEALTHY

The augmentation and enhancement of global medical knowledge, as might be anticipated to result from BSNP, **instantaneously-effectible-genetic-self-re-engineering** (IEGSRE), MPEC-BBP circulation and MPEC-BBP internet, especially when and if MP-circulation/internet might be interfaced or internetted with a global computer Internet, its successors or other future derivative developments, could possibly entail advances in medical treatment that would be substantial and comprehensive enough to encompass everyone comfortably within the category of being thoroughly healthy. Additional and more instantaneously-impressive **universal-good-health-promoting-and-maintaining phenomena** and, in particular, **processes** might be entailed in ways implicit as follows.

The aforementioned education-augmenting and -enhancing modalities might accelerate and magnify the trend toward development of micro-, mini-technology, describable as nanotechnologization, or proliferation of nanotechnologies, to such an extent as to engender conception and implementation of microscopes and imaging modalities so much more powerful than any currently available that we might actually be able to literally **see** (or, otherwise, **perceive**) molecules, atoms and even subatomic particles. Consequently, we might be enabled to literally **see** and otherwise perceive **individual minds** (i.e., conscious experiencers or experiencing entities, conceptualized herein as **mind-particle-consciousness** experiencers, MP-CONEXES). Then, we would be seeing what we **really** look like, that is, how our respective essences of individual identity (MPs) actually appear and what each and everyone's objectively-viewed, measurable, quantifiable boundaries of self can accurately be delineated as. It would be astonishing, but not altogether inconceivable, that we (our MPECs) might be discerned as manifesting some significant degree(s) of resemblance to the macroscopic people we, respectively, observe in our mirrors.

With vastly increased powers of observational magnification accessible to us, we might be able to literally **see** or otherwise **perceive** (at each and every three-dimensionally-specified and -located point in the human body) exactly **how**, that is, precisely what are the **mechanisms** whereby molecules, atoms, subatomic particles and waveforms interact with each other in such ways as to constitute or mediate diseases and disordered conditions and dysfunctional processes.

Consequently, we might be able to readily deduce, directly from our perceptual observations, how we might most beneficially, even curatively design, create and deliver medications and other therapeutic interventions and modalities, rather than formulating medical treatments based on relatively indirect, often tenuous, experimental and **clinical** inference and reasoning, as is necessary when crucial mechanisms of disease cannot be actually, directly observed or perceived.

151

HOW EVERYONE MIGHT BE ANOREXIA-, OBESITY-, INSOMNIA-FREE,

ETC.

By means of **selective activation** and/or **deactivation**, i.e., **excitation** and/or **inhibition** of **appropriate site(s), pathway(s)** or **structure(s)** in the brain or elsewhere in the nervous system, **brain stimulation/neural** (possibly, **pacemaking** or **pacesetting) prostheses** (BSNP) might give rise to and enable relatively **de-effortized** and reliable **dieting**, which would readily empower anyone to easily, reliably and predictably lose or gain as much weight as desired. There might be **no** reason or occasion to experience the stressful, strenuous hardship and unreliability of needing to generate and sustain will power or to experience dietary **deprivation**, hunger or **food-craving** to any degree or in any way whatsoever.

Effort-free weight control, modification and maintenance **might** be attained to/achieved by stimulatively (activatingly or deactivatingly) focusing on the brain's ostensible (a) feeding/**dietary-appetization**-subserving and/or (b) **dietary-satiation**-subserving regions or **centers**, such as **may**, respectively, be located in the (a) lateral and (b) ventromedial hypothalamic nuclei (113).

Additionally, if one were displeased with one's (own) body-shape, contours or body habitus, as associated with some particular pattern or distribution of body fat, then, perhaps without there being any need for or appropriateness of changing dietary intake, one might be able to use (surgically-) noninvasive **focused electromagnetic, acoustic/sonic, thermal, particulate** (consisting in one or more particle(s) of some type(s)), or some **other kind(s)** of stimuli that would be directable to volumes or pockets of relatively large accumulations of fat in such way(s) as to (1) **selectively increase** the rate of effective, local fat **metabolism** or (2) decrease the efficiency of localized absorption of fat-storing nutrients, either way (1 or 2), so as to cause attrition of fat-storage/deposition only within the narrowly- or selectively-circumscribed body-areas where one were to feel one might have too much adipose tissue. Effective techniques might be capable of expeditiously, maybe even instantaneously, dissolving, melting or otherwise reducing and re-contouring the self-determined, body-topographically-relatively-localized or distributively- disproportional, excess adiposity, without affecting those areas of the body with respect to which one might feel the amount of fat deposition is aesthetically optimal or, at least, acceptable to oneself.

Conversely, if someone were to feel there were some part(s) of one's (own) body wherein there were not large **enough** accumulations of fat (for example, in **too-thin** legs), one might be able, here, also, without any change in dietary intake being necessary, to direct preferably (surgically-) noninvasive stimuli that would be modified, in terms of those aspects mentioned in the preceding paragraph, in such ways as to (a) **decrease** the rate of localized fat metabolism or (b) **increase** the efficiency of localized absorption of fat-storage-deposit-augmenting nutrients, either way, or in either case (a or b), so as to **increase** the amount of adipose deposition and bring about the associated, desired change(s) in body habitus.

BSNP might also facilitate full pleasurization and defortation (de-effortization) of all kinds of bodily-exercising and body-building. Hence, we, most of us anyway, might have more muscular and generally better-maintained, better-toned bodies. An

153

additional, perhaps BSNP-mediated, efficiency-of-time-utilization-improving benefit

might be that a person would possibly be able to **simultaneously** (a) automatically,

unconsciously or subconsciously, virtually entirely defortizedly (effortlessly) **exercise**,

or perhaps be passively exercised, perhaps by means of functional electrical

stimulation, **FES** (61), of one's body musculature and other body-components, such as

pulmonary, cardiac and vascular aspects **while** (b) the person's **brain** and **mind** (i.e.,

mind-particle-experiencer-consciousness, designatable as MP-CONEX, MPEC,

MPEX or MP) might be actively, fully-consciously engaged in valuable, constructive

and readily-marketable learning and working. Also of possibly valid relevance to the

overall area of concern/pursuit in respect of well-developed body musculature may be

the notion of being able to increase and improve body-muscle mass, strength and

condition via specially-developed drugs capable of **increasing muscular**

development perhaps even in the absence of, that is, **without** any **exercise** being

necessary (114).

Perhaps by means of BSNP-mediated focusing on, exciting or suppressing of

appropriate brain or neural site(s), regions or pathways, it might be **readily, easily,**

painlessly, and virtually instantaneously **possible** for anyone to **stop being addicted**

to any substance(s) without having to invoke or sustain difficult-to-maintain self-

denial, resistance to ceaseless temptation, and without having to endure (1) the

physical-dependence-associated symptoms of **withdrawal,** (2) **tolerance** (the need

to progressively increase the dosage or intake of many or any medicinal or other

substance(s) in order to achieve the same remedial effect), (3) the **mental-**

dependence-associated symptoms of craving the addictive substance or (4) even the feeling of being depressed by reason of being deprived of something strongly desired.

BSNP might be used to alleviate motion sickness and nausea (in general) **whenever it might occur**, such as can be mediated by the vestibular apparatus of the internal or inner ear. For example, nausea might be relieved by means of inhibitory stimulation or deactivation of the "vomiting center" located within the medulla region of the brain (113, 115, 116) known as the **area postrema**, where there is no appreciable **blood-brain barrier** (116), to act as an obstacle to medication or any other therapeutic agents or modalities.

And BSNP might also eliminate or markedly diminish the hurtful aspects of receiving criticism, so that we would possibly be better able to benefit from it, without being traumatized in any way(s). Moreover, BSNP might help the blind to see (39, 43, 117-119) and the deaf to hear (39, 43, 113, 118, 120). BSNP might be therapeutically valuable for anyone who has been deprived of the use of any of a number of various bodily functions, for example, by dint of stroke(s) (61, 73, 113, 119-122) or injuries (123, 124). It might significantly help them with their lost or diminished faculties or functions by activating or deactivating functionally appropriate and useful site(s), structure(s), or pathway(s) in the brain, elsewhere in the nervous system or even outside of the nervous system. The prospects of **BSNP-mediated** or **BSNP-facilitated** compensatory or alleviative treatments, if used together with other methodologies that might bring about neurogenesis, nerve-regeneration, other kinds of cellular, histologic or whole-organ replacement/ redevelopment, perhaps via pluripotent, neural or other types of stem cells, tissue transplants (105-109, 121), etc.

might be applicable in such ways so as to be observed to be of notable value to neurologically-deprived or otherwise medically-challenged/impaired individuals.

BSNP medical devices might contain variable, rheostat-like and ON-OFF-switch-alarm-clock-like, modulating mechanisms, effective with respect to alertness-vigilance versus sedation-relaxation levels, so as to provide the following benefits. In particular, one valuable possibility might be any person's instantaneously-implementable, self-willed, self-controlled, merely BSNP-mediated induction and selected modes of maintenance of deep, neurophysiologically more-than-adequate, even **replete** sleep. The sleep-inducing and -regulating mechanisms might be expected to be thoroughly dependable.

Accordingly, anyone could obtain such high-quality sleep virtually any time, anywhere, for precisely as long (and no longer a period of time) as the individual might need or want it, in order to attain full refreshment and reinvigoration. And this BSNP approach could be feasible despite any and all circumstances and concerns as are conceivable as being currently capable of unduly and maladaptively interfering with and undermining a person's quantity or quality of sleep and degree of restedness.

Sleep-inducing BSNP, perhaps entailing focused, targeted substances/chemicals/particles (pharmacologic/medicinal agents) and/or electromagnetic, acoustic, etc. focused fields, waveforms, beams, streams or, perhaps, tidy "lines" of precisely-aimed molecules, atoms, ions, subatomic particles, etc. (125) might conceivably involve activation of a small cluster of cells in the ventrolateral preoptic (VLPO) area of the brain's hypothalamus (126), which has been referred to as a "pinpoint (ON/OFF) sleep switch." These cells, when they become active, send inhibitory signals to the brain's arousal/alertness-producing/-subserving system and thereby bring about sleep. Other approaches to reliably producing health-sustaining/improving sleep might entail relatively diffuse stimulation of neuroanatomic sites functionally entailed in spontaneous, unassisted sleep and stimulation, conceivably, of **some** neuroanatomic sites used in general anesthesia.

Moreover, most kinds of physical/bodily pain and suffering, irrespective of pathogenesis (for example, in association with "advanced carcinoma," as per page 225 of ref. 20) and irrespective of the nature of specific symptoms that have been observed and reported (20, 23, 96-102), have been found to be substantially remediable with BSNP. Mental pain and suffering also seem to be encouragingly responsive to this mode of treatment (4, 19, 20, 22, 23).

Noteworthy prospects as potential components or aspects of processes that might prove useful in conceptualizing and applying systems of BSNP might include adaptations of electromagnetic, acoustic, biochemical, and pharmacologic media, modalities and approaches, as might be used in such ways as to provide effective, highly focused (or, as appropriate, relatively **diffuse**) treatments or performance-/outcome-enhancers (125) for various medical conditions, diseases, disorders, syndromes and pathogenic mechanisms involving, occurring or functioning in any neural or non-neural anatomic regions, body-tissues, structures or organ(s') system(s).

Hence, such prospects might potentially constitute categories of therapeutic formulations or treatment methodologies that might be designated as function-modifying pharmacologic, electronic or otherwise characterizable means of neuronal, neural, or non-neural modulation.

Micro-miniaturized therapeutic or otherwise beneficial (such as performance-improving) robots, nano-robots (42) or, referring to a term used by Raymond Kurzweil (43), "nanobots" might be conveyable and deployable as strategically useful, neuroanatomically or otherwise anatomically precisely-positioned entities. Passageways of body-entry might include those of inhalation, injection, permeation of **inter-molecularly**, even **inter-atomically-sharply-focused penetration/propulsion** (125) that is, passageways that would be targeted and utilized for good-health-conducive or bodily-function-improving substances (e.g., particles) or waveforms. Via BSNP, instantaneously-**effectible**, **genetic-self-re-engineering (IEGSRE)** and MPEC-BBP-circulation-internet, virtually all diseases, disorders and other afflictions might be anticipated to be **viably-escapable** (that is, any afflicted individual MP-CONEX/MP/MPEC/MPEX might be able to deathlessly or undyingly escape from the afflicted BB/BBP and transfer to a healthy, unafflicted BBP) even if the afflication itself (of the original BB) were not readily, effectively treatable or curable.

TO BE WHATEVER WE WANT TO BE, WHENEVER WE WANT TO BE

By means of the methodologies included in the preceding paragraph, each and every one of us (each mind-particle-experiencer-consciousness, MPEX, or mind-particle-consciousness-experiencer, MP-CONEX) might be able to inhabit or, synonymously, be bonded to brains and bodies that fit **whatever** descriptions we want them to fit, **whenever** we want them to apply. We might be able to change any mental or physical characteristic(s) we want to change, perhaps instantaneously, via precisely-targeted waveforms and/or substances, in almost any way and to almost any degree we might possibly desire (104).

Hence, each of us (MPEXes) might be able to (possibly, instantaneously) **morph** (i.e., **change** the characteristics of the BBP we find ourself, respectively, ensconced in, that is, change into **any form** or change any aspect(s) of the overall morphology, structural minutiae and/or physiological functioning of) any (or even all) of the attributes, internal components, clinically-, cognitively-, or adaptively significant processes or external parts of any **brain-body pair** (perhaps by genetic splicing, insertion, deletion, activation, deactivation or, perhaps, by **other kinds of techniques**) at any time during any portion or throughout any period of our (MP's) occupancy of, being bonded or bound to, or implanted within any brain-body in question or under consideration.

CAN COMPUTERS BE CONSCIOUS?

Let us suppose a **mind** or (in other, but equivalent, words, a mind particle, consciousness-experiencer, MPEC, MPEX or, simply, abbreviatedly) an **MP can be** bound, bonded to or implanted within **a computer**. In particular, let us suppose an MP **can** be attached therein in such a way as to be able to **follow** the direction of **flow of information** within **and keep pace** with such rapid flow of information, as generally occurs within a modern computer. Then, the answer to the question of whether or not **computers can be rendered** conscious would apparently be revealed to be "**yes,**" computers can (perhaps by being implanted with an MP) become conscious. Then you, I or anyone else might be able to find out directly (by **firsthand**

159

experience) what it would be like, what it would **feel** like to actually lead the life of a (conscious) computer. Such an opportunity might occur as a consequence of your, my or anyone else's (MP's) allowing and facilitating the implantation of our respective mind (that is, consciousness or MP) into the confines of some kind(s) of chemical, physical bond(s) within (at least, **some** components of) a computer, for some appreciable period of time, perhaps hours, weeks or years. Then the conscious computer might be regarded, at least by some people, as a new life-form on earth.

Being disembodied and separated from its human brain-body, it would probably seem incongruous, at least to some people, to regard a computer-implanted human mind (MPEX) as a veritable human being. Yet it would probably be relatively easy to regard an MPEX-containing computer as being **alive** (hence, **some** kind of **form of life**), **by reason** of its **experiencing** (various phenomena, collectively, constituting) a **life**, even though neither an animal's nor a plant's nor any other conceivable kind of organism's **biologically**-based type of life. So, the answer to the question of whether or not computers can be or can become conscious, perhaps as reasoned directly above, is possibly, "yes."

HOW WE MIGHT ALL BECOME RELATIVELY UNSELFISH

Anyone who is desirous of becoming relatively more unselfish might be able to do so by using BSNP to enhance compassion for and empathy with others (26). Voluntary genetic self-re-engineering (perhaps of an instantaneously-effectible kind) might be expected to add another dimension of capability to the possibility of attainment to a goal of relatively increased unselfishness. MPEX-BBP circulation and virtual circulation (MP-internet) by their **very** mutually (**interactive**) **nature** would almost unavoidably enable or induce all participating MPECs to become **more empathetic, sympathetic** and **unselfish** than we currently are.

These increases in unselfishness might occur as readily understandable consequences of, and in direct connection with all **MPEC-BB circulation-internet** (that is, MPEX-BBP circulation and/or virtual circulation, MP-internet) **participants'** cycling through the entire population of participating MPs, BBs, and computers included in the MP-BB circulation/internet loop, over and over again, and thereby directly **experiencing** the needs and wants of MPECs in addition to our, respective, self and the strengths, weaknesses, and problems of all of the BBs (in addition to the one each of us was, respectively, **born** into) and of all of the loop-included computers, far more convincingly-vividly and tangibly than is possible with each of us MPECs being confined and biochemically-biophysically-medical-scientifically bonded (in some yet-to-be discovered way) within the single, individual brain-body pair, BB, in which we, each of us, respectively, generally seem to find ourself quite thoroughly contained.

HOW WE MIGHT PROCEED TO RESEARCH AND DEVELOP BRAIN STIMULATION/NEURAL PACEMAKING, NEUROPROSTHESES, MIND-PARTICLE-EXPERIENCER-CONSCIOUSNESS DETECTION, ISOLATION AND CIRCULATION/INTERNET

Electrical/electronic brain stimulators, neural pacemakers/pacesetters or stimulating electrodes/microchips have been and are currently in effective use as surgically implanted devices, as well as functioning, in some cases, as completely

surgically-non-invasive devices/equipment of various types, designs and composition.

They have already been or are at present being used to treat a variety of different

medical problems (4, 16, 20, 22-25, 27-29, 31-37, 43, 54, 56, 61, 96-102, 117, 118,

120-124, 126-130) including Parkinson's disease, multiple sclerosis, cerebral palsy,

idiopathic tremors, epilepsy, spinal cord or other neurological injuries, paralysis,

such as, paraplegia and quadriplegia, (especially, **chronic**, relatively intractable)

pain, depression, anxiety, schizophrenia, strokes, "locked-in" syndrome, etc. The last

explicitly-listed medical entity (syndrome) characteristically presents clinically as a

condition in which a person (patient), generally/usually as a consequence of stroke(s),

has lost all abilities to communicate thoughts, feelings, desires and needs to the

surrounding environment, usually including every other person therein.

Consequently, it might be readily understandable that it might not be

unconscionable to **treat** or to clinically/therapeutically minimize in stimulative ways,

such as those referred to above, **extreme, substantial** or otherwise untreatable

significant neurological-disease-related or injury-caused **dementia** or markedly

disabling, deteriorative **impairment**, such as can be caused by trauma, multiple

infarcts and cognitive-function-undermining disease processes of diverse kinds,

including, conceivably, at least, some aspects or symptoms of Alzheimer's disease.

The preferable use of macroscopically, surgically entirely noninvasive brain/neural

stimulative devices/equipment might usefully entail: a) electromagnetic fields/waves,

b) acoustic/sonic, e.g., ultrasonic fields/waves and/or c) pharmaceutical/medicinal

substances, some or all of which might be delivered in precisely-focused ways, as conceptualized to be within the broad-based category of BSNP. Such approaches, as reported and reflected on in the above list of references, might reasonably be expected to yield clinically and therapeutically worthwhile results in terms of patients' responses.

The increasingly diverse research application of surgically-**noninvasive** treatments (such as in relation to depression and anxiety disorders, including obsessive-compulsive disorder (4), for example, transcranial magnetic (brain) stimulation (**TMS**), repetitive or rapid-rate TMS, **rTMS**, cranial or, virtually equivalently, transcranial electrostimulation (CES or TES), suggest various modes of access to research and development of effectively therapeutic methodologies. Electromagnetic, acoustic (e.g., ultrasonic), pharmacologic and other kinds of stimuli (as noted below) might, with suitable values of stimulus parameters and appropriate target foci, induce or contribute to the induction of reward or **pleasure responses** that might, conceivably, be of **higher intensity** than those generally associated with **sexual** and **eating-linked** indulgence and gratification (20, 23). And such stimuli might be found to be especially noteworthy and clinically valuable with respect to research and development of effective, remedial BSNP, especially in terms of the pleasurization/enjoyitization and de-effortization of learning and work(ing).

As suggested by the following quotations (a-f), examples of technologies that might be useful (4, 19, 34, 129, 133, 134) in the research and development of learning and work-skills' facilitative (LWF) and other modes of helpful/therapeutic brain stimulation/neural prosthetic functional modifiers/pacemakers (BSNP) might include (perhaps, repetitive) transcranial magnetic (brain) stimulation (TMS or rTMS), vagal nerve stimulation (VNS), cranial or (also known as) transcranial electrical stimulation (CES or TES) (131), and deep brain stimulation (DBS) (132).

(a)   On page 50 (34), "Left prefrontal rTMS was associated with a mildly improved mood and greater mental alertness."

(b)   On page 57 (4), under experimental conditions different from those entailed in quotation (a), "Left prefrontal TMS results in slight increases in subjective sadness, whereas right prefrontal repetitive TMS (rTMS) causes increased happiness" (133).

(c)   On page 57 (4), under experimental conditions different from those involved in quotation (b), "Left prefrontal rTMS has been observed to have antidepressant effects" (133).

(d)   On page 58 (4), "TMS at specific (neuroanatomic) regions, (stimulus/stimulation) intensities and frequencies might serve as a new treatment option for a host of conditions and might have applications for enhancing or modifying normal functions such as memory or (employment-related/work) skill acquisition" (133).

(e)   On page 70 (134), "A feeling of relaxation" was noted in association with left vagal stimulation.

(f)   On page 58 (4), the reproducibly observed and noted "anticonvulsant action of vagal nerve stimulation (VNS)" has been adequately significant such that "Now VNS is FDA approved for the treatment of epilepsy and about 3,000 people in the US have these generators implanted" (133). And continuing observations are such as to facilitate the inference that the device "offers hope to epileptics" (129).

(g)   Also on page 58 (4), "VNS parameters can affect learning and memory" in facilitative ways (133) and (19) "could have far-reaching effects, such as enhancing memory or treating obesity by curbing appetite...because the vagus nerve sends messages to the brain" that can signify that the "stomach is full."

Mind-particle/consciousness-experiencer (MP/MPEX/MPEC or MP-CONEX) research (coincidentally, having research implications for BSNP) might begin with the highest possible resolution or detail-revealing imaging modality/ies being used in such ways as to focus on a circumscribed point or area (maybe a **moving** target or center) of maximal activation that may - or may not - be observed to travel around, throughout the brain, elsewhere in the nervous system and, conceivably, even elsewhere in the body, outside of the nervous system. Functional magnetic resonance imaging (fMRI), magnetoencephalography (MEEG or MEG) (38), and computer-analyzed electroencephalography (CEEG) might, possibly, be seen as (being, at least, among) the **current** technology/ies of relative choice, with which to initiate a search for a mind (particle).

A research project centering on a search for a potentially-**perceptible MPEC** might **instrumentally involve** selective applications and adaptations of technologies, principles, properties, processes and other phenomena at least as diverse as the following list (and, undoubtedly, more so):

cytoskeletally-associated microtubules (135) as might comprise a **tubular, tunneling rapid transit system** for mind particles, superposition principles, including both constructive and destructive interference, particle accelerators, particle detectors, photomultipliers, scintillation counters, cloud or bubble chambers, possibly "noncontact," contactless or, contact-free ultrasound (i.e., "a noncontact ultrasound device that can work as far as two inches from the skin, (because) the investigators added layers of material to the sound emitter, thereby matching its impedance to that of air") (68), infrasound, acoustic/sonic adaptations of laser's principles (55), holographic principles, tomographic principles, shock-wave-like acoustic phenomena, for example, low energy **extracorporeal shock wave therapy** (ESWT) (136), pulsed, variable, static or continuous waveforms, discrete or discontinuous waves, components of supersonic compression waves, hypersonic waves, echoencephalography, sonar, Doppler ultrasonography, three-dimensional (3D) ultrasonography, echolocation, diverse electromagnetic phenomena, including intersecting laser beams, diamagnetic and antimagnetic materials, infrared spectroscopy, thermal infrared cameras, thermography, radar, transceivers, transponders or other kinds of transmitter-receivers, transducers, microwaves, ultraviolet light, Cerenkov radiation (involving electromagnetic waves that are analogous to supersonic compression waves), transcranial magnetic stimulation (TMS), repetitive TMS (rTMS), magnetic resonance imaging (MRI), functional MRI (fMRI), superconductivity, superfluidity, superconducting quantum interference devices (SQUIDs), Josephson junctions, magnetic levitation, the Meissner-Ochsenfeld effect, quantum tunneling, antimatter, positron emission tomography (PET) scanning, single photon emission computed tomography (SPECT) imaging, electron beam computed tomography (EBCT), electron-beam analysis, digitization, analog/digital interconversion, genetic engineering of "smarter" mice, possibly involving N-methyl-D-aspartate (NMDA) receptors, medicinal substances injected or permeated into an individual's circulatory system that might be activated by sharply focused physical modalities, such as precisely-targeted sonic/acoustic and/or electromagnetic phenomena, (for example, lasers), only **whenever** and **wherever** they reach, permeate and engage in the process of passing through one of more therapeutically-optimal sites in any cases of disease/disorder-afflicted BBPs (137), "smart pills" perhaps entailing chemicals that can infiltrate neurons and stimulate an over-production of "memory protein (a form of CREB," that is, "Cyclic AMP Response Element Building Protein" (138), "time-reversal acoustics" (41), i.e., **sequence-reversal** acoustics, focusing mirror-assemblies, reflectors, fiber optics, optical computing technologies, neural networks, very large scale integrated circuits (VLSI), microcircuits, minimicrocircuits or nano-circuits, mini-microprocessors/nanoprocessors, centrifugal or centripetal forces, gravity and anti-gravity, ballistics, antiballistics, wind, solar, geothermal (139), hydrogen-derived (140) and other kinds of power/energy, electromyography (EMG), anatomic/neuroanatomic regional blood flow analyses, electrocorticography, computer-spectral-analyzed electroencephalography (CEEG), evoked potentials (EPs), "artificial neurons," (combining both digital and analog processing) "that either excite or inhibit each other," depending on "feedback from other neurons" (141), electroconvulsive therapy (ECT), neuro- or other bio-feedback, virtual reality, vagal or vagus nerve stimulation (VNS) (4), nerve regeneration, synapses, neurotransmitters, partial cloning of specialized body parts, neural and possibly other kinds of stem cells, tissue-, partial- and whole organ re-growth, re-specialization/-differentiation, "neuron transistors" (39, 43), field effect transistors (FETs) (62-67), nanotransistors including single-molecule transistors (69) (anti-angiogenesis or) angiogenesis-related methods (142, 143), alternative medicine such as acupuncture and herbalism, non-invasive, non-implanted superficial or deep brain stimulation, macroscopically-surgically **noninvasive** devices or mechanisms, quantum electronic devices, carbon and other kinds of nanotubes, DNA- (e.g., gene chips, that is, DNA-coated microchips) or other kinds of micro-chips or micro-arrays, phased arrays or beam antennas, osmosis, percutaneous or transdermal permeation, iontophoresis (76, 144), electrophoresis, ionic (molecular, atomic or subatomic) propulsion systems, molecular diodes, molecular ratchet motors, "smart" drugs or pharmacologic agents with built-in, engineered mechanisms by which to affect and interact only with specifically-identified cells, cell receptor types, reflective interfaces between superconductors and normal conductors, particle and waveform beams of diverse kinds, interferometry, scanning sensors of various types, "biophotonics," that is, biologically-/medically-applied "photonics," which refers to a combination of **light**-entailing and electronic technologies, nanotechnologically-microminiaturized, microscopic-sized bubbles (145-146) that transport discrete packets, packaged **doses**, streams of medicinal substances or biochemically-/biophysically-active and effective agents/modalities directed to any particular site(s) or structurally-/functionally-significant anatomic destinations, a way of "nudging" and potentially transporting individual atoms to specific anatomic/neuroanatomic sites, involving adaptations of scanning tunneling microscopes (147), neuromodulators, pacemakers/pacesetters and other (neuro-)

prostheses of numerous different kinds, robots, microminiaturized pharmacologic

and/or electronic nanorobots/"nanobots" (39, 43), other means by which to enable and

bring about **transmission** of therapeutic agents or stimuli in macroscopically

nondisruptive ways, hence, effectively, **noninvasively from anywhere outside** of a

patient's (or other category of help-seeker, such as student or work-skills-job-seeker's)

body **to anywhere**, that is, any specific location(s) inside the person's body, etc.

This list, in terms of its actual literal contents as well as what else may be

inferable from it **might** barely begin to anticipate some of many different approaches

and numerous yet-to-be-envisioned and devised methods that could possibly provide

valid mechanistic vehicles or pathways of constructive potential, whereby it might be

feasible to conduct and implement appropriate research, development and application

of both BSNP/neural prostheses and MPEX-related phenomena. There may emerge

many beneficial methodologies, modalities and practical applications that might

facilitate fulfillment of either or both of these categories of potential (BSNP **and**

MPEC-circulation, MPEC-virtual circulation-internet), which **may** be markedly

strengthened and diversified by genetic strategies which, in and of themselves, seem to

have reached significant levels of attainment of knowledge and seem to promise

impressive heights of prospective quality-of-life-improving wherewithal and well-

being.

Mind-particle-consciousness-experiencer-circulation/virtual circulation-

internet (MPEX-CVCI) might validly be anticipated to be several or many years or

perhaps several decades away from a time when their research and development might possibly come to fruition and their potential promise might be fulfilled. In contrast with these probably protracted prospects, brain-stimulation-neural-prosthetic-pacemaker/pacesetter functional-modulation-modifiers might possibly be brought to substantial fruition at any time between the present moment and several years (conceivably, depending on the pace of relevant, appropriate research and development, less than ten years) from now. The notion that brain stimulation, neuroprosthetically-mediated-**learning** and **work-skills' facilitation** (BSNP-LWF) might already be technologically fully feasible seems **significantly supported by** the emerging BSNP-type or BSNP-like treatment modalities that are already being assessed and used (albeit in **early** phases of research and development) as therapeutic modalities for (symptoms of) Parkinson's disease, multiple sclerosis, idiopathic tremor, epilepsy, cerebral palsy, otherwise untreatable bodily pain, anxiety, depression, etc.

BSNP, genetic therapeutic methods, and MP-CONEX circulation/virtual-circulation-internet might help to ensure that, in the not-very-distant future, or (at any rate) eventually, virtually everyone might be broadly, deeply and diversely well educated. And the following quotation from a recent article (148), seems to render transparently appreciable that it might behoove each individual (current and potential) patient to become medically (and, by extrapolation, if not by implication, also otherwise) well educated.

> "The most underused resource in the health care system is the patient's time. I have begun suggesting that my patients look up their diseases on the Internet, (thereby) learning about therapeutic options, drug side effects, necessary

testing and monitoring. Compared to me, they have much more time and a greater incentive to research their disease(s), especially the particulars specific to them. I tell them they will soon know more than I do, and that that is good."

REFERENCES

1. Andres J.C., Director, Family Practice Residency Training Program, Niagara Falls Memorial Medical Center, Niagara Falls, NY; personal communication: late '99, early 2000.

2. Spangler R.A., Assoc. Prof., State Univ. of NY at Buffalo, Depts. of Physiology and Biophysics: personal communication, late, '99.

3. Butler S.R., Giaquinto S. Technical note: stimulation triggered automatically by electrophysiological events. Med & Biol Engng, now, Med Biol Eng Comput, 1969; 7: 329-331.

4. George M.S., Nahas Z., Lomarov M., Bohning D.E., Kellner C. How knowledge of regional brain dysfunction in depression will enable new somatic treatments in the next millennium. CNS Spectrums 1999; 4: 53-61.

5. Gevins A.S., Morgan N.H., Bressler S.L. et al, Human neuroelectric patterns predict performance accuracy. Science 1987; 235: 580-585.

6. Williamson S.J. How quickly we forget - magnetic fields reveal a hierarchy of memory lifetimes in the human brain. Science Spectra 1999; 15: 68-73.

7. Walgate J., Wagner A., Buckner R.L., Schacter D., Sharpe K., Floyd C. Memories are made of this. Science & Spirit 1999; 10, 1:7.

8. Connor S. Thanks for the memory. The World in 1999. The Economist Publications, 1999: 110-111.

9. Goetinck S. Different brain areas linked to memorization. The Buffalo News, final edn., Sun., June 13, 1999, Science Notes: H-6.

10. Hall S.S. Journey to the center of my mind, brain scans can locate the home of memory and the land of language. They may eventually help to map consciousness. The New York Times Magazine, June 6, 1999; section 6: 122-125.

11. Neergaard L. Studies shed new light on memory/studies take close look at brain's memory process. Buffalo News 1999; Fri., Aug. 21: A-10.

12. Sullivan M.M. (Editor). Task-juggling region in brain pinpointed. Buffalo News 1999; Sun., May 23: H-6.

13. Fox M. Test on rats turns thought into action. Buffalo News 1999; Sun., June 27: H-6.

14. McCrone J. States of mind, learning a task takes far more brainpower than repeating it once it's become a habit, could the difference show us where consciousness lies, asks J.M. New Scientist March 20, 1999; **161**: 30-33.

15. Pinker S. Will the mind figure out how the brain works? Time 2000; **155**: 90-91.

16. Jacques S. Brain stimulation and reward: "pleasure centers" after twenty-five years. Neurosurg 1979; **5**: 277-283.

17. Heath R.G. Modulation of emotion with a brain pacemaker. Journal of Nervous and Mental Disease 1977; **165**: 300-316.

18. Langford K.H. of the Univ. at Birmingham, Dept. of Surgery/Neurosurgery, Birmingham, Ala., USA, personal communication, Aug. 10, 1987.

19. Neergard L. Brain pacemaker helps treat depression. Buffalo News 1999; Tues., Oct. 12: A-4.

20.   Heath R.G. Pleasure response of human subjects to direct stimulation of the brain: physiologic and psychodynamic considerations. The Role of Pleasure in Behavior: Harper & Row, 1964: 219-243.

21.   Wanecski E.J.E., 1988 graduate of State Univ. at Buffalo/Niagara County Community College co-sponsored electroencephalography technology training program and recipient of 1988 Graphic Controls Corp. award for EEG tech. excellence, personal communication, Mon., March 27, 2000. Also, please see ref. 22, which was received from/via E.J.E. Wanecski.

22.   Callinan T.E. (edtr). Relief believed ahead for schizophrenia. Rochester Democrat and Chronicle, March 24, 2000; **168**: 2A.

23.   Bishop M.P., Elder S.T., Heath R.G. Attempted control of operant behavior in man with intracranial self-stimulation. The Role of Pleasure in Behavior: Harper & Row, 1964: 55-81.

24.   Sem-Jacobsen C. W. Effects of electrical stimulation on the human brain. Electroencephalogr Clin Neurophysiol 1959; **11**, 379.

25.   Olds J. Pleasure centers in the brain. Sci Am, 1956; **193**: 105-116.

26.   Mancini L. Brain stimulation to treat mental illness and enhance human learning, creativity, performance, altruism and defenses against suffering. Med Hypotheses 1986; **21**: 209-219.

27.   Barker A.T., Freeston I.L., Jalinous R., Merton P.A., Morton H.B. Magnetic stimulation of the human brain. J Physiol 1985; **369**: 3P.

28. Barker A.T., Freeston I.L., Jalinous R., Jarratt J.A. Magnetic stimulation of the human brain and peripheral nervous system: an introduction and the results of an initial clinical evaluation. Neurosurg 1987; **20**: 100-109.

29. Bickford R.G., Guidi M., Fortesque P., Swenson M. Magnetic stimulation of human peripheral nerve and brain: response enhancement by combined magnetoelectrical technique. Neurosurg 1987; **20**: 110-116.

30. Ebenbichler G.R., Erdogmus C.B., Resch K.L., et al. Ultrasound therapy for calcific tendinitis of the shoulder. N Engl J Med 1999; **340**: 1533-1538.

31. George M.S. Brain activation involving mood and mood disorders, transcranial magnetic stimulation. Audio-Digest Psychiatry 1995; **24**: Side B.

32. Talan J. Personal magnetism. Experimental method of treating depression helps 2 patients improve. Newsday, Tues., Nov. 21, 1995: B23, B26.

33. George M.S., Speer A.M., Wassermann E.M., et al. Repetitive TMS as a probe of mood in health and disease. CNS Spectrums 1997; **2**: 39-44.

34. Greenberg B.D., McCann U.D., Benjamin J., Murphy D.L. Repetitive TMS as a probe in anxiety disorders: theoretical considerations and case reports. CNS Spectrums 1997; **2**: 47-52.

35. Sherman C. Magnetic stimulation may offer ECT alternative. Clinical Psychiatry News 1998; April: 9-10.

36. Wassermann E.M. Repetitive transcranial magnetic stimulation: an introduction and overview. CNS Spectrums 1997; **2**: 21-25.

37. Stein L., Belluzzi J.D., Ritter S., Wise C.D. Self-stimulation reward pathways: norepinephrine versus dopamine. J Psychiatr Res 1974; **11**: 115-124.

38. Clayton J. Caught napping: depression, Parkinson's and obsessive-compulsive disorder may have a common cause. They could all be triggered when a tiny part of the brain dozes off. New Scientist 2000; **165**: 42-45.

39. Kurzweil R. The Age of Spiritual Machines: When Computers Exceed Human Intelligence. Penguin Books, 1999: 52,80, 120, 124, 127-128, 205, 220, 221, 279, 300, 307-308, 313, 314.

40. Damasio A.R. How the brain creates the mind. Sci Am 1999; **281**: 112-117.

41. Fink M. Time-reversed acoustics. Sci Am 1999; **281**: 91-97.

42. Rotman D. Will the real nanotech please stand up? Technology Review, MIT's Magazine of Innovation 1999; **102**: 44-53.

43. Kurzweil R. Live forever. Psychology Today 2000; Feb.: 66-71.

44. Neergaard L. Researchers testing rub-on medicines: 'skin enhancer' creams, gels may eventually replace ingested drugs. Buffalo News 1998; Tues., Sept. 29: A-6.

45. Charlier J.C. Tiny pipes with a big future. Science Spectra 1999; **17**: 64-69.

46. Fry W.J. Electrical stimulation of brain localized without probes - theoretical analysis of a proposed method. J. Acoust Soc Am 1968; **44**: 919-931.

47. Fry F. J. (brother of the late W. J. Fry; please note ref. no. 46), of the Indianapolis Center for Advanced Research, Indianapolis, Indiana, USA, personal communication, May 27, 1987.

48. Barker A.T. of the Department of Medical Physics & Clinical Engineering at Sheffield University, Sheffield, England, personal communication, Jan. 8, 1990.

49. Spangler R.A. of the Department of Biophysical Science and Physiology, School of Medicine and Biomedical Sciences, State University of New York at Buffalo, Buffalo, New York, USA, personal communication, Oct. 18, 1991.

50. Fink M., Prada C. Ultrasonic focusing with time-reversal mirrors. Advances in Acoustic Microscopy Series. Edited by A. Briggs and W. Arnold. Plenum Press, 1996.

51. Fink M. Time-reversed acoustics. Physics Today 1997; **50**: 34-40.

52. Kuperman W.A., Hodgkiss W., Song H.C., Akal T., Ferla C., Jackson D.R. Phase conjugation in the ocean: experimental demonstration of an acoustic time-reversal mirror. J Acoust Soc Am 1997; **102**: 1-16.

53. Fink M. Ultrasound puts materials to the test. Physics World 1998; **11**: 41-45.

54. Rinaldi P.C., Jones J.P., Reines F., Price L.R. Modification by focused ultrasound pulses of electrically evoked responses from an in vitro hippocampal preparation. Brain Res 1991; **558**: 36-42.

55. Watson A. Pump up the volume, what lasers do for light, sasers promise to do for sound - once you can work out the best way to build one. New Scientist March 27, 1999; **161**: 36-40.

56. Oldham J. Thoughts control a computer. Popular Mechanics 1999; **176**: 28.

57. Sullivan M.M. (Editor). Atom-size circuits envisioned. Buffalo News 1998; Sun., Aug. 30: H-6.

58. Vogel M. Big minds gather to think small, really small. Buffalo News 1998; Sat., Oct. 24: C-5.

59.   Fox M. Test on rats turns thought into action. Buffalo News 1999; Sun., 6-27: H-6.

60.   Kurzweil R. The coming merging of mind and machine: the accelerating pace of technological progress means that our intelligent creations will soon eclipse us - and that their creations will eventually eclipse them. Sci Am 1999; **10**: 56-60.

61.   Chase V.D. Mind over muscles: when two emerging technologies meet, paralyzed people can move their limbs - just by thinking about it. Technology Review: MIT's Magazine of Innovation 2000; **103**: 38-41, 44-45.

62.   Schatzthauer R., Fromherz P. Neuron-silicon junction with voltage-gated ionic currents. European Journal of Neuroscience 1998; **10**: 1956-1962.

63.   LaBar K.S., LeDoux J.E. Partial disruption of fear conditioning in rats with unilateral amygdala damage: correspondence with unilateral temporal lobectomy in humans. Behavioral Neuroscience; **110**: 991-997.

64.   Watson A. Why can't a computer be more like a brain? Science 1997; **277**: 1934-1936.

65.   Taubes G. After 50 years, self-replicating silicon. Science 1997; **277**: 1936.

66.   Service R.F. Neurons and silicon get intimate. Science 1999; **284**: 578-579.

67.   Vassanelli S., Fromherz P. Transistor probes local potassium conductances in the adhesion region of cultured rat hippocampal neurons. The Journal of Neuroscience 1999; **19**: 6767-6773.

68.   Brown P.G. Q-bits, don't touch. The Sciences 2000; **40**: 10.

69.   Oldham J. (Ed.). One-molecule transistors. Popular Mechanics 2000; **177**: 24.

70. Brooks M. Quantum clockwork. New Scientist 2000; **165**: 28-31.

71. Zeilinger A. Quantum teleportation. Sci Am 2000; **282**: 50-59.

72. Yerkes D. (Editor). Webster's New Universal Unabridged Dictionary. Barnes & Noble Books, Random House Publishing, Inc., 1996: 645-646, 1482.

73. Crystal D. (Editor). The Cambridge Encyclopedia, 2nd edn. Cambridge University Press, 1994: 1163.

74. Irvine M. Virtual reality changing the way doctors learn. The Buffalo News, June 18, 2000: H-6.

75. Davis H.L. Hand on the future: UB is developing virtual reality glove. Buffalo News 2000; Thurs., 6-29: B-1.

76. Walker P.M. (Editor). Chambers Dictionary of Science and Technology. Chambers Harrap Publishers, 1999: 877, 1190, 1240.

77. Dennett D.C. Consciousness Explained. Toronto, Little, Brown & Company, 1991; 101-102, 430.

78. Wade N. Brain may grow new cells daily. The New York Times 1999; Fri., Oct. 15: A-1 & A-21.

79. Talan J. The infinite mind. Psychology Today 1999; **32**: 16.

80. Sinha G. Memory Expansion. Popular Science 2000; May: 44.

81. Hales D., Hales R.E. The brain's power to heal, major advances in the '90s: the most dazzling discovery is that the brain can generate new cells. Buffalo News, Parade Magazine 1999; Sun., Nov. 21: 10.

82. Squire L.R. Memory and Brain. Oxford University Press, 1987: 115-117.

83. Restak R.M. The Brain. Bantam Books, 1984: 245-269.

84. Gazzaniga M.S. The split brain revisited. Sci Am 1998; **279**: 50-55.

85. Hamer D., Copeland P. Living with Our Genes: why they matter more than you think, 1st edn. New York: Doubleday, 1998: 18.

86. Davis H. WNY (Western New York) gene pool. Buffalo News 2000; Weds., 6-28: A-1, A-7.

87. Neergaard L. Apes minds may shed light on evolution. Buffalo News, Weds., 6-28: A-1, A-7.

88. Wrangham R., Peterson D. Demonic Males, Boston: Houghton Mifflin Company, 1996: 40-41.

89. Wilson J. Miracles of the next 50 years. Popular Mechanics 2000; **177**: 52-57.

90. Winston R. Twins. The Learning (television) Channel (TLC). British Broadcasting Corporation late May, 1999.

91. Hall C.S., Nordby V.J. A Primer of Jungian Psychology. Mentor, Division of Penguin Books, 1973: 24-25, 38-41, 123.

92. Norton A.L., Ed. Dictionary of Ideas. London: Brockhampton Press, Helicon Publishing Ltd, 1994: 105.

93. Aspect A., Dalibard J., Roger G. Experimental test of Bell's inequalities using time-varying analyzers. Physical Review Letters 1982; **49**: 1804-1807.

94. Coyle M. Time travel: a scientific possibility? UFO Magazine, 1999; **14**: 50-55, 60.

95. Walker E.H. The Physics of Consciousness: Quantum Minds and the Meaning of Life. Cambridge, MA.: Perseus Books, 2000: 120-129.

96.   Meyerson B.A., Boethius J., Carlsson A.M. Percutaneous central gray stimulation for cancer pain. Appl Neurophysiol 1978; **41**: 57-65.

97.   Akil H., Richardson D.E., Hughes J., Barchas J.D. Enkephalin-like material elevated in ventricular cerebrospinal fluid of pain patients after analgesic focal stimulation. Science 1978; **201**: 463-465.

98.   Hosobuchi Y. Periaqueductal gray stimulation in humans produces analgesia accompanied by elevation of beta-endorphin and ACTH in ventricular CSF. Modern Problems in Pharmacopsychiatry 1981; **17**: 109-122.

99.   Dieckmann G., Witzmann A. Initial and long-term results of deep brain stimulation for chronic intractable pain. Appl Neurophysiol 1982; **45**: 167-172.

100.   Tsubokawa T., Yamamoto T., Katayama Y., Hirayama T., Sibuya H. Thalamic relay nucleus stimulation for relief of intractable pain. Clinical results and B-endorphin immunoreactivity in the cerebrospinal fluid. Pain 1984; **18**: 115-126.

101.   Young R.F., Kroening R., Fulton W., Feldman R.A., Chambi I. Electrical stimulation of the brain in treatment of chronic pain. Experience over 5 years. J Neurosurg 1985; **62**: 389-396.

102.   Blumenkopf B. Chronic pain relief with deep brain stimulation. The Psychiatric Times/Medicine & Behavior 1988; Sept. 8-9.

103.   Thomas K.R., Folger K.R., Capecchi M.R. High frequency targeting of genes to specific sites in the mammalian genome. Cell 1986; **44**: 419-428.

104. Mancini L. Riley-Day syndrome, brain stimulation and the genetic engineering of a world without pain. Med Hypotheses 1990; **31**: 201-207.

105. Stover, D. Growing hearts from scratch. Popular Science 2000; **256**: 46-50.

106 Mooney D.J., Milos A.G. Growing new organs. Sci Am 1999; **280**: 60-65.

107. Recer P. Neural stem cells in mice are found to grow organ, muscle, other tissues. Buffalo News 2000; Fri., 6-2: A-6.

108. Howland D. Organs grown using cells from animals. Buffalo News 1997; Weds., 7-23: A-1, A-4.

109. Petranek S.L. (Editor). Growing organs. Discover 2000; **21**: 112-113.

110. Bilger B. Metamorphoses: hair-raising feats in cell biology. The Sciences 1999; **39**: 6-7.

111. Friedman R., Ed. The Life Millennium, The 100 Most Important Events & People of the Past 1,000 Years: Life Books, Time, Inc., 1998: 188.

112. Keesling B. Beyond orgasmatron. Psychology Today 1999; **32**: 58-60, 62, 84-85.

113. Carpenter M.B. Core Text of Neuroanatomy, Baltimore: Williams & Wilkins Co., 1972: 74, 94, 180.

114. Zorpette G. Muscular again: within a decade or two, scientists will create a genetic vaccine that increases muscle mass - without exercise. Sci Am 1999; **10**: 27-31.

115. Hoffmann-Wadhwa N.I., 1981 graduate of St. George's Univ. Schl of Medicine, Grenada, West Indies, personal communication, Thurs., June 15, 2000.

116. Stensaas S., Stensaas L., Depts. of Anatomy and Physiology, Univ. of Utah, Salt Lake City, Utah, personal communication, Mon., June 19, 2000.

117. Ritter M. Blind man navigates whole new world of vision by using tiny camera wired directly to his brain. Buffalo News 2000; Mon., Jan 17: A-14.

118. Mead C. Analog VLSI and Neural Systems. Addison-Wesley Publishing Co., Inc. 1989: 229, 257, 279, 294.

119. Peterson S. Ultrasound breakthrough offers hope blind may see. Buffalo News 1992; Weds., Jan. 15: A-1.

120. Kwiatkowski J. Sweet sounds: breaking into the new world of hearing with the sometimes controversial cochlear implant. Buffalo News 2000; Tues., Feb. 22: C-1, C-2.

121. Fischer J.S. Tweaking nature's repair kit: one's own cells may be the best medicine. U.S. News & World Report 2000; **128**: 55.

122. Brenner M.J. The new Atlantis and the frontiers of Medicine. JAMA 2000; **283**: 2296.

123. Editorial staff. Quadriplegic students may be walking before this summer's sunshine ends. Medical World News 1982; **23**: 58-59.

124. Brand C. Computer chip helps paralyzed man to walk: paraplegic walks, thanks to computer implant. Buffalo News 2000; Tues., 3-21: A-1, A-2.

125. Sullivan M. M. (Editor). Tidy line of molecules could mean much to science. Buffalo News 1997; Sun., Feb. 16: H-6.

126. Friend T. Scientists pinpoint brain's 'sleep switch.' USA Today 1996; Fri./Sat./Sun., Jan. 12-14: 1-A, 1-D.

127. Moon M.A. Electrical stimulation tempers advanced Parkinson's, subthalamic nucleus implants. Internal Medicine News, Clinical Rounds 1999; Jan.: 14.

128. Douma A. Cause of tremors remains unknown. Buffalo News 1999; Fri., 10-29: B-15.

129. Davis H.L. Implant offers hope to epileptics. Buffalo News 1999; Mon., 3-8: B-1.

130. Sullivan M.M. (Editor). System helps paralyzed write using brain waves. Buffalo News 1999: Thurs., 3-25: A-4.

131. Stinus L., Auriacombe M., Tignol J., Limoge A., Le Moal M. Transcranial electrical stimulation with high frequency intermittent current (Limoge's) potentiates opiate-induced analgesia: blind studies. Pain 1990; **42**: 351-363.

132. Andy O., Jurko F. Thalamic stimulation effects on reactive depression. App Neurophysiol 1987; **50**: 324-329.

133. Privitera M.R., Clinical Associate Professor, Dept. of Psychiatry, Strong Memorial Hospital, Mood Disorders Center, Rochester, New York 14627, personal communication, 8/16/99.

134. Upton A.R.M., Tougas G., Talalla A. et al. Neurophysiological effects of left vagal stimulation in man. Pace 1991; **14**: 70.

135. Penrose R., Shimony A., Cartwright N., Hawking S. The Large, the Small and the Human Mind. Cambridge University Press 1997, paperback 1999: 128-143.

136. Douma A. Painful bone spurs gradually go away. Buffalo News, Sat., June 17, 2000: B-21.

137.   Tsien J.Z. Building a brainier mouse. Sci Am 2000; **282**: 62-68.

138.   Weed W.S. Smart pills: how about a little Viagra for your memory? Discover 2000; **21**: 82.

139.   Sullivan M.M. (Editor). A crisis of will, not energy. The Buffalo News 2000; April 3: B-2.

140.   Sullivan M.M. (Editor). New way to make hydrogen gas seen promising. The Buffalo News 2000; Sept.: H-6.

141.   Fordahl M. It's not Hal but new circuit mimics the way the brain works. Buffalo News, Thurs., June 22, 2000: A-1, A-4.

142.   Folkman M.J. Can Conventional Anti-Cancer Therapies be Improved by Inhibition of Angiogenesis? Centennial Symposium Cancer Genetics & Biology, Oct. 9, 1998. Roswell Park Cancer Institute, Buffalo, New York, USA. Re: M.J. Folkman, Andrus Professor of Pediatric Surgery & Professor of Cell Biology, Harvard Medical School, Children's Hospital, Boston, MA.

143.   Hanrahan D. Induction of Angiogenesis and Acquired Resistance to Apoptosis along Pathways of Multistep Tumorigenesis. Centennial Symposium Cancer Genetics & Biology, Oct. 9, 1998. Roswell Park Cancer Institute, Buffalo, New York, USA. Re: D. Hanrahan: Dept. of Biochemistry & Biophysics, Hormone Research Institute, Univ. of California, San Francisco, CA.

144.   Douma A. Stress can aggravate excessive sweating. The Buffalo News, 2000. Sat., June 10: B-1.

145.   Davis H.L. Shedding light on the future. Buffalo News, Sun., April 2, 2000: A-1, A-12.

146. Prasad P.N., of the Depts. of Chemistry and Physics and the Institute for Lasers, Photonics (optical technologies) and Biophotonics at the State U. of N.Y. at Buffalo, N.Y., USA, personal communication, Oct. 25, 1999.

147. Sullivan M.M. (Ed.). A new way to nudge individual atoms. The Buffalo News, Sun., April 23, 2000: H-6.

148. Merrill M. Overworked hospital staff should learn to put patients to work. The Buffalo News, June 25, 2000: H-1.

First update: a minimal update on one potentially important aspect of the first of this book's

two essays (the essay completed on April 7, '03)

This update is dedicated to Louise

An article titled "Stimulating the brain: activating the brain's circuitry…" (reference one,

directly below) seems especially relevant to the first essay. This article explains how

transcranial magnetic stimulation (TMS) (a shortened version of "transcranial magnetic **brain**

stimulation"), possibly entailing a magnetic coil configuration "that is designed to generate

sufficient magnetic field strength to stimulate neurons deep inside the brain mass" (page 72),

might be **useful for** the purpose of **teaching** (any person(s)) "a **new**…" conceivably relevant-to-

employment and, therefore, valuable "…**skill"(s)** (page 68). And, of course, **new skills** could

entail an abundance of new jobs.

In a subsequent article (ref. 2, page 73, below), it is mentioned that the author of the

article referred to directly above, (Dr. Mark) "George, is even willing to entertain the possibility

that such methods could someday stimulate the brain's pleasure centers. (Mr. – Woody – Allen,

your Orgasmatron is on its way.)"

References

1. George M.S. Stimulating the brain: activating the brain's circuitry with pulsed magnetic
   fields may help ease depression, enhance cognition, even fight fatigue. Scientific American,
   2003; special issue, Sept., **289**(3): 66-73.

2. Zolli A. Best of what's next: Popsci resident futurist Andrew Zolli spotlights five
   technologies you won't want to wait for. Pescovitz D. Your wits: pampered and sharp. At
   the "brain spa" of the future, transcranial magnetic stimulation and memory-enhancing drugs
   will clear your mind of forgetfulness and flabby thinking. Popular Science, 2004, May,
   264(5): 69-79.

A second minimal update (concerning the danger of choking and

another **hypothetical** way to relieve it),

written on October 8, '03:

This update is dedicated to Margaret

In an earlier publication (reference one, directly below) it is suggested that by applying a (possibly, specifically-**modified**-for-intended-purpose) transcranial magnetic stimulation (TMS) coil to the skin directly over (that is, overlying) a choking individual's larynx, it might **thereby** be **possible to stun** the larynx in such a way as to **distract** the choking victim's attention and simultaneously relax and relieve the intensely concerted, spasmodically-maladaptive state of neuromuscular-laryngeal contraction and tension, so as to relieve the choking emergency.

However, this emergency might **more readily** (and more reliably) be **relieved** by applying the stimulus coil (or otherwise describable) apparatus to a one-to-three-centimeter-diametric (roughly) circular area directly over (that is, above) both the right and the left ears. This approach might be preferable (to a direct laryngeal approach) because the superficial areas of the brain directly beneath these two areas of the head and skull (being the neuroanatomically-identifiable laryngeal-control areas of the primary motor cortex of the brain) **might** in the relatively near future be determined to **be the most readily accessible**, hence, most feasibly **interruptible** of all **of the links** in the **chain of** dysfunctional neuromuscular **events** that occurs when an individual (human or other kind of being) is experiencing the extremely distressing emergency state associated with choking on food or any other ingested object(s) or material(s).

Clearly, however, thorough and unequivocally-persuasive research and testing would need to be done before **anyone** should think of applying either approach in a real-life choking emergency, in which case **only** the Heimlich Maneuver should be attempted/done/implemented.

Reference

1. Mancini L.S. short note: A magnetic choke-saver might relieve choking. Medical Hypotheses, 1992; **38**: 349.

Instant Learning, Reverse (Mental) Relativity,

$$L = E \times (PL)^2,$$

Compressed or Enveloped Medicinal Substances

Readily Affordable Body-Scanning Equipment

You're a Particle Attached to Your Body,

Plus: A Closing Note

This fourth update is dedicated to:

My classmates, reunion companions and friends:

Erica-Joani, Dick (Richard), Liz, Karel, Melinda, Liz-Ruth, Peter, Franz-Peter,

Dick (Richard), Wendy, Graham, Don, Karen, Kit, Christopher-Jacques,

Laura-Louise, Lolly and Ruth-Naomi

Figure One below is a diagram of How Human (and Animal) learning ability might be quickly improved, so that employment and job-related skills might **also** be improved and diversified. Figures Two through Eleven are illustrative cartoons by my classmate and friend, Erica-Joani.

Explicit explanations of how a) learning/education, b) employment-related skills and c) financial/economic and fiscal processes/phenomena might be quickly (almost instantaneously) and simultaneously improved, augmented and diversified are contained in the two relatively long essays that together comprise the crux of this book (at this time: June 30, '04).

The essence of an intuitive grasp of how these three categories of phenomena might be rapidly, synchronously and mutually-interactivatingly amplified and strengthened consists in the notion that if almost any person could learn almost any new job skill(s) in almost no (amount, that is, very little or **almost zero amount** of) time, then no individual(s) would be able to monopolize high-paying job(s) of any kind(s). And virtually any individual person(s) could readily supply whatever job skill(s) that the surrounding economy might demand in connection with (a) actual needs or significant desires and (b) readily and easily producible/providable supplies of goods/merchandise and/or services.

Reverse (Mental) Relativity

or more simply put:

Reverse Relativity

According to Einstein (according to Dr. Michio Kaku's book, Hyperspace, ref. one) the brains and the **mental processes** (of passengers in a rocketship/spaceship traveling at near-light speeds) would be **slowed down** to the point of rendering these individuals "slow-witted." Conversely, travel-speed-related effects on the brain's functioning speed such as might be expected to consist in **accelerated** or **sped-up mental processes**, can be inferentially imagined. However, a discussion of the nature of these effects will be postponed until the writing of some other, that is, some future update.

But for this context, please let it be said that the brain's mental processes might be optimally accelerated and effectively speeded-up **by way of** actively **rewarding**, that is, by positively-**reinforcing** (via pleasurable brain stimulation or other modes of enjoyable mental activation) **only** those neurophysiological **indicators/detectable** manifestations or physiological signals **of fastest – (possible)** – paced (!) mental processes **for any given brain-stimulation** (or other mental-activation-modality-mediated paradigm-) **recipient**. Such positive reinforcement might be delivered to any number of (potentially) ultra-fast-paced, rewarding-stimulation/activation-receiving students, workers, medical patients, etc.

$$L/W = E \times (PL)^2, \text{ where } L = \text{Learning, } W = \text{Work/Working, } E =$$

Effort and PL = Pleasure. Incidentally, the letter 'L' might

adequately-logically be construed to mean 'Labor' or 'Laboring'

Initially, please consider the following simple mathematical (and psychological)

relationship or expression (i.e., an admittedly oversimplified but heuristically-instructive

equation).

$$L/W = \frac{E \times PL}{PA}, \text{ where PA} = \text{pain (and/or suffering)}$$

In other words, the amount(s) of learning and/or work(ing) that might get accomplished

by virtually any individual, for example, a student or worker/laborer is a) **proportional** (as might

be denoted by the symbol 'oc', followed by a multiplicative 'proportionality constant') even **if**

not, strictly speaking, b) **equal** to the amount(s) of effort expended and pleasure experienced

(i.e., **interest** taken in the subject matter or task(s) 'at hand' or in question) and (**inversely**

proportional to the amount of (mental and/or physical) pain (such as stress) experienced by the

individual (e.g., student, worker or patient) in the context of any mode(s) of learning and/or

working being considered here.

Due to the phenomenon of **reciprocal inhibition** (refs. Two through four), the brain's

and mind's pleasure or 'reward' tends to inhibit the brain's (and mind's) pain or 'aversiveness'

and vice versa (i.e., the brain and mind's displeasure/pain-suffering tends to inhibit the brain and

mind's pleasure). The following inversely interrelated basic mathematical and neuro-

psychological/psychodynamic relationship is relevant and applicable to this discussion:

$$PA = \frac{1}{PL} \quad \rightarrow \textbf{Pain} \text{ and } \textbf{Pleasure} \text{ are inversely–proportionally interrelated. In other}$$
words, they are **reciprocally-inhibitory to each other.**

Next: substituting 1/PL in place of PA in the preceding L/W-based equation yields the

following:

$$L/W = \frac{E \times PL}{\frac{1}{PL}} = E \times (PL)2$$

PL

Hence, we now have before us:

L/W = E x (PL)^2, as delineated directly above (in the section heading)

L/W = E x (PL)^2 bears a suggestive similarity to Einstein's famous equation, E – mc^2. For this context, let's please allow the similarity to merely be noted without accompanying this notation with any (necessarily far-flung cosmological) explanation as to how and why this similarity is **not** merely a coincidental one.

The Potential Therapeutic Implications of Compressed And/or Electrostatically-neutrally-Enveloped Medicinal Chemicals/Pharmacologic Agents

When and if it might become possible to either (a) compress medicinal substances, perhaps by using pressure-transmission fluids (refs. 5,6) or a combination of Bose-Einstein condensates and compressed laser pulses (ref. 7) (and/) or (b) envelop medicinal chemicals in **electrostatically-neutral (neutral** so as **to avoid being** either **obstructed or pulled off-course** by various positive and negative charges as are virtually omnipresent throughout the human (and every other kind of animal's) body(/-ies)) possibly-membranous (?) **sheaths, then** it might be **possible to deliver these therapeutic agents (chemicals,** i.e., **drugs, elemental atoms, subatomic particles,** nano-robots, that is, synonymously speaking, micro-miniature robots, cloned or genetically engineered bacteria, viruses, other kinds of biological, biochemical, biophysical entities, etc.) **to any** x-, y-, and z- coordinates'-bodily-spatially-specifiable point(s) in any (medical/surgical) patients' body/-ies without needing to negotiate, be encumbered by or worry about electrostatic or electrodynamic obstacles and distractions, or about painstaking details of oral, intravenous (IV), intramuscular (IM), transdermal or other conceivable, relatively conventional, parenteral routes of therapeutic substance (or entity) delivery.

Instead, doses of such compressed and/or enveloped therapeutic entities might be delivered simply by accelerating, directing and propelling them not only through the air but also through the **empty spaces within** the **atoms** and **molecules** that make up any patient's body and from there (various intracorporeal empty intramolecular and intra-atomic spaces) into the therapeutically-optimal, delivery-receptive anatomic site(s) within the diseased, structurally- and/or functionally-impaired patient'(s') body (-ies).

Readily-Affordable
Body-Scanning Equipment

One (of very, very many) possible examples of a useful pairing of different technologies might consist in a combination of (a) T-Ray(s) (ref. 8) (i.e., electromagnetic, "deep-infrared," 'T' for terahertz, with the **combining form** or (virtual) prefix 'tera'- meaning trillions and referring to trillions of waves per second, positioned within the electromagnetic spectrum just before/below the region where wavelengths begin to stretch into the microwave range) **or T-wave(s)** and (b) functional magnetic resonance imaging (fMRI). They **might** together constitute a relatively safe, especially safe-for-doing-daily-or-otherwise-frequently, cancer-and-other-disease-seeking/screening or scanning modality, as compared with (c) CT, i.e., cross-sectional X-rays and (d) positron emission tomography (PET), because a and b, unlike c and d, would not entail the medical risks and hazards that are anxiety-engenderingly imposed by exposure to harmful ionizing radiation.

The problem of there being "little control over the spread of costly technology" (ref. 9) might be alleviated by the yet-to-be-developed **capability of** virtually **any** individual **person(s)** (as a consequence of or in connection with pleasurable learning/work-facilitative brain stimulation or other mode(s) of mental activation/empowerment) **to readily** and relatively quickly **learn** to build, operate and maintain any and all kinds(s) of **body-scanning equipment.**

You're a Particle
Attached to Your Body (for a Lifetime)

Because Your mind (and mine, too) seems to be what makes You an **individual**, that is an indivisible entity, it would seem to stand to reason that there must be some **individual physical entity** that **is** You. Since the human brain (and the rest of the human body, too) is/are made up of **billions of** component **parts, You,** being an indivisible, singular conscious entity cannot possibly be (equated with or consist in) Your brain (and/or any other part(s) of Your visible, touchable body).

Instead, it seems to make more sense to think of **You** (as opposed to Your brain and body) as **an individual**, indivisible **physical** or biophysical **particle** (that might potentially vary in size between the submicroscopic, smaller-than-a-nanometer) range and the gargantuan larger-than-planet-earth-size range of magnitudes, depending on the overall summation of Your personal circumstance). So you are a particle that You (and the rest of us humans) cannot readily see or have the experience of touching, perhaps either because **it** (i.e., **You,** the particle) are currently too small to be seen or perceptibly touched **or** because it (i.e., You) exist(s) in a set of three dimensions (of space) that is different from the three that Your brain and the rest of Your body exist/reside in.

This idea is examined relatively intuitively and broadly in the longer of the two main essays contained in this book. And **if** it, sooner or later, proves to be a valid and correct idea, then it might prove to be a very practically **useful** idea as well. If it is a valid idea, then **the**

reason why You (the individual, indivisible particle, who dwells within a relatively large, complicated human body) cannot see or otherwise perceive Your unitary, particulate self **might** be because **the particulate You** resides in some dimension(s) of space **other than** the readily perceptible commonplace three dimensions (1. height or length, i.e., the Y-axis or component of the analytic geometric coordinate system, 2. width or breadth, i.e., the X-axis or component of the coordinate system, and 3. depth or thickness, i.e., the Z-axis or component of the coordinate system) within which **Your visible** and otherwise **perceptible, complicated body** resides.

This notion would fit in well with string or superstring (i.e., string plus supersymmetry) theory (a particle-physics theory, refs. 1, 10-13) which aspires to become a "theory of everything," that is, a Unified Field Theory that **might** correctly reconcile among each other all of the equations (via one set of internally-consistent equations), that is a theory that describes the essential nature and interactive behavior of the four basic forces of Nature in the known universe (i.e., the strong nuclear force, the weak nuclear force, electromagnetism and gravity).

String/superstring theory seems to require at least six more spatial dimensions than the three (x, y, and z, as noted above) that We humans are perceptibly familiar with. So, **one possible** reason why You cannot perceive Your unitary, particulate self (which could be as large or even much larger than the body You're trapped inside of!) might be that Your particulate self resides in one or more of the six (or more) additional spatial dimensions which are postulated in the context of String Theory) that We humans seem incapable (so far, at least) of obtaining any perceptible information about.

My own contention would be that there are actually an **infinite number** of **spatial dimensions** (as well as an infinite number of temporal dimensions) and that sooner or later, in due time, We will discover and/or invent ways in which to obtain perceptible access and direct experiential information about all (or many) of the infinite numbers of dimensions of both space and time.

Some suggestive evidence (ref. 14) that the mind and the brain are **two physically separate** and distinctly different (biochemical, biophysical and anatomical) **entities**, even though they are intimately bonded to each other for a lifetime (apart from any possible genuine out-of-body or near-death experiences) **can be** inferred from the observations that "motor **activity (in the brain)** precedes our **(mind's)** awareness of the intention to move" (page 358). And the "brain is gong full speed ahead well before a person experiences the conscious intention (in their mind) of moving (page 360). Moreover, "neural motor **(brain)** activity (is) well in the works by the time a person('s **mind**) feels an intention to act (in any way)" (page 365).

An Incidental Note to this Update; one that can be Interpreted as Empirical Evidence in relation to Brain Stimulation and its Conceivable Potential

According to a recent personal communication from three knowledgeable colleagues and friends (ref. 15), that is, a delivery that was conveyed to me on Tuesday, June 15, '04: By simply placing some electrodes on the surface of the brain, four volunteers have already been able to play video games using only their thoughts…." These people are not moving their limbs. It seems they learned (in a matter of only several minutes) how to move computer cursors using **previously-untrained brainpower alone**. These observations would certainly seem to bode well for the human (or other animal-)-to-machine interface.

Moreover, a new book (ref. 16), titled: Brain Stimulation in Psychiatric Treatment explains the methods, rationale and currently available evidence on the safety and efficacy of four new potential psychiatric treatments: (1) transcranial magnetic stimulation (TMS), (2) magnetic seizure therapy (MST), (3) deep brain stimulation (DBS), and vagus nerve stimulation (VNS).

References
(for fourth update)

1. Kaku M. Hyperspace: A Scientific Odyssey through Parallel Universes, Time Warps, and the 10th Dimension: Doubleday, Anchor Books, 1994: 359 pages; Please see pages 83-84, 87-88, 151-177.

2. Stein L., Belluzzi J.D., Ritter S., Wise C.D. Self-stimulation reward pathways: norepinephrine versus dopamine. J Psychiatr Res 1974; 11: 115-124.

3. Stein L. reciprocal action of reward and punishment mechanisms. The Role of Pleasure in Behavior: Harper & Row, 1964: 113-139.

4. Heath R.G. Pleasure response of human subjects to direct stimulation of the brain: physiologic and psychodynamic considerations. The Role of Pleasure in Behavior: Harper & Row, 1964: 219-243.

5. Sullivan M.M. (Editor) Molecule expands when compressed. The Buffalo News 2002; Sun., Jan. 6: F-6.

6. Lee Y., Vogt T., Hriljac J.A., Parise J.B., Artioli G. Pressure-induced volume expansion of zeolites in the natrolite family. J. Am Chem Soc 2002; 124: 5466-5475.

7. Hau L.V. Frozen light: slowing a beam of light to a halt may pave the way for new optical communications technology, tabletop black holes and quantum computers. Sci Am, May 31, 2003; 13 (1): 44-51.

8. Arnone D. T-rays. Technology Review: MIT's Magazine of Innovation, Feb. 2004; 107 (1): 42, 44.

9. Sullivan M.M. (Editor). Little control over the spread of costly technology. The Buffalo News 2004; Thurs., June 3: A-2.

10. Musser G. The future of string theory. Sci Am, Nov. 2003; 289 (5): 68-73.

11. Crystal D. (Editor). The Cambridge Encyclopedia, 2nd edn. Cambridge University Press, 1994: 1069.

12. Walker P.M. (Editor). Chambers Dictionary of Science and Technology. Chambers Harrap Publishers, 1999: 1131.

13. Isaacs A. (Editor). A Dictionary of Physics, Oxford Paperback Reference, 3rd edn. Oxford Univ. Press, 1996: 410, 414-145.

14. Sukhvinder S.O., Haggard P. Free will and free won't: motor activity in the brain precedes our awareness of the intention to move, so how is it that we perceive control? American Scientist, July-Aug., 2004; 92 (4): 358-365.

15. Bucki M., Trifan R., Spangler R.A., Assoc. Prof., State Univ. of NY at Buffalo, Depts. of Physiology and Biophysics: personal communication, June 15, '04.

16. Lisanby S.H. Brain Stimulation in Psychiatric Treatment: American Psychiatric Publishing, Inc., 2004: 172 pages.

APPENDIX

12 Keywords

to make the book easy to find

in a bookstore search

1. Money

2. Stress

3. Depression

4. Pain

5. Death

6. Love

7. Sex

8. Rich

9. Famous

10. Education

11. Jobs

12. Employment

20 word

Book marketing statement or keynote

"…Everyone could be Rich, Famous,…" explains how everybody could become an immortal wealthy celebrity…, and includes a potential business item.

Veterans
Administration

April 15, 1986

TO WHOM IT MAY CONCERN:

RE: Lewis Mancini, M.D.

I'm writing this letter on behalf of Dr. Lewis Mancini. I had the opportunity to work with Dr. Mancini during his rotation in Consultation/ Liaison Psychiatry Service at the Buffalo VA Medical Center from January to June of 1985.

Dr. Mancini demonstrated initiative, cooperative team spirit and empathy in dealing with patients, families and staff. He was highly motivated in pursuing his own research.

I do hope you will consider his application seriously.

Sincerely,

Fern E. Beavers, R.N., M.S.
Clinical Nurse Specialist/Psychiatry

UNIVERSITY AT BUFFALO
STATE UNIVERSITY OF NEW YORK

Department of Biophysical Sciences
School of Medicine and Biomedical Sciences

18 October, 1991

To Whom It May Concern:

This is to certify that Dr. Lewis Mancini has successfully completed a program in independent study with me during the Spring semester, 1989. The objectives of this program were that of exploring various physical modalities by which a small region of the human CNS could be selectively and non-invasively stimulated.

The problem of safely and conveniently stimulating restricted regions of the brain, primarily for purposes of pain control, is one in which Dr. Mancini has long held an interest; I first spoke with him in this regard about five years ago, early in his psychiatry residency. Since then his appreciation and knowledge of the physical mechanisms likely to be involved -- electromagnetic and ultrasound fields --has evolved substantially. It is my understanding that Dr. Mancini intends to pursue research in this area in conjunction with or subsequent to his completion of training in psychiatry. Alternatively, Dr. Mancini is well-prepared, I believe, to undertake training in bioengineering prior to his re-entry into a psychiatric residency program in order to research and develop this specific interest in techniques of brain stimulation.

Over the course of the previous semester, Dr. Mancini reviewed the theoretical basis of magnetic fields. Clearly, a purely electromagnetic phenomenon cannot be sufficiently focussed sufficiently distant from generating coils or electrodes to allow adequate selectivity in stimulating a small portion of the CNS. Electromagnetic induction, in combination with another physical process, however, seems to offer a possible method of achieving adequate focussing. One such technique is that proposed by W. Fry, based upon the use of superimposed electric and ultrasound fields, both of the same frequency. Given a finite dependence of electrical conductivity upon pressure and/or temperature, the focussed ultrasound generates partial rectification of the alternating electrical field, leading to neural stimulation in that region. The small magnitude of the conductivity's pressure/temperature coefficient makes the fields necessary to achieve stimulation (theoretically) prohibitively high, however. The basis and ramifications of Fry's proposed method were extensively discussed.

A more likely methodology growing out of the discussions held during the semester is based upon the observations of several

Russian authors that sufficiently intense ultrasound alone can result in neural stimulation. Dr. Mancini proposes to couple this effect with magnetically induced currents within the brain. While the precise mechanism whereby ultrasound achieves stimulation remains to be established, it may well involve alteration of membrane properties through direct mechanical action on the neural membrane at the molecular level. It is an interesting and plausible prospect that this effect would enhance the sensitivity of the neural tissue to magnetically induced electrical currents. Were this hypothesis proved true, the ultrasound field could be used to define the region to be stimulated, with the electromagnetic field providing a mechanism for stimulation at reasonable field strength of each.

In view of these considerations, it is plausible that adequately localized deep brain stimulation could be achieved by means of an external device using ultrasound at energy levels considerably lower than those suggested by Fry. In order to pursue reasearch along these lines, I have suggested that Dr. Mancini explore opportunities at laboratories outside the Buffalo area, since this application of ultrasonics to brain stimulation is not the primary focus of any laboratory in the city.

At the conclusion of the independent study program, Dr. Mancini prepared a paper exploring these potential techniques of brain stimulation, based upon his review of the relevant literature.

Sincerely,

Robert A. Spangler, M.D., Ph.D.
Associate Professor, Biophysics

UNIVERSITY AT BUFFALO

STATE UNIVERSITY OF NEW YORK

Department of Biophysical Sciences
Faculty of Health Sciences

3 February, 1992

To Whom It May Concern:

Dr. Lewis Mancini is currently enrolled in Independent Study (BPH600) with me. The objective of his independent study program is that of continuing to broaden his knowledge concerning ultrasound and its possible direct effects upon CNS function, and the EEG. Building upon his previous experience and training, Dr. Mancini is eager for an opportunity to obtain practical research experience in these and related areas of research in an appropriate laboratory setting. His interest and longstanding enthusiasm concerning these investigations will be a valuable asset in the exploration of a range of potential applications of these physical modalities.

4 May, 1992

To Whom It May Concern:

This is to certify that Dr. Lewis Mancini has successfully completed the program of independent study as indicated above. During the course of the semester, Dr. Mancini continued to broaden his knowledge of the potential physical basis for non-invasive focussed brain stimulation by ultrasonic energy through library research and communication with researchers in this field. His ideas concerning such direct stimulation and its possible applications are being refined and written up in a manuscript which, at present, is envisioned to form the basis of two books for which he has developed detailed outlines.

Sincerely,

Robert A. Spangler, M.D., Ph.D.
Associate Professor of
Biophysical Sciences

pseudonym of Lewis Mancini 230

WAITING HOPEFULLY
by Nemo T. Noone

From the time of earliest recollection, both my mother and physician father expressed definite expectations that I should become a physician. Early on, it became obvious to everyone involved that it takes me at least twice as much time as most people to learn any subject matter or accomplish any task. The problem was incomprehensible not only to my parents and teachers, but also to me.

During my junior and senior years of college, I became significantly depressed. The prospect of disappointing my parents as to career choice seemed unconscionable. On the other hand, the necessary brain power for a medical career simply didn't seem available to me. Suddenly, one day during July 1972, as I was dozing off in organic chemistry class, a cogent and somewhat reassuring understanding of the basic problem popped into awareness; the reason for the abnormal slowness is twofold:

1. An *attention deficit* associated with excessive daydreaming and rumination.

2. An abnormally high level of (learning- and work-related) *performance anxiety*, associated with an extreme fear of failure and fear of making mistakes.

Hence, due to deficit attention and intense anxiety, concentration becomes markedly impaired and progress toward goals becomes obstructed.

As soon as the optimistic notion of finding a therapeutic way of simultaneously enhancing attention and diminishing anxiety began to circulate through my mind, the depression began to diminish appreciably. This notion or prospect constituted a bright light at the outlet of a depressive tunnel, a clear sparkle of hope.

Although it was fairly apparent that professional help might entail the most effective possible pharmacologic or behavior-modification therapy, at the time, there was neither sufficient financial wherewithal nor security of self-esteem to take the necessary steps to obtain such help. Consequently, the only readily accessible (admittedly less than optimal) treatment method seemed to be a regimen of increased daily caffeine intake (increased from one to five or six cups a day).

By virtue of the fact that the megadoses of caffeine improved the attention deficit (by enhancing alertness) much more markedly than they worsened the anxiety, a significant net benefit was acquired. This benefit, while not dramatic, was enough to facilitate passing grades in all premedical course work.

Having mediocre grades, of course, I didn't gain admission to an US medical school, but was fortunate to receive an acceptance from a foreign medical school. In the context of psychiatry residency, (initiated in '83), my day's work typically stretched from 8:30 or 9:00 a.m. till midnight or beyond. I was getting very burned out, very quickly. My bosses noticed this. And in '85 they laid me off with an indeterminate return date.

I went on to total psychiatric disability with a diagnosis of obsessive-compulsive disorder (OCD), substantiated by various symptoms, including many hours spent each day praying and engaging in superstitious rituals of many different kinds, intended to ward off evil influences.

Time-wasting rituals included excessively meticulous and repetitious grooming (five to six hours to get ready to leave the house, including a full hour in the shower to ensure "adequate" cleanliness). Adherence to ideas that certain colors, numbers and positions of objects in the physical environment were either good or evil, resulted in arranging and, almost incessantly, rearranging them, in my mind or in space in highly idiosyncratic ways to maximize superstitious advantages and minimize superstitious disadvantages. Another major problem was checking and rechecking, over and over again, to ascertain that no errors were made in context of any tasks undertaken.

In 1985 an electroencephalogram (EEG or brain wave test) demonstrated abnormal neurological function, in particular, abnormal slow activity on the left side of the brain. Every plausibly appropriate medication and virtually every conceivable kind of behavior modification were determined (by the psychiatrist and two clinical psychologists) to be ineffectual. So, from a practical standpoint, what the OCD diagnosis and abnormal EEG seemed to signify was both a form of attention deficit disorder (ADD) and learning disability (LD). These inferences were confirmed in '92 by a psychologist who administered a comprehensive battery of psychometric tests.

At this point, I'm hopefully and patiently awaiting the emergence of a "wonder" drug that'll simultaneously enhance alertness and attention, while diminishing task-related performance anxiety. Another possibility might be some therapeutic adaptation and application of the kinds of physical phenomena, such as ultrasound and electromagnetic forces, which are in widespread use for medical imaging and diagnosis.

If they can be used noninvasively (that is, nonsurgically) to visualize and analyze minute details of *structures* of anatomic areas of medical interest, then isn't it conceivable they might also be used to therapeutically and noninvasively influence their *functions*? This is a question which can only be answered by way of extended amounts of time and considerable outlays of effort. In the meantime, I'm waiting patiently and doing the best I can. ❑

THE "FRAGILE PATIENT"
by Ramon Montes-Deoca

I presently work at a mental health group home. Being in a good position to observe those with a no-fault brain disease, I find "my clients" are "fragile". Things that I can easily do, they need more time for. Or they may just not be able to do something at all. We must do *all* we can to help them. Even the small things they ask us for can be a great big thing in their lives. Just because their illnesses are not visible does not mean they're not ill. The illnesses have greatly impaired their minds.

I'm only 21 years old, but many of my friends have been victimized by mental illnesses. I watched some of my very athletically talented friends turn into people who wanted to stay in bed all day. Those who enjoyed life were suddenly crying, wanting to end it all. Let's stop looking at the mentally ill as a bad mark on society. All of them are someone's parents, children, brothers, sisters, wives and husbands. Let's treat them as people. People who may be "fragile." And let's work toward meeting all their needs. Most of all, let's not give hope that mental illnesses may be wiped out someday, a disease of the past. ❑

Full length or other alternate title(s):

How Everyone

could be

Rich, Famous,

Painless, Deathless,

Well Educated,

Sexually Liberated,

Etc.

Full length title of a Potential Book Series

Beginning with this (Book Number) One:

How Everyone could

Be Rich, Famous, Etc.,

How all Diseases

(including Death)

could be Cured

and

Waiting <u>Your</u> Turn

to be Vice-President of the Universe

Other alternate or Future Update Titles:

1. Everyone is <u>POTENTIALLY</u>

Equally and Infinitely Intelligent

(and <u>EQUALLY UNIQUELY GIFTED!</u>)

2. How Everyone could be a

Wealthy, Immortal Celebrity,

etc.

3. Love Equals Money times Sex

Times Fame times Compassion

(L = M x S x F x C)

4. How Everyone could be Rich and Famous,

not just "for fifteen minutes," but Forever!

How Poverty, Your Financial Stress, etc.

could possibly be Alleviated by

Medicine, Science and Technology

Lewis S. Mancini

completed on April 7, 2003

This is a potentially practical theoretical essay dedicated to Herbert, Mary, Grace, Herb's mother, Bernice, and to his family members who were present at the hospital Emergency Room, referred to ~~below~~ *above and below.*

How Poverty, Your Financial Stress, etc.

could possibly be Alleviated by

Medicine, Science and Technology

Summary

The Basic Idea at a Glance

It might prove helpful or useful to stimulate or activate one or more pleasure-subserving sites(s) in the brain or elsewhere in the body **if** and **only if, when** and **only when**, and for **as long as** and **only** for **as long as** the stimulation-recipient emits some kind(s) of physiologically-correlated signal(s) that indicate that this recipient is engaging in high-level mental and/or physical activities, such as learning or (skillfully) working. Consequently, it would be possible to readily enable this recipient to **associate pleasure with** and **therefore** take an interest in/**find interesting** any (preferably, **high-paying** – or other) kind of **working** or **employment**. The stimulation mechanism might be a circuit or otherwise-describable device(s), modality/-ies, media or means that deliver(s) the pleasurable stimulation/activation whenever the stimulation recipient emits the learning-linked and/or working-linked (characteristic) signal(s). The stimulation modality might be electromagnetism (EM), sound waves (for **example**, ultrasound), particle beams, pacemakers, pharmacologic agent(s) or some other biological, chemical, physical, engineering, technological or otherwise scientifically-describable phenomena. Being as versatile and productive as this pleasure-based paradigm might enable any person to be, this person would be unlikely to suffer from poverty or even financial stress.

The basic idea inherent in the methodology proposed herein is simply an adaptation of the psychologist, B.F. Skinner's operant conditioning. A device or other kind(s) of mechanism(s) that would utilize this principle as suggested above could probably be developed in less than one (to five) years' time, at a cost of several million dollars, which would be a minuscule investment in comparison to the many billions of dollars worth of increased human productivity and improved work skills it might facilitate.

The Basic Idea: An Overview

It would be appropriate to use (a) a **pleasure-inducing stimulation modality** or

mechanism, such as electromagnetism (EM) (for example, possibly, neuroanatomic-**regionally-**

focused **transcranial magnetic** brain **stimulation**, TMS) (refs. 19, 20) or some other kind(s) of specific-neuron/nerve-cell-targeted or otherwise anatomically-precisely-aimed stimulator(s) or pacemaker(s), possibly entailing sound waves, for **example**, ultrasound (US) or infrasound, shock waves, particle beams, such as, for example, beams of subatomic particles, ionized gas particles, "nano-particles," nanorobots or other nano-technologized entities (with "nano-" meaning, essentially, "micro-miniature" or ultra-**small**) (refs. 21, 22), laser-drug photodynamic therapy, molecular carriers capable of squeezingly compressing pharmacologic agents, nanometer-size particles capable of condensing medicinal substances within/inside of them (ref. 23) other biological/chemical/physical/technological/engineering-related media, substances or processes **AND/OR SOME OTHER KINDS OF (OR OTHERWISE DESCRIBABLE) PHENOMENA that might** (or might **not**) **be** narrowly focused, **targeted** and applied (preferably, but **not necessarily**, e.g., implanted microchips-?) entirely from outside of the head and possibly from outside of the rest of the body as well, that would be, altogether extracorporeally-applied.

Incidentally, the same or **similar** technologies as might prove useful for imaging and stimulating specific sites anywhere in the body might also be useful (particularly if different input parameters and values are used) for curing, eradicating or, at least, effectively treating disease-mediating entities as can and do occur anywhere in the body, almost entirely regardless of the type of disease-producing phenomena that are involved in undermining any individual's health (e.g., cancer, cardiac, vascular, genetic, infectious, immuno-deficient such as AIDS-related, autoimmune, post-traumatic-stress induced, pain-induced, psychiatric, etc.). For example, radiofrequency ablation of cancer has been viewed as a promising medical tool (ref. 24).

It would be appropriate to use (a) a pleasure-inducing stimulation modality together with (b) a relatively simple and straightforward circuit (perhaps describable as a feedback or biofeedback circuit, possibly similar to the circuits noted and delineated in references numbers 25 and/or 26), whereby a person would obtain (c) pleasurable stimulation or activation of one or more reward pathway(s), structure(s) or site(s) in the brain (or elsewhere in the body) **if and only if, whenever and only whenever,** and for **as long as** and **only** for **as long as** this person were engaging in (d) **high-level mental** and/or **physical activities** or processes, such as learning, reading, problem-solving, memorizing, remembering/recollecting or (skillfully) working, as **instrumentally indicated** and **signaled** by (e) this person's emission of one or more detectable, monitorable physiologically-correlated brain wave/electroencephalographic (EEG), magnetoencephalographic (MEG) (ref. 27) functional magnetic resonance imaging (fMRI) (ref. 27), Doppler ultrasonographic scanning (ref. 28), electromyographic (EMG) (ref. 28), evoked-response-derived (ref. 28), echoencephalographic (ref. 28), **OR OTHER** KIND(S) of **occurrence-of-high-level-mental-or-physical-activity-or-process-indicative signal(s)** (refs. 29-39) that would necessarily and instrumentally be used by the stimulation circuit, device, agent (substance) or mechanism as the **TURN-ON** and **MAINTAIN-** or **STAY-ON signal**(s) for the pleasurable brain (or other anatomic-site-directed) stimulation. **Consequently:** (f) these high-level activities/processes/phenomena would be or come to be experienced by the stimulation-receiving person as intensely **pleasurable and therefore interesting** and therefore likely to occur often and for long periods of time.

What is meant by **"high-level"** activities, processes or phenomena is activities, processes or phenomena that require or entail high levels of sustained, relatively intense and focused attention, mental concentration and/or mental and/or physical (bodily) exercise. **These activities** or processes, by reason of their association with the enjoyable stimulation, in particular, for example, by means of their possibly being simultaneous (or nearly simultaneous) with the pleasurable brain (neural, or elsewhere, otherwise-anatomically-located) stimulation or by dint of their, at least, being chronologically intermittently juxtaposed with or otherwise in close temporal proximity with the enjoyable stimulation (with the details of timing depending on the stimulus parameters used, neuro- or other anatomic pleasure-delivery sites focused on, etc.), **consequently, these activities** or processes would be loaded with pleasure, pleasure-loaded or **pleasurized**, hence, interesting and likely to occur often and for long periods of time.

By virtue of being able to pleasurize (in the way delineated directly above) and thereby to render any (preferably, **high-paying**) mental/physical activity/ies or subject matter interesting to anyone, that is, stated in different terms, by means of **rewarding** (i.e., pleasurizing) and **thereby rendering interesting only correct performance** of technical or other procedural details of skilled behavior, (refs. 29-39) as would be prerequisitely indicated (a prerequisite in order to receive or a prerequisite for receiving the pleasurable stimulation) by the occurrence-of-high-level-mental-or-physical-activity-process-phenomena-indicative signal(s) (refs. 29-39), consequently anyone could become interested in, knowledgeable about the overview as well as the details and competent in the performance of skilled behavior in any area(s) of endeavor this person might choose to become interested, knowledgeable and competent in relation to.

And being so productive and versatile (as this method would enable virtually anyone, who chooses to do so, to be/become, that is) any person could virtually always quickly and effectively change vocation(s)/job(s)/nature of employment/career(s)/area(s) of expertise in accordance with/according to whatever kind(s) of employment/job opportunities happen to **pay well** (or, at least, **well enough to live comfortably**, if not lavishly) during any particular period of time and within any given environment or set of environmental circumstances. Being so productive and **employmentally-versatile**, any person would be unlikely to suffer from/be afflicted with financial stress, poverty, hunger or any other lack-of or shortage-of-money-related adversity.

It is conceivable that these effects could all be produced without involving any contact between the stimulator and the person being stimulated. In any case, not only might there be no surgery, pain or discomfort involved, but, quite possibly, there would be no tactile (or other) sensory perceptions(s) of any kind(s). As a result of (a) these high-level activities becoming abundantly infused with pleasure and (b) this infusion effectively **bypassing**, surpassing or effectively **removing** the **barrier** or **obstacle** of **performance anxiety** (this barrier may be considered analogous to (part of) the **activation energy** in a chemical reaction (refs. 1,2)) in relation to these high-level activities, (the consequence would be that) the activities would or might be expected to readily be experienced, by the stimulation-recipient, as not merely being pleasureful in some amusing way, but also as being **interesting** (by dint of some increased accessibility of, or in relation to, the **intrinsic pleasure of knowledge**, together with an effectively decreased preponderance of the intrinsic pain and frustration of ignorance or lack of knowledge) in terms of their actual learning/working/vocationally-relevant content.

As a consequence of these high-level activities' being rendered both **pleasureful** and **interesting** (in a deeper sense than mere hedonistic pleasurefulness), one might reasonably expect the stimulus-recipient to participate in these brain/neural-stimulation-facilitated, high-level activities and processes **often and for long periods of time.** Hence, **learning** and **skilled-work-related activities/processes** (having been significantly or even substantially pleasurized) might reasonably be expected to occur **frequently** and **for long periods of time.**

The basic idea inherent in the method proposed herein is simply an adaptation or modification of the late (1904-1990) psychologist, B.F. Skinner's **operant conditioning** (refs. 26,40,41).

The only significant difference between (a) Skinnerian operant conditioning and (b) the stimulation paradigm or principle being suggested here is that with (a), whenever the subject (individual) in question produces a particular **behavioral** phenomenon (for example, pressing a lever), the individual **gets rewarded** (for example, with a sweet beverage) whereas with (b) whenever the subject in question produces a detectable, identifiable **neurophysiologically-related** phenomenon (for example, emitting a particular EEG or functional magnetic resonance, fMRI manifestation), this individual **gets rewarded** (with pleasurable brain stimulation or some other directly neurologically-targetable, pleasure-mediating modality/-ies or functionally-facilitative physical and/or chemical/pharmacologic agent(s)).

A device that would utilize this principle, as suggested above, could probably be developed in one to five years' time, at a cost of **several million** U.S. dollars, which would be **a small investment in comparison to** the billions (or, conceivably, even trillions) of dollars worth of increased (per capita, as well as aggregate or total) human productivity, in terms of both services and goods, and new, improved and diversified work skills and high-quality workmanship it might facilitate.

How One Might De-effortize and Pleasurize One's Learning Processes and Work Skills' Performance

One possible way in which to initiate the research and development (R&D) of a methodology by means of which poverty and anyone's (or **almost** everyone's) financial problems (or stress) could (possibly) virtually-**readily** be alleviated might be as follows. If You were to enlist the assistance of some of the patients who are **currently/already** being treated (for pain, depression, obsessive-compulsive disorder, OCD, etc. **and**) who (might) **already have** surgically-implanted or otherwise somewhat invasive brain pacemakers (refs. 3,4,42) then (despite the **probable preferability** of **completely noninvasive** pacemakers/stimulators/ activators/inhibitors) You **might be readily** able to get started with the R and D by doing the following.

It might prove helpful to (a) modify the stimulation/stimulus parameters, such as waveform shapes, pulse train, stimulus frequency, interstimulus intervals, etc. and (b) position or re-position the pacemakers' stimulating electrode(s) or other **already-implanted** stimulation equipment/apparatus in one (or more than one) appropriate pleasure centers. These pleasure centers (sites, structures or pathways) should be **appropriate for working** and **learning,** that is, for mental, studious/scholastic, athletic, artistic, etc. processes and gratification as (conceivably, **possibly**) opposed to bodily/physical processes and gratification, such as eating/tasting, sexual-impulse-related processes and gratification.

It might then prove useful and helpful to add on (probably entirely onto the **outside** of the stimulation-recipient, that is, **extracorporeally**) an, i.e., one (or possibly more than one) non-surgery-necessitating and otherwise noninvasive-to-the-structural-integrity-of-the-stimulation recipient, possibly feedback-type loop(s) or circuit(s)/circuit component(s) that might (or **might not**) be functionally similar to a couple of possibly conceptually suitable circuits/circuit types that come to mind (refs. 25,26) (and that were referred to above in a slightly situationally different – **no already operational brain pacemakers involved** – context and regard). Then You might be able to do the following. You might be able to remove, eliminate, at least markedly reduce, or take the effort, stress and strain out of learning as well as out of the processes of (mental and physical) working in the way(s) delineated below.

The reader might pose the question, "If the patient/student/worker/recipient were given access to **direct, unconditional** pleasureable stimulation, **apart from** any contingency in relation to high-level mental/physical activities/processes, would this person lose all interest in and motivation toward these high-level activities/processes and spend most of their time pleasurably self-stimulating while simultaneously engaging in (nothing any more valuable than) aimless, low-intensity mental/physical activities?" What is meant by "low-level" activities and/or processes is activities and/or processes that do **NOT** require or entail high levels of sustained, relatively intense and focused attention, mental concentration and/or mental and/or physical (bodily) exercise or other use, but instead entail the mind and body merely drifting pointlessly and purposelessly, e.g., daydreaming, relaxing or ruminating apparently unproductively.

The probable, tentative answer to the question is "no." And the reason why not may be twofold:

1) the patient/student/worker would be aware and understand that engaging in, or participation in high-level mental and/or physical activities/processes would or might entail the rewarding properties of a pathway to **high-paying employment**, whereas participation in low-level activities/processes would not entail these rewarding properties, and

2) knowledge as well as employment-related capability in relation to practical skills are inherently pleasurable/rewarding/interesting in their own respective rights, that is, intrinsically, even **apart from economic considerations**, whereas ignorance as well

as employment-related **in**ability in relation to practical skills are inherently displeasurable/punishing/uninteresting in **their** own rights, that is, intrinsically. So, there are the intrinsic pleasures of knowledge and vocational competence/capability and the intrinsic displeasures of ignorance and incompetence/inability. Their existence is substantially rooted in the apparent fact that knowledge and capability enhance any person's self-esteem, self-confidence and optimism.

If the burden of effortful stress and strain that typically accompany learning and working could be eliminated or minimized (as suggested below), then the human mind could take a (relatively effortless and stress/strain-free) short-cut or, **electrical-engineering-analogously** speaking, relatively, at least, **resistance-free** pathway to very substantial knowledge and work skills' mastery. Please read on.

The present human condition seems to be such that when we succeed at a task, we feel moderate to high-intensity pleasure, but when we fail at a task we generally feel high-intensity to **very** high-intensity displeasure/pain. Moreover, whether we succeed or fail at a task, the task seems to require what we call "effort," which, in essence, amounts to a euphemism for pain (i.e., strain, stress, etc.) including the following two kinds of pain: (1) performance anxiety and (2) the "uphill battle" feeling or work/burden of actually doing the (learning, work-related) task. These two kinds of pain, considered together, as one additive entity (together, as one dichotomous phenomenon) might be viewed as being analogous to the entirety of the "activation energy" of a chemical reaction (refs. 1,2).

By modifying the circuit conception mentioned above in appropriate ways, when You would **succeed** at any given task, You would get rewarded with **high-intensity** pleasurable brain (or other) stimulation, whereas when and if You were to fail at a given task (instead of being punished by the "natural" feelings of disappointment, dismay and self-criticism), You would, instead, get **mildly** rewarded with (and feel) **low-intensity** pleasurable stimulation. And when You would succeed at a task, as opposed to when You would fail at a task, the success (or failure) would show up distinctively in the brain waves or other physiologically-correlated index/indices/signal(s) (refs. 29-39).

At this point, the question "How does (even low-intensity) pleasurable stimulation" eradicate the experiencing of mental/physical pain/effort? The answer lies in the phenomenon of **reciprocal inhibition** (refs. 43-45), the neurological phenomenon whereby activation of the brain's/body's "pleasure centers" tends to deactivate the brain's/body's "displeasure/pain centers" (and vice versa).

"Striking and immediate relief from intractable physical pain was consistently obtained with stimulation to the septal region [of the brain] of three patients with advanced carcinoma (cancer), two with metastases from primary breast [cancer] to bone and one with [cancer] of the cervix and extensive local proliferation" (ref. 46).

Moreover, regarding mental pain/suffering, "with septal stimulation the patients brightened, looked more alert, and seemed to be more **attentive to their** environment during and for at least a few minutes after, the period of stimulation. With this basic affective change, most subjects spoke more rapidly, and content was more productive; changes in content of thought were often striking, the most dramatic shifts occurring when prestimulation associations were pervaded with depressive affect. Expressions of anguish, self-condemnation, and despair changed precipitously to expressions of optimism and elaborations of pleasant experiences, past and anticipated. Patients sometimes appeared better oriented; **they could calculate more rapidly and** generally, **more accurately** than before stimulation. **Memory** and recall were

enhanced or unchanged. ....Only rarely was there objective evidence of sexual arousal" (ref. 46).

Sem-Jacobsen (ref. 47) reported that "We have been able to obtain feelings of comfort, relaxation, joy and intense satisfaction... In the ventromedial part of the frontal lobe, regions of pleasure and relaxation are lower and more internal than those mediating anxiety and irritation. The responses of relaxation and comfort obtained from stimulation of the frontal lobe are so intense that psychotic episodes have been broken up in less than one minute on several occasions.... Stimulation of the **ventromedial** part of the **frontal lobe** has a calming effect, as does stimulation of the **central region** of the **temporal lobe**."

Neuroanatomic sites, structures and pathways that might prove valuable in relation to the goals expressed herein might (or might not) include some of the following: the septal region and its principal outflow pathway, the medial forebrain bundle, interpeduncular nuclei of the mesencephalic tegmentum (ref. 46), the nucleus accumbens, ventral prefrontal cortex, amygdala, arcuate nucleus, hippocampus, ventral tegmental area, locus coeruleus, cerebellum, inferior and superior colliculi, periaqueductal gray area, thalamus, sensory cortex, etc. (refs. 46,48,49).

Regarding the prospect of adaptations of brain-stimulation-mediated therapy for treatments in relation to bodily illness, Mathias Fink, in his November, 1999 article titled: "Time-reversed acoustics: arrays of transducers can re-create a sound and send it back to its source as if time had been reversed," (Fink) points out that the process can be used to destroy kidney stones, detect defects in materials and communicate with submarines." Then, he proceeds to make the following relevant-to-physical-health observation and statement: "Porous bone in the skull presents an energy-sapping challenge to focusing ultrasound waves on a brain tumor to heat and **destroy** it. A time-reversal mirror with a modified playback algorithm can nonetheless focus ultrasound **through skull bone** onto a small target" (ref. 50).

Moreover, another article titled: "Rivals form brain tumor treatment center" (ref. 51) would seem to emphatically suggest that there may be more than one good and reliable way to effectively eradicate brain tumors, other neoplastic entities, as well as diseases of non-cancerous, non-neoplastic pathogenesis. If brain tumors, **despite the obstacle of the skull,** can be extirpated, then it might stand to reason that tumors, both malignant and benign, and cancerous cells located anywhere (else) in the body (outside of the head, that is, with these other neoplasms not even being burdened with the obstacle of the skull) could just as easily, or even more easily, be extirpated. Indeed, radiofrequency (just one kind of a potentially large number and variety of kinds of **electromagnetic**) ablation (facilitated by ultrasonic probe guidance) has been observed to destroy cancerous tissue in the liver (ref. 52). It is conceivable that many different kinds of diseases (beside cancer) might be effectively treated by the kinds of therapeutic approaches suggested herein or similar hereto.

Returning to the primary line of reasoning that centers on the alleviation or minimization of frustration and dismay as routinely occur in the face of failure at any given task(s), the result of the approach delineated above (i.e., intense pleasure for success and mild pleasure – but no significant frustration or consternation in response to failure), the result of such an approach would be analogous to using a rectifier/rectifying circuit to convert alternating electrical current (a.c.) (with a.c. being analogous to alternating between what is often **high-intensity pleasure and pain**) to direct current (d.c.) (with d.c. being analogous to alternating only between the lesser extremes of, i.e., narrower range or lesser difference between the highs of high-intensity pleasure/pleasurable stimulation and the lows of low-intensity pleasure/pleasurable stimulation).

So, the necessary modification(s) in circuit design that this high-intensity versus low-intensity (but painless, pain-avoidant, pain-alleviative, reciprocal-inhibition mediated) pleasure paradigm would entail, might be expected to effectively eliminate the need for and the purpose of the role of effort/pain and thereby optimally, fully de-effortize/pleasurize the processes of learning and working.

Another way of delineating this analogy is as follows. In the case of alternating current (a.c.), the current flows in one direction (let us call it direction A) during one short interval of time and then in the **opposite** direction (let us call it direction B) during the next short interval of time. And the current continues to alternate between directions A and B.

In the case of direct current (d.c.), the direction of current flow is always in the same direction (let us call it direction A). After the insertion of a rectifier/rectifying device/rectifying mechanism into an a.c. circuit, from the moment of insertion onward, the current changes from alternating between A and B to consistently/only flowing in direction A. So, if we conceptualize pleasure as direction A (pleasure = A) and effort/pain as B (effort/pain = B), then it becomes clear that by replacing the commonplace human situation of intermittently alternating between pleasure (A) and pain (B), according to whether we succeed at any given task (and feel pleasure) or fail at any given task (and feel pain), that is, by replacing this situation, as follows, a worthwhile purpose might be served.

By replacing this situation (via pleasurable stimulation) with the situation of intermittently alternating between (high-intensity) pleasure (A) and (low-intensity) pleasure (A), according to whether we succeed at any given task (and feel high-intensity pleasure) or fail at any given task (and feel low-intensity pleasure), we might be doing something analogous to rectifying a.c. in order to render it as d.c. And, more importantly from a human perspective or

227

standpoint, it might become readily possible to almost entirely eliminate effort/pain from the human experience. And this elimination of pain (and effort) would not necessarily compromise survivalist adaptability or undermine safety, as hypothesized previously (ref. 7).

What we would be doing here, if we can visualize an analytic geometric, Cartesian coordinate system entailing two directional coordinates in a plane with the horizontal or X-axis (the abscissa) representing time, t, and the vertical or Y-axis (the ordinate) representing pleasure above the X-axis and pain/effort below the X-axis, then by using the high-intensity versus low-intensity pleasure/reward dichotomy for success versus failure as opposed to the pleasure/dismay dichotomy for success versus failure in relation to any given mental/physical task, You would be **rectifying** the human (effort-strained and pain-drained) condition so that **all** values on the Y-axis would be in the pleasure range, i.e., above the X-axis. This approach might markedly improve (the quality of) life as we know it, by eliminating values of Y below the lower limit of pleasure (Y=0) or analogously and more tangibly by virtually eliminating the need for and occurrence of effort/pain.

The **pleasurization/de-effortization** (methods delineated herein) with "de-effortization" synonymously expressible as 'deeffortization,' 'deffortization,' or even 'defortation,' of **learning** and **working/work skills' acquisition** and implementation/application or exercise/utilization-use thereof would be analogous to **substantially reducing** (possibly by means of a catalyst) the **activation energy** of a chemical reaction wherein "activation energy" may be defined as the "minimum energy required for a chemical reaction to take place" (ref. 2).

Also, according to ref. 2 (pages 11,12), "the activation energy is the difference between the maximum energy" (level, i.e., the apex or highest value of the energizing waveform needed for the reactants to actually react) "and the" (immediately-pre-re-action) "energy" (level) "of the reactants, i.e., it is the **energy barrier** that has **to be overcome** for the reaction to proceed." The analogy to the pleasurization, defortation methods proposed herein can be well appreciated by substituting the (extended-) term, "performance-anxiety, burdensome-work/stress-strain/pain/ effort, for **BOTH** the word "barrier" and for "activation energy" in the quotations just cited, directly above.

In accordance with this analogy and substitution of words and their meanings, is the notion that the activities or processes of learning and working are analogous to the processes of chemical reactions, such as might be conceptualized in the chemistry dictionary in question (ref. 2) or any similar such dictionary. Being relieved of the stress and the need for mobilization or actuation of effort and being helpfully facilitated by pleasure-mediated, absorbing interest, concentration and attention (in relation to whatever subject matter the patient/student/worker chooses to learn and chooses to become knowledgeably competent in the performance and application of), consequently, this person (patient/student/worker) could suddenly concentrate-on intensely and pay unwavering attention to any subject matter or set of work skills that leads to (preferably) **high-paying** employment/jobs.

Hence, (assuming that suitable pleasure pathways, sites or centers **and** appropriate stimulus parameters were being used) high-level, **high-paying**-employment-related mental and physical activities might be expected to become significantly or intensely pleasurable/enjoyable from the experiential standpoint of the stimulation-recipient, so that this individual might be/become readily and easily motivated to frequently (and for long periods of time) engage in the high-paying **activities** chosen (by the person in question) to be engaged/involved and absorbed in. The particular mode of mental and/or physical activity that might be chosen by a student/worker/stimulation-recipient/participant would be a direct reflection of this person's own self-decided choice but would, undoubtedly, also be, to some significant degree, a reflection of what particular mode(s) of vocational/employment-related activity might be expected to entail high-paying employment/jobs.

When a person is engaging in high-level, mental and/or physical, learning and/or work-skills related activity/ies, this person's brain waves (electroencephalographic, EEG phenomena), etc. and other detectable physiological emissions and manifestations are discernibly and characteristically different than when this person is simply relaxing and allowing their mind to carelessly drift wherever and ruminate on whatsoever subjects it spontaneously will (refs. 29-39).

These brain waves and other kinds of detectable manifestations of various mental and physical/behavioral functions could possibly readily be used as the necessary and sufficient activator (i.e., switch-closing or TURN-ON) and sustainer (i.e., switch-closed, maintenance or STAY-ON/KEEP-ON) **signals** for the **pleasurable** brain/nervous system/other modes of anatomic (such as muscular) **stimulation circuit** in a context of learning-facilitation and work-skills' acquisition and performance enhancement.

The specific pleasure-mediating **modality/ies** or **mechanisms** might be implanted brain pacemaker electrodes, nerve/neural/neuronal stimulation, or surgically-noninvasive modalities/methods such as transcranial magnetic stimulation (TMS) (ref. 19), acoustic/sonic (such as, for example, ultrasonic, sonar, or infrasonic stimulation), electromagnetic (for example, microwaves, radiofrequency/radar adaptations, lasers, etc.), particle-beam stimulation, as might be mediated by fluid optics (ref. 53) or "time-reversal" mirrors (ref. 50) and/or particle detectors/accelerators, iontophoresis, DNA or other kinds of microchips, superconductors/superconducting materials, such as superconducting quantum interference devices, known as SQUIDS, methods that involve electromagnetic fields, combinations of laser beams, magnetic fields and radio waves (ref. 54), other optical methods entailing photonics/biophotonics (55,56) (biologically interactive photons, i.e., light particles), targeted, microminiature robotic entities, intravascularly or extravascularly traveling extremely small therapeutic entities, etc., with 'etc.' implying **any** (very large or virtually infinite) **number** of medical/technological treatments and modalities that are not referred to above.

Consequently, virtually regardless of a person's age and/or any other extraneous variable(s), this person could quickly become **de-effortized** (using this term to mean freed or rendered free of/from strenuous, stressful effort) and intensely **pleasurized** (using this term to mean imbued with pleasure in relation to, hence meticulously/deeply and broadly/extensively interested in the details of) and comprehensively/thoroughly well-educated in any area(s) of endeavor or vocational pursuit/employment that this person might choose, perhaps simply because it pays a good high wage or salary. Hence, this person could relatively readily become knowledgeable, work-skills-relatedly capable and effortlessly pleasurized in relation to any endeavor in question.

If anyone and virtually everyone could relatively suddenly and quickly become extensively and deeply knowledgeable about any kind(s) of subject matter or practical skill(s) that happen(s) to pay generous or ample money, then anyone and everyone could relatively suddenly secure a hold on or gain access to, that is, get a high-paying job or high-paying employment. Hence, the **"minimum" wage** (by dint of there being genuinely enhanced work-skills' performance, easy educability/flexibility, and genuinely increased per capita productivity and tangible output as opposed to mere economic inflation), as a minimal cost-of-living indicator, (the minimum wage) could be expected to readily and very substantially increase in amount, perhaps by factors/multiples of tens or hundreds.

Therefore, by virtue of markedly increased real earning power, rooted in increased employment-related versatility, flexibility and productivity, coupled with a notable and highly significant increase in minimum wage, and by reason of almost everyone (or almost everyone who wants or, situationally-speaking, **needs** to be in a position or condition of) having a relatively high-paying job, no one would be living in poverty (or even in financially stressed or strained circumstances) anymore.

Hence, poverty and financial stress could readily become, almost entirely, problems of the past. Money and all of the things it can buy or, at least, all of money's ability to afford a reasonably comfortable lifestyle's actual requirements, such as adequate food, shelter, clothing, etc. as well as modest luxuries such as intermittent vacation and personal hobby-indulgence periods, perhaps almost or **somewhat** like the air's ability to provide the full complement of the oxygen that we need and **freely** breath, could conceivably, comfortably and realistically be taken for granted and no longer be associated with disturbing anxiety, stress and depression in anyone's life. Within the context of a scenario such as the one delineated herein, the phrase "job skills training" might take on a new and usefully different meaning.

Closing Comments and Incidental Afterthoughts

With numerous and diverse new technologies, treatments modalities, and therapeutic methods emerging at a seemingly very rapid rate, it would probably be incorrect to heavily rely on, bet on, or predict the success of **any one** particular technology, therapeutic approach or methodology. For example, in consideration of two short publications, one in relation to a conceivably possible magnetic way to **relieve CHOKING ON FOOD** (a terrifying emergency when it happens) (ref. 9) and the other in relation to a conceivably possible ultrasonic way to relieve depression (ref. 8), it behooves me to freely admit (and I **do** admit) that the best way to relieve **choking on food (etc.)** might **not** be a magnetic way and the best way to relieve very severe depression might **not** involve ultrasound.

In any event, one needs to always be open to and receptive of new ideas and suggestions, new technologies, new therapeutic treatment, approaches, processes, methods, methodologies, and other new, modified or (old-?) **re-discovered** processes or phenomena. In other words, an open mind is almost always admirable and often helpfully useful.

One major reason why the possibility of any person's choking to death has generally "always" been especially frightening to me might be that when I was 10 or 12 years old, my mother told me about how, when she was only 12 year old, despite her not having had any formal training in First Aid, she saved her 12-year-old foster-sister (Agnes) from choking to death, when no one, other than the two of them, was at home. She recounted guiding Agnes down into a sitting position on the floor, then swiftly delivering a series of blows to the upper back area between the shoulder blades, so as to suddenly dislodge the obstacle from the airway, from which it shot out with projectile force.

Incidentally, returning to the subject of my (late) friend and neighbor, Bernice (Herb's 100-year-old mother), she was admitted to the hospital and died gracefully on August 22, 2002. She was a seemingly perpetually dignified, friendly and optimistic soul. And the expression of fascination I saw on her face (approximately an hour after her demise) definitely seemed to me, at least, to convey an optimistic signal for those of us who are hopeful in relation to the prospect of a blissful, **suffering-free** afterlife.

A Relevant Afterthought

As an ostensibly relevant afterthought it occurred to me that the following content might appropriately be attached to the end of this essay. As a consequence of a friend (Lyman) spotting an article titled: "Ultrasound breakthrough offers hope blind may see; discovery also may ease pain, mental illness" (ref. 57), I visited the ultrasound laboratory of Dr. Joie Pierce Jones at the University of California at Irvine, California (and spent the week of June 22, 1992 there), where he, some of his colleagues and I had some very stimulating and edifying conversations on the subject of the prospects of useful "artificial vision" and virtual-eyesight for the blind. Let it suffice to say that it seems to be a considerable privilege to have had relatively close contact with two (mutually independent) leaders (Drs. Dobelle and Jones) within the artificial eyesight for the blind/visually-impaired research and development movement/community. A letter of recommendation that Dr. Jones was kind enough to write for me is included in the appendix.

REFERENCES

1. Lehninger A.L. Biochemistry: Worth Publishers, 1970: 152-153.

2. Daintith J. (Editor). A Dictionary of Chemistry: Oxford University Press, third edition, 1996: 11-12.

3. Carmichael M. Healthy shocks to the head, magnets that move moods. Newsweek, June 24, 2002: 56-57.

4. Manning M. A Shock to the system, when Martha Manning found herself in the grip of extreme depression,she decided to undergo a little-understood treatment of last resort. Rosie (magazine), Aug., 2002: 117-126.

5. Mancini L.S. How learning ability might be improved by brain stimulation. Speculations in Science and Technology 1982; 5(1): 51-53.

6. Mancini L.S. Brain stimulation to treat mental illness and enhance human learning, creativity, performance, altruism, and defenses against suffering. Medical Hypotheses, 1986; 21: 209-219.

7. Mancini L.S. Riley-Day syndrome, brain stimulation and the genetic engineering of a world without pain. Medical Hypotheses, 1990; 31: 201-207.

8. Mancini L.S. Ultrasonic antidepressant therapy might be more effective than electroconvulsive therapy (ECT) in treating severe depression. Medical Hypotheses, 1992; 38: 350-351.

9. Mancini L.S. A magnetic choke-saver might relieve choking. Medical Hypotheses, 1992; 38: 349.

10. Mancini L.S. A proposed method of pleasure-inducing biofeedback using ultrasound stimulation of brain structures to enhance selected EEG states. Speculations in Science and Technology, 1993; 16(1): 78-79.

11. Mancini L.S. (written under the pseudonym: Nemo T. Noone). Waiting hopefully. Western New York Mental Health World, 1995; 3(4), Winter: 14.

12. Mancini L.S. How Everyone might be Rich, Famous, Pain and Death Free (Immortal), Well-Educated, Sexually Liberated, Unselfish, Healthy, Free of Anorexia, Obesity, Nausea, Blindness, Deafness, Paralysis, Insomnia, etc. via Brain Stimulation, Neural Prostheses, Pacemakers, Mind Particle Internet, Circulation, Cloning, Genetic Engineering, Conscious Computers, etc. Copyright © 2001; contained in this book as Essay number one.

13. Irwin C. (Managing Director). First artificial eye. Guinness World Records 2001: Mint Publishers, 2000: 179.

14. Cunningham A. (Managing Editor). Most successful artificial eye. Guinness World Records 2002: Mint Publishers, 2002: 27.

15. Dobelle W.H., Mladejovsky M.G., Girvin J.P. Artificial Vision for the blind: electrical stimulation of visual cortex offers hope for a functional prosthesis. Science, Feb. first, 1974; 183:440-444.

16. Ritter M. Blind man navigates whole new world of vision by using tiny camera wired directly to his brain. Buffalo News, Mon., Jan. 17, 2000: A-14.

17. Whitaker M. Light for the blind. Newsweek, 1974; Feb. 11: 48.

18. Bergstrom B. Inventor of dialysis machine, 91, now working on lung. Buffalo News, Sun., Nov. 10, 2002: H-6.

19. George M.S., Belmaker R.H. TMS, Transcranial Magnetic Stimulation in Neuropsychiatry: American Psychiatric Press, 2000: 298 pages.

20. Lemonick M.D. The power of mood: lifting Your spirits can be potent medicine. How to make it work for You. Time, 2003; special issue, Jan. 20: 64-69.

21. Crichton M. Could tiny machines rule the world? Buffalo News, Parade Magazine 2002; Sun., Nov. 24: 6-8.

22. Garcia B. Enormous potential, nanotechnology may hold key to future. Buffalo News 2002; Tues., Nov. 26: D6-D7.

23. Langer R. Where a pill won't reach, how to get drugs where they need to go: implanted microchips, embedded polymers and ultrasonic blasts of proteins will deliver next generation medicines. Scientific American, 2003; April: 50-57.

24. LoCascio N.J.T. Clinical instructor, State Univ. of NY at Buffalo, Dept. of Neurology; personal communication regarding radiofrequency ablation, via ultrasonic guidance probe, of cancer tumors and individual cancerous cells, late 2002.

25. Butler S.R., Giaquinto S. Technical note: stimulation triggered automatically by electrophysiological events. Med & Biol Engng, changed to Med Biol Eng Comput, 1969; 7: 329-331.

26. Siegel J.M., Sterman M.B., Ross S. Automatic detection and operant reinforcement of slow potential shifts. Physiology and Behavior 1979; 23: 411-413.

27. Park A. Postcards form the brain. Time, 2003; special issue, Jan. 20: 94-97.

28. Berkow R. (Editor-in-Chief). The Merck Manual of Medical Information. Pocket Books, Simon & Schuster 1997: 312-314.

29. Gevins A.S., Morgan N.H., Bressler S.L. et al, Human neuroelectric patterns predict performance accuracy. Science 1987; 235: 580-585.

30. Williamson S.J. How quickly we forget - magnetic fields reveal a hierarchy of memory lifetimes in the human brain. Science Spectra 1999; 15: 68-73.

31. Walgate J., Wagner A., Buckner R.L., Schacter D., Sharpe K., Floyd C. Memories are made of this. Science & Spirit 1999; 10, 1:7.

32. Connor S. Thanks for the memory. The World in 1999. The Economist Publications, 1999: 110-111.

33. Goetinck S. Different brain areas linked to memorization. The Buffalo News, final edn., Sun., June 13, 1999, Science Notes: H-6.

34. Hall S.S. Journey to the center of my mind, brain scans can locate the home of memory and the land of language. They may eventually help to map consciousness. The New York Times Magazine, June 6, 1999; section 6: 122-125.

35. Neergaard L. Studies shed new light on memory/studies take close look at brain's memory process. Buffalo News 1999; Fri., Aug. 21: A-10.

36. Sullivan M.M. (Editor). Task-juggling region in brain pinpointed. Buffalo News 1999; Sun., May 23: H-6.

37. Fox M. Test on rats turns thought into action. Buffalo News 1999; Sun., June 27: H-6.

38. McCrone J. States of mind, learning a task takes far more brainpower than repeating it once it's become a habit, could the difference show us where consciousness lies, asks J.M. New Scientist March 20, 1999; 161: 30-33.

39. Pinker S. Will the mind figure out how the brain works? Time 2000; 155: 90-91.

40. Skinner B.F. Contingencies of Reinforcement: a Theoretical Analysis. Appleton-Century-Crofts 1969: 319 pages.

41. Crystal D. The Cambridge Encyclopedia. Cambridge University Press, 2nd edition, 1994: 1347 pages; p. 1021.

42. Hall S.S. Brain pacemakers: surgeons re implanting tiny electrodes in the brains of patients suffering from everything from Parkinson's disease to obsessive-compulsive disorder. Soon, these devices may be as common as heart pacemakers. Technology Review: MIT's magazine of innovation 2001; 104(7): 34-43.

43. Stein L. Reciprocal action of reward and punishment mechanisms; pages 113-139 in the book, The Role of Pleasure in Behavior (editor: Heath, R.G.) Harper & Row, New York, 1964.

44. Stein L., Belluzzi J.D., Ritter S., Wise C.D. Self-stimulation reward pathways: norepinephrine versus dopamine. J Psychiatr Res 1974; 11: 115-124.

45. Mancini L.S. Practical Implications of Learning and Cognitive Facilitation Theory. Term paper similar to a "senior thesis" written during the second half (semester) of my senior year at Trinity College, Hartford, Connecticut under the auspices of Dr. George Doten of the Psychology Dept., 1973; unpublished manuscript.

46. Heath R.G. Pleasure response of human subjects to direct stimulation of the brain: physiologic and psychodynamic considerations, pages 219-243, with quotations from pages 224 and 225 within the book titled: The Role of Pleasure in Behavior (Heath R.G., editor), Harper & Row, New York 1964.

47. Sem-Jacobsen C.W. Effects of electrical stimulation on the human brain. Electroencephalography and Clinical Neurophysiology 1959; 11: 379.

48. Begley S. How it all starts inside Your brain. Newsweek 2001; Feb. 12: 40-42.

49. Cowley G. Our bodies, our fears. Newsweek 2003; Feb. 24: 42-49.

50. Fink M. Time-reversed acoustics: arrays of transducers can re-create a sound and send it back to its source as if time had been reversed. The process can be used to destroy kidney stones, detect defects in materials and communicate with submarines. Scientific American 1999; Nov.: 91-97.

51. Davis H.L. Rivals form brain tumor treatment center. The Buffalo News 2003; March 29: B-8.

52. Spangler R.A. Professor, State Univ. of NY at Buffalo, Dept. of Biophysics/Physiology; personal communication regarding radiofrequency ablation, via ultrasonic guidance probes, of cancer-mediating mechanisms located anywhere in the body, late 2002.

53. Buderi R. Fluid optics. Technology Review: MIT's magazine of innovation 2003; March, 106(2): 20.

54. Hau L.V. Frozen light: slowing a beam of light to a halt may pave the way for new optical communications technology, tabletop black holes and quantum computers. Scientific American 2003; 13(1): 44:51.

55. Davis H.L. Shedding light on the future. Buffalo News, Sun., April 2, 2000: A-1, A-12.

56. Prasad P.N., of the Depts. Of Chemistry and Physics and the Institute for Lasers, Photonics (optical technologies) and Biophotonics at the State Univ. of N.Y. at Buffalo, NY, personal communication, Oct. 25, 1999.

57. Peterson S. Ultrasound breakthrough offers hope blind may see; discovery also may ease pain, mental illness. The Buffalo News 1992; Jan. 15.